War Despatches

1971

OTHER OCCAM MILITARY TITLES

March to Justice: Global Military Law Landmarks
Navdeep Singh, Frank Rosenblatt

Once Upon a Time in RIMC
Brig Jasbir Singh, SM

The Fighting Fourth: A Personal Narrative of the History of 4 Kumaon
Brig Jasbir Singh, SM

War Despatches
1971

From Young Army, Navy and Air Force Officers Commissioned for Combat (along with the June '66 Batch)

Edited by Brig B.S. Mehta

OCCAM

an imprint of BluOne Ink

Title: War Despatches 1971: From Young Army, Navy and Air Force Officers Commissioned for Combat (Along with the June '66 Batch)
Editor: Brig B.S. Mehta

ISBN: 978-93-92209-12-3
Edition: 1

Published by:
BluOne Ink LLP

Publisher's Address:
306, Tower-I, Assotech Business Cresterra,
Plot No. 22, Sector 135, Noida.

Website: www.bluone.ink
Email: publisher@bluone.ink

Printed in India at Thomson Press (India) Ltd.

OCCAM

an imprint of BluOne Ink

To the National Defence Academy, the schools of instruction of the Indian Army, Navy, and Air Force, and to the brave hearts who remind us every day with their supreme sacrifice: Nation first

Editorial Team

Balram Mehta (Editor)
Arvind Sharma
Narinder Dhand
Manohar Ramtri
Satish Kukreja
Pradeep Sharma
C.P.C. Nath
Trigunesh Mukherjee (Photo Editor)

Contents

Preface 11

I Introduction

The War in Retrospect Maroof Raza 17

Background to the Conflict: An Insider's View Pradeep Sharma 30

II Eastern Theatre

The Burinda Bash Balram Singh Mehta 42

My Most Memorable Learning Experience R.S.K. Kapur 58

Snippets from the First Mission Virender Budhwar 65

1971: An Eventful Year Sukhdev Singh 71

Letters to My Wife Shimi Kanbargimath 89

The Kilo Flight: A Chronicled Personal Account Arun Karandikar 99

The Battlefield Blues Balram Singh Mehta 110

The Solitary Sapper Pradeep Sharma 118

The War in the East: Through the Eyes of a Pigeon Arvind Sharma 134

A Nation is Born Trigunesh Mukherjee 142

Airman or Tankman? Balram Singh Mehta 158

III Western Theatre

A Battle After the Ceasefire: The Case of Pul Kanjri Tarlochan Singh Kalra 164

Bloodied on Raising P.P.S. Bhandari 173

The Naval Operations: Action in the Arabian Sea by the Western Fleet S.S. Sethi 182

A Page from My Diary S. Balasubramanian 198

A Naval Story from Southern Naval Command E. Jai Chacko 206

From the Battle Zone of Longewala Ram Chandra Chhetri 209

From Hinterland to War Zone Ujjal Dasgupta 218

Battle of Shakargarh M.I. Jaisinghani 227

From the Diary of a Prisoner of War K.C. Kuruvilla 233

Some Recollections of 1971 Satish Kumar Kukreja 241

A Flashback Mohinder Puri 249

The Capture of Southern Mamdot Bulge K.K. Nanda 255

SIGINT during the 1971 War C.P.C. Nath 273

Battle of Jarpal: An Action Journal Mahendra Singh Joon 281

The Capture of Mamdot Bulge Vijay Rai 294

The War as I Saw it P.J.S. Sandhu 314

Tribulations of Ammunition Supply Chain in War Subash Bindra 321

Forward Maintenance Area in Barmer C.P. Tewari 330

IV Appendix

Captain R.N. Gupta, VrC Mohinder Nath Mahajan 340

Captain G.G.K. Panicker Pradeep Sharma 346

Captain Daljinder Singh Gautam Tandon 350

Honours, Awards and Achievements Arvind Sharma 356

Citations 364

In Fond Memory... 369

Preface

This book is a collection of articles written by officers of the Indian Army, Navy and the Air Force who fought in the War of 1971. The idea to write it took root in August 2020 in a periodic virtual meeting of officers from an email group. Conscripted by pandemic restrictions, we were interacting amongst ourselves when one of us mentioned the likelihood of a Golden Jubilee Celebration of this war in 2021. Brigadier Balram Singh Mehta, one of the members of this group, suggested that we consider publishing a book to commemorate the war. As all members of this group were veterans of the Armed forces, we decided to write an account each based on our experience of the war.

The email group was created in 2006 and comprised officers of the 28th Course of the National Defence Academy, Khadakwasla, who had joined the academy in July 1962 (this included cadets of the Army, Navy and Air Force). The membership was subsequently enlarged to include Army officers who were part of the batch commissioned on

15 June 1966 from the Indian Military Academy, Dehradun (this also included those from the 28 NDA Course). All accounts in this book are contributions of this group of soldiers.

While we were extremely enthusiastic about this book, the realisation that one would have to rummage through old papers, books, personal and public records, among others, in order to recall events, authenticate details and indulge in coherent narration of events and incidents of the War did wane our initial joy. In many a case, old war diaries, sequence of events and records held by units where one was posted during the War had to be referred to, all five decades vintage! It merits mention here that while all officers of the Armed forces are trained in communication skills to fulfil their responsibilities towards their combat groups, we were fully aware that we were not professional writers or journalists. Nevertheless, an editorial team was constituted, which managed to persuade a reasonable number of course mates to put pen to paper and produce articles, with some photographs and sketches where available, to present to the reader the contribution of this batch of officers to the War of 1971. Since this war has been a historical landmark for the Indian Armed forces, one that is unlikely to be surpassed in the foreseeable future, a number of books have been written on it. These books cover detailed research on the history, geographical aspects, cultural and ethnic ties, economic and social aspects of Pakistan. We, thus, took a deliberate decision to restrict ourselves to the narration of experience(s) of the combatants of the War. As most of the officers at that time were in the service bracket of four to five years, the articles cover events at the tactical level only and mostly at the level of a company or a battalion. It, however, merits mention that it is winning the small wars that eventually results in bigger victories.

Our batch of officers comprised over 400 soldiers. At the time of the War, a fairly large number of officers of our batch were in schools of instruction, attending specialist courses of long duration. By the time they rejoined their units, the war was almost over. Many others were posted in units and formations which were not part of the order of battle of the war and were deployed to counter enemy designs elsewhere, and thus were not a part of the war effort. Some of those who participated in the 1971 operations are no longer with us. Despite all the above, the articles cover the entire spectrum of war—the land, sea and air battles.

In 1971, the Indian Armed forces achieved a glorious victory, busting the myth that a nation could exist as a single entity when its two parts were more than a thousand kilometres apart. Bangladesh was born as a consequence of the War, with 93,000 Pakistani prisoners of war (POWs) and over ten million refugees, who could return to their homeland.

All cogs of the wheel have a job to perform wherefrom the vehicle moves smoothly on its path. Thus, every account is not only a factual first-hand unfolding of events but also an honest expression of the soldier's state of mind in the event of a war—it is here that we laugh, we cry, we lose, we gain, we reminisce, we mourn, and through it all, we carry on. In his article *From the Diary of a Prisoner of War*, Air Commodore K.C. Kuruvilla recounts his aircraft being shot while attacking an enemy convoy and being taken prisoner of war thereafter. Air Commodore Arun Karandikar in *The 'KILO' Flight: A Chronicled Personal Account* narrates his experience of doing the unthinkable—single-handedly operating a transport aircraft and flying at night without night navigation aids in the Eastern Sector. Captain S.S. Sethi revisits aspects of the Naval operations in the War which paralysed the Pakistan Navy, in his article titled *The Naval Operations: Action in the Arabian Sea by the Western Fleet*. Brigadier Balram Singh Mehta, Colonel K.K. Nanda, Major Pradeep Sharma and Lieutenant General P.P.S. Bhandari narrate staggering accounts of their providential escape during the War. Other articles shed light on the significant aspects important to win a war. Adhering to the military ethics and values of '*veer bhogya vasundhra*'—the Earth is for the brave', we salute those who made the supreme sacrifice for the nation!

It was primarily due to the effort of the members who contributed the articles that the book has been compiled. Besides the authors, we are also grateful to the editorial team who spent valuable time in giving shape to the book. Finally, Lieutenant Colonel C.P.C. Nath and Brigadier Balram Singh Mehta deserve special mention, as the book is their child, conceptualised and nurtured by both all through its journey to print.

Lieutenant General Arvind Sharma

I
Introduction

The War in Retrospect

Maroof Raza

The Indo-Pak war of 1971 was a consequence of many events and factors. Pakistan was an artificial entity that came into being with the partition of India following the demands for a nation for the Muslims of the Indian subcontinent. But as the events leading to the 1971 Indo-Pak war and the emergence of Bangladesh were to show to the world, Islam per se wasn't a bonding adhesive enough to the two entities of West and East Pakistan, separated by the huge land mass of India. Although the tensions between the Bengali population of East Pakistan and the dominant Punjabi elites of West Pakistan had taken root just after the creation of Pakistan, it gathered momentum from 1966 when the military leadership of West Pakistan refused to accept the 'Six-point Programme' for the autonomy of East Pakistan, championed by the Bengali leaders led by the Awami League's Sheikh Mujibur Rahman. This came about when the Bengalis in East Pakistan were tired of being treated as second class citizens and of being economically exploited. For instance, all the jute and tea grown in East Pakistan earned most of Pakistan's foreign exchange, but this was used to develop Pakistan's western wing. The more populous East Pakistan was even denied protection from floods and cyclones, which brought periodic devastation to life and property in their wake. Besides their differences of language and cultural habits from that of the West Pakistanis, the Bengalis wanted autonomy for themselves in the eastern wing of Pakistan.

The rift between the Bengalis and the West Pakistanis had become public when the Bengali leaders were jailed and tried for conspiracy and treason, and India was blamed for allegedly aiding them. In fact, Pakistan's military rulers were ill-informed about Bengali sentiments as their intelligence agency, the ISI, had no clue of the deeply embedded Bengali resentments and the revolts that were to follow in East Pakistan, which were a manifestation of the arrogance and greed of West Pakistan. Furthermore, the first ever general elections held in Pakistan since its independence after delays on 7 December 1970 for the 300 constituencies of their National Assembly, threw up results that surprised Pakistan's ruler, General Yahya Khan. The results gave the Awami League in East Pakistan 160 out of 162 seats, while the Zulfikar Bhutto led Pakistan People's Party had 81 seats (plus 5 reserved for women), thus undoing Bhutto's plan to become prime minister. Despite the appointment of a veteran Bengali politician, Nurul Amin, temporarily as prime minister, who had sought to attain a compromise between the Awami League and the PPP, the delay in the inauguration caused great resentment in East Pakistan. First, the Awami league's leader Sheikh Mujib launched a non-violent non-cooperation movement. This led to protests in the streets of Dacca, and eventually the hoisting of a flag of 'independent' Bangladesh at the University campus. Even as the rapid unfolding of events in March 1971 across East Pakistan took the Pakistani military leadership by total surprise, the firing at an Awami League procession in Rangpur, by pro-Pakistan Biharis and encouraged by local administration, made matters go out of control.

Soon thereafter, Rawalpindi sent in Lieutenant General Tikka Khan, earlier known notoriously as the 'Butcher of Baluchistan', to be appointed governor of East Pakistan. This took tensions to the highest levels. He could not be sworn in as the new Governor initially, as the Chief Justice of East Pakistan, Badruddin Ahmed Siddiki, refused to swear him in. Hence, the Chief Justice of West Pakistan was flown in to swear him in! Thereafter, the administration of East Pakistan, including the police, refused to obey the orders of an establishment loyal to West Pakistan. Instead, they chose to report to Sheikh Mujibur Rahman, who had declared the start of the liberation struggle. By the time the President General Yahya Khan arrived in Dhaka on 15 March, for what became his last visit, much of East Pakistan was under Mujib's absolute sway. General Yahya and Sheikh Mujib did meet along with their aides, over the next few days to thrash out a solution to the crisis, but nothing came out of it. On 21 March, Zulfikar Ali Bhutto, who was following his own ambitions, also arrived in Dhaka following the invitation of Yahya Khan. These tripartite negotiations involving the Awami League, the Pakistan People's Party and the army brass went on till 23 March, when the Bengalis observed Pakistan Day by hoisting Bangladesh's flags atop homes and offices. Thereafter, there seemed to be no turning back for Sheikh Mujib and the Bengali movement for freedom from Pakistan.

Once Yahya Khan left Dacca on the night of 25 March 1971, instructing Lieutenant General Tikka Khan to 'sort them out', the Pakistan army launched 'Operation Searchlight' in East Pakistan. They went on a killing spree across East Pakistan (now Bangladesh), after which at least 7,000 people were found dead the next day in Dacca. Residential areas, the local police lines, Dacca University's halls of residence and girls hostels on campus were all targeted. But Zulfikar Bhutto, who had stayed back, to see Dacca burn, left on 26 March. Before leaving, he had patted Lieutenant General Tikka

Khan's back and assured him and his partners in the genocide that he would reward them someday! Thus, when Bhutto manoeuvred his way to the top of Pakistan's political heap after the War of 1971, Tikka Khan was made Pakistan's army chief, and his colleague Lieutenant General Farman, the head of Fauji Foundation, Pakistan's biggest business entity.

As the atrocities of the Pakistan army continued, it led to a large exodus of bewildered refugees into India. By the end of May 1971, India had about 10 million Bengali refugees, and soon there were refugee camps all across eastern India, with a Bangladeshi government in exile in Calcutta. The financial burden of this refugee relief effort was estimated by the World Bank, (as quoted in *The New York Times*), at about $700 million in a full year. This was roughly half of India's defence budget in 1970. This financial drain created political pressure on India's Prime Minister, Mrs Indira Gandhi, for India to first seek global support for humanitarian assistance to deal with this refugee crisis as also to put pressure on Pakistan to stop the genocide in East Pakistan. But as there was little international support for India initially, Mrs Gandhi wanted an Indian military intervention in East Pakistan, following much pressure from the chief ministers of the Indian states that had to house the refugees, to liberate parts of it and to push the refugees back at the first instance. However, the Indian military commanders suggested a more calibrated approach. General (SHFJ) Sam Manekshaw, the Indian army chief, having conferred with his two counterparts, the naval chief, Admiral S.M. Nanda and Air Chief Marshal P.C. Lal, and after much deliberation at the Military Operations (MO) Directorate, cautioned against haste, since many factors were involved. The subcontinent had, by then, stepped into the summer of 1971, and thus the harvested grain needed to be moved across the country. Also, the trains and road transport could either ferry the grain or the troops to battle, and once the monsoons would follow, the movement of India's military units would be hampered, especially in the riverine terrain of East Pakistan. Moreover, the Indian armed forces needed to upgrade its military inventories with new weapons and platforms to confront Pakistan's better armed forces that had received superior war fighting systems mostly made in the US, since Pakistan was part of the US led alliance(s) against the USSR; India's capabilities with Centurion tanks, Hunter aircrafts and many naval vessels needed to be upgraded, never mind the better training and strong morale of India's force. Additionally, the one certain way to ensure that a Chinese intervention across the Himalayas could be held back was to go into a conflict after mid-November, when the heavy winter snowfall would severely restrict Chinese movements.

Above all, General Manekshaw, though a decorated hero of the Second World War, hadn't been in command of troops in the 1947–1948, 1962 and the 1965 wars, and was thus keen to ensure that the battles unfolded as planned. (The veterans of this war who have contributed with their staggering accounts to *War Despatches 1971* know it all too well that the best laid plans go up in smoke once a war begins!) Moreover, General Manekshaw had also secured the support of India's two other service chiefs to launch a winter campaign. But it is also to Mrs Gandhi's credit that despite a strong personality that resented dissent and political pressures at home, she saw merit in the military's suggestions. She was also aware of how the meddling by her father, Pandit Nehru, and his defence minister, Krishna Menon, in the military's plans had led to the military debacle of 1962. Thus, heeding the military's advice, she decided to let the armed forces do what they are best at—to fight a war and win it. Sam Manekshaw had apparently promised her that given the time, he could help her 'make history and even geography', as I recall him saying at the first Infantry lecture at Vigyan Bhawan in October 1994. Thus, even as the armed forces began to prepare for what truly became a historic victory, Mrs Gandhi took up the job of winning the world's support for India's humanitarian initiative in East Pakistan. This wasn't easy, with the US clearly supporting Pakistan, more so after Pakistan had helped President Nixon's National Security Adviser, Henry Kissinger, to open a diplomatic dialogue with China in July 1971. This eventually led to China's economic rise, but that's another story.

Thus, recognising the importance of global backing for its military campaign, Mrs Indira Gandhi along with her foreign minister Swaran Singh, visited many world capitals in 1971, including Washington D.C., where she was cold-shouldered by the Nixon-Kissinger combine because of America's strategic interests in Pakistan—a CENTO & SEATO ally. But it was finally in August 1971 when her diplomatic efforts bore serious fruits—New Delhi had signed the 'Indo-Soviet Treaty of Peace, Friendship and Cooperation' with Moscow. In the years preceding that, Russia (then USSR) had in the past supported China indirectly, when it invaded India in 1962, and had kept Pakistan humored to stall any US-Pak military adventures into Central Asia, which Moscow saw as its soft underbelly. Not only was India's diplomatic initiative a significant departure from the Nehruvian obsession with non-alignment, but it was Russia's support at the many sessions in the United Nations that stalled pro-Pakistan resolutions at the initiative of Washington, when Indian troops rolled down the plains of East Pakistan. Though the War officially started on 3 December 1971, following simultaneous Pakistani air raids on Indian air bases in north and west of India, military operations along the borders of East Pakistan had started in the last week of November 1971.

Following the months of training imparted to Bengali guerillas of the Mukti Bahini and some other groups—who had come into India with the refugees—military operations had picked up considerable momentum by November. After the Indian Air Force's Hunters of the 37th Squadron had begun to carry out aerial reconnaissance missions in October and November, 'India's military involvement increased substantially in the first three weeks of November 1971' writes Air Vice Marshal Arjun Subramaniam in his detailed account of India's Wars, quoting from historical accounts of R. Sisson and L.E. Rose. He further adds that while earlier on, 'India's forces did hit objectives in East Pakistan and then withdrew back into Indian territory, after the night of 21 November 1971, Indian tactics changed in a significant way. Thereafter, India's forces did not withdraw... the Indian Army's divisions were divided into smaller tactical units that launched simultaneous military actions on all key areas of East Pakistan, with armour and air support.' Some of the fascinating first-hand accounts in this volume tell us about these operations. And at least two famous battles, the Battle of Garibpur on 21 November and the Battle of Hilli on 22 November occurred before the war was officially declared!

Once the war officially started, a lot of attention shifted initially to India's western front with Pakistan. There were many reasons for this. India's devastating naval attack on Karachi Harbour, that scared the Pakistan Navy away for the rest of the war, took place on 4 December 1971, and a major Pakistani offensive that was stalled at Longewala on 4/5 December 1971 had attracted a lot of attention among the military brass hats; whereas on India's eastern front a lot of synergy between the three services had to be developed and troop readjustments by the Indian Army had to be made before what led eventually to the blitzkrieg towards Dacca. Few people knew, at least in the winter of 1971, that General Manekshaw continued to insist that the Chinese could force India to engage on two-fronts and spoil India's race to Dacca, even though there were no intelligence intercepts to back Manekshaw's concerns. It was only much later that Manekshaw had agreed to release additional troops from the Sino Indian border, though by then, Major General Jacob had managed to get troops from the Himalayan formations moved, without Manekshaw's knowledge but with help from Major General Inder Gill, the DMO.

Apparently when Sam did learn of this, he gave Inder Gill a dressing down, but things were moving so fast that the focus shifted to Dacca, says General Jacob in his autobiography *An Odyssey in War and Peace*.

All through, the US was pushing the UN for a ceasefire, even as Moscow and some other Indian friends were holding out for India. But they couldn't do so forever. If that had happened, then all the military gains would be literally 'back to square one'. Thus, New Delhi was in a hurry to at least establish a free Bangladeshi government, fearing a UN ceasefire, in the port towns of Khulna and Chittagong. But as the operations unfolded and gathered momentum, India's eastern command went ahead with a plan, to capture Dacca. A CIA memo, later declassified, had summed up India's aims as: a) the liberation of (East Pakistan) Bangladesh, b) the incorporation into India of the southern areas of POK, and c) the destruction of Pakistan's armour and its air force. Thus, the Indian Army, ably assisted by the Indian Air Force raced to Dacca. The IAF quite literally bombed the daylights out of the Pakistan Air Force. Soon the skies were clear of any Pakistan fighters: they lay wrecked on their airfields. And then a heli-borne operation was initiated—the first of its kind since independence—that put troops across the vast Meghna river and the many rivers that had until then, given Dacca a natural defence. This was followed by the first ever Indian airborne drop of paratroopers at Tangail. On India's western front, some fierce battles were also fought as the Pakistani army was eager to exploit their advantages with Patton tanks and Sabre jets. But Indian troops held their positions against Pakistani efforts. A counter offensive by India across the Shakargarh Bulge led to the famous battles of Jarpal and Basantar. The exploits and the demanding challenges on India's brave officers and the men they led are in this unique collection of essays: *War Despatches 1971*.

En route to Dacca, the Indian Army heard many accounts of the atrocities of the Pakistan Army, and of the massacre of thousands of Bengalis. The evidence of that was unearthed in the nearly 40 mass graves, and also there were reports of the rape of about 2,00,000 Bengali women. It was shockingly encouraged by the Generals Tikka Khan, his successor, Niazi, and his senior officers. By 15 December, Indian troops had surrounded Dacca. Then during a short lull in the war, Major General Jacob—then chief of staff at HQ eastern command—received a call from General Manekshaw, who said: 'Jake, go and get a surrender'. A draft surrender document was quickly prepared, and then he proceeded to Dacca to meet Lieutenant General A.A.K. Niazi, MC, the overall military commander in East Pakistan. Once there, General Jacob saluted him and asked if he was willing to accept an unconditional surrender. General Niazi was in no mood to surrender, since 26,400 Pakistani soldiers were still in Dacca, while only 3,000 Indian soldiers were nearby. Thus, a pompous General Niazi was enjoying the winter afternoon over beer and lunch, with all silver laid out in their officers mess, when Jacob met him, and he dismissed the proposition of a surrender with the wave of his hand, stating: 'Who said I am surrendering? You have only come to discuss a ceasefire and withdrawal as proposed by me.' Apparently still hopeful that even then, a ceasefire would soon be ordered by the UN, and could save him and his army a humiliation.

But General Jacob was persistent, and said to him that he had 30 minutes within which he'd ask him thrice whether he'd accept to surrender. If Niazi still didn't respond, he couldn't guarantee the safety of Pakistani families (as the Bengali rebels were waiting to lynch them all). Moreover, he'd ask for the resumption of bombings on Dacca. Since Lieutenant General Niazi had refused to respond to Major General Jacob's demand for a surrender, General Jacob picked up the document and held it up to say: 'I take it as accepted'. Tears rolled down General Niazi's cheek, as he hung his head in shame. Other Pakistani officers glared at Niazi in disbelief, as General Jacob got up, and asked General Niazi to prepare for the surrender, wrote

General Jacob in his autobiography. Lieutenant General Niazi had set one pre-condition before he surrendered on 16 December 1971 with 93,000 Pakistani military officers and soldiers and allied elements at the Race Course in Dacca. It was that Pakistani soldiers be allowed to keep their weapons even after the surrender—something which isn't done once a soldier surrenders—fearing that he and his men would be lynched to death by the angry mobs of Bengali men and women! They were allowed to do so, to prevent an additional crisis, and perhaps because Niazi and his Indian counterpart—Lieutenant General J.S. Arora, India's eastern army commander—were batch mates from the IMA, Dehradun! Moreover, India wanted the end of an end to bloodshed, not have more of it, and a quick return to normalcy. The next day, a tearful Niazi on signing the surrender document, removed his badges of rank and handed his pistol to General J.S. Arora, before being whisked away by India's senior officers. He needed to be kept alive to tell the world that he wasn't mutilated to surrender, but did so for the world to see, at Dacca parade ground.

Thus, Pakistan's darkest day was the surrender of 93,000 Pakistanis in Dhaka on 16 December 1971. Nearly 81,000 prisoners of war were from the Pakistani armed forces (with some Bengali soldiers who had chosen to remain with the Pakistani Army) and another 12,000 odd civilians including collaborators. And though everyone associates the fall of Dacca (as Dhaka was then known) to then army chief, General Sam Manekshaw (who had no doubt a larger than life presence in South Block), a closer reading of one of the few accounts of how it all happened (since official records in Calcutta were shredded at General Arora's orders) shows that credit must also go to a few others like then Major General J.F.R. Jacob, who was Chief of Staff at HQ Eastern Command in Calcutta, who was involved in the planning and meticulous implementation of the operations in East Pakistan along with Major General Inder Gill, who was then the Director of Military Operations (as there was no DGMO then), and Lieutenant General Sagat Singh, who led the race to Dacca with his IV Corps from Assam and Tripura, as also to Air Marshal H.C. Dewan and Vice Admiral N. Krishnan. That war was the finest example of inter-service cooperation, and credit must also go to the naval chief, Admiral Nanda who had the foresight to move India's only aircraft carrier, INS *Vikrant*—despite resistance from naval brass hats—to the Bay of Bengal, and Air Chief Marshal P.C. Lal who had set up an advance HQ in Calcutta to coordinate the efforts of the two air commands in the eastern sector.

The fall of Dacca—the crowning moment of the war—had come about essentially as Pakistan's generals hadn't expected the Indian Army to do what it did. As the Pakistan Army spread its forces on the East Pakistan long borders—in all three Pakistan Army divisions to fight Bengali guerillas and the offensive operations of the three corps of the Indian Army—Pakistani forces were fortified around its garrison towns, that led to some fierce battles around them, but there was a simultaneous Indian drive to get to Dacca. A simple tactical lesson taught to every officer in the army is never to re-enforce a failure, and thus those areas of Pakistani resistance were bypassed, even as the Pakistan's army generals were confident that three factors wouldn't allow any worthwhile success to the Indian armed forces in East Pakistan. First, their well-armed military machine in West Pakistan would be enough to threaten India's strategic states of Punjab and J&K. Second, a Chinese military build-up along the Himalayas would tie down enough of the Indian Army, and thus disallow India's commanders to move troops to capture East Pakistan. Lastly, they were banking on the US to intervene militarily if Indian operations became difficult for Pakistan to contain. Washington did choose to send in its 7th fleet into the Bay of Bengal. It not only reached too late to stall the Indian effort, but also found that the Indian Navy had blockaded East Pakistan's coastline.

On 20 December 1971, Pakistan's bumbling President General Yahya Khan resigned and handed over power in the truncated country to Zulfikar Ali Bhutto, who it is said, had orchestrated the delays at the UN for a 'ceasefire order' that Yahya had hoped would prevent the fall of Dacca. Bhutto was the eternal political chameleon, and thus on 8 January 1972, when Sheikh Mujibur Rahman was freed to fly to London from Rawalpindi to return to a free Bangladesh, he was seen off by Z.A. Bhutto (the new leader of a truncated Pakistan), to be escorted by an Indian team back to Dacca, to take over as the first leader of Bangladesh. But India's gains of this stunning military victory were squandered with its inability to extract anything more than a promise from Z.A. Bhutto to settle the long standing dispute over Kashmir, in a meeting with Mrs Gandhi in Simla in the summer of 1972. The Simla Accord failed to achieve what India's leadership wanted; that, however, is the subject of another study. But how the 1971 war unfolded is the subject of *War Despatches 1971*, a collection of essays by the gallant officers of the Indian armed forces from the 28 NDA, 37 IMA and 21 Tech course of the three Services, who were commissioned on 15 June 1966. They were all young warriors in the service bracket of 5–6 years, but they saw it all and often went beyond the call of duty. We must salute them for giving India its finest moment since Independence. Their essays will not only add to the limited literature on the War of 1971, but will inspire the coming generations of warriors.

Maroof Raza is a former Indian Army officer, educated in India and the UK. A commentator on military and security issues, he is now the Consulting Editor (Strategic Affairs) of Times Television Network in India, on which he appears and hosts the weekend strategic affairs television show 'Latitude' (Times Now). He presently hosts 'The Defenders' on Sansad TV. He lectures on a range of security issues in India and abroad, has co-authored *Kashmir's Untold Story: Declassified* (published by Bloomsbury in 2019), and *Contested Lands: India, China and the Boundary Dispute* (published recently by Westland/Amazon.com).

Background to the Conflict
An Insider's View

Major Pradeep Sharma

Most storms gather in hours, some in a day or two. The one that led to the War of 1971 had been brewing for over two decades. When Pakistan emerged as a nation in 1947, its two regions, the East and West, were split along cultural, geographical and linguistic lines. The people in East Pakistan, being part of erstwhile East Bengal, were like those in West Bengal, both culturally and linguistically, and quite different from their countrymen in West Pakistan. The Bengali-speaking majority of East Pakistan turned violent when Urdu was made the sole national language of Pakistan, sparking huge protests. The students at Dhaka University and other colleges organised a general strike on 11 March 1948. Public meetings and rallies were banned. In 1952, when Prime Minister Khwaja Nazimuddin declared in Dhaka that 'Urdu will be the State language', students of Dhaka University revolted and held a massive demonstration against the announcement. The police and paramilitary forces resorted to the use of brutal force and killed six students. The deaths sparked widespread civil unrest led by the Awami Muslim League. After years of conflict, the central Pakistani Government relented and granted official status to the Bengali language in 1956.

Discriminatory Policies against East Pakistan

It would seem that the West Pakistanis had done just about everything they could to stoke animosity in their Eastern Wing instead of trying to assuage feelings of alienation. The problems between the Western and Eastern wings of Pakistan were deep-rooted—physical separation, different languages and lack of trust. The popular joke in the subcontinent was that the two wings were separated by a thousand miles but united by only three things—Islam, English, and the Pakistan International Airlines. The long-standing discriminatory and exploitative policies led to a sense of alienation. A feeling of victimisation permeated due to disparity in Bengali representation in civil services, defence forces and managerial positions. To make matters worse, the West Pakistanis scorned the Bengali 'Bingo' as weak and unfit for soldierly duties. Even the Urdu-speaking Biharis did not merge with the Bengalis, instead maintaining closer relationships with the West Pakistanis.

The Six-point Proposal

After the defeat of Pakistan in the War of 1965, the general feeling in East Pakistan was that they had been left at the mercy of India with only one infantry division protecting East Pakistan. Fearing that the eastern half of Pakistan was getting alienated, opposition leaders in West Pakistan called for a national conference on 6 February 1966. Sheikh Mujibur Rahman (Mujib), along with some members of the Awami League (AL), reached Lahore to attend the conference. The next day, Mujib placed a Six-point Proposal before the conference. The proposal was rejected, and Mujib was identified as a separatist.

This led to Mujib boycotting the conference.

On 21 February, the Six-point Proposal was unanimously re-affirmed by AL in Dhaka. It was envisaged that the Constitution should provide for a Federation of Pakistan with the Federal Government dealing with only defence and foreign affairs, the residual subjects being vested in the federal states. It also demanded two distinct freely convertible currencies, adding that if this was not feasible then there should be one currency, with effective constitutional provisions, to stop the flight of capital from East to West Pakistan. The proposal also laid down the demand for two separate accounts for the foreign exchange earnings, the provision for both wings to establish trade links with foreign countries, and the power of taxation and revenue collection to be vested in the federal units which would provide a share of these to the Federal Government. It further proposed that East Pakistan should have a separate military or paramilitary force and that the naval headquarters should be based in East Pakistan.

Agartala Conspiracy

Another trigger was the Agartala Conspiracy Case—a sedition case foisted on Mujib and other leaders of AL by the Government of Pakistan in 1968. This resulted in protests, the upsurge and hostility, which forced Ayub Khan to withdraw the sedition case. When Mujibur Rehman returned from West Pakistan to Dhaka after a prolonged stay in jail, he was accorded a hero's welcome, and thereafter anointed with the endearing salutation of *Bangabandhu*. The upsurge contributed to the increasing Bengali nationalism. In 1969, political unrest, agitations and General Ayub's health compelled him to ask General Yahya Khan, the Chief of Army Staff (COAS) to quell the unrest. General Yahya insisted that Ayub abrogate the Constitution and impose martial law. While the world and media believed that General Ayub had handed over power, in reality, General Yahya had conducted a 'silent coup'.

Revised Constitution

In March 1970, General Yahya announced national and provincial elections under the Legal Framework Order. This stipulated the principles to be honoured under the new Constitution, which would provide fundamental rights to citizens, an independent judiciary, provincial autonomy, and the removal of economic disparities between the two wings. The Constitution would stipulate an Islamic Republic under which laws repugnant to the Quran and the Sunnah would not be admissible. The other major change was the removal of the Principle of Parity between the two wings by introducing universal adult franchise which favoured the Bengalis of East Pakistan.

Impact of Cyclone Bhola

In the 12 months leading up to the liberation and birth of Bangladesh, several other events took place, that hastened the complete disaffection of the population in the East. On 11 November 1970, cyclone Bhola lashed East Pakistan. The gales shrieked at 150 miles per hour followed by monstrous tidal waves of over 20 feet. Death and devastation were widespread.

As per some estimates, the lives of over two lakh people ended in a watery grave. Total neglect by the West Pakistani military junta became the final straw for an emotional break. The AL converted this widespread negative disposition into a mass movement. The clash had virtually become 'civilian vs military', 'Bengali vs West Pakistani', 'popular democracy vs military dictatorship', 'non-violent vs violent'. While the East was immersed in fighting death, disease, epidemic, and starvation, the West wing was toasting the emergence of Zulfiqar Ali Bhutto.

Elections and Aftermath

General elections were held in Pakistan on 7 December 1970 to elect members of the National Assembly. It was the first general elections in the 23 years since the independence of Pakistan, based on the principle of universal adult franchise. Voting took place in 300 constituencies, of which 162 were in East Pakistan and 138 in West Pakistan. The result was a victory for the AL, which won an absolute majority of 160 seats, all of which were in East Pakistan; the Pakistan People's Party (PPP) of Bhutto won only 81 seats, all of which were in West Pakistan. In the provincial elections held ten days later, the AL again dominated in East Pakistan, while PPP was the largest party only in Punjab and Sindh. Other parties emerged victorious in the sparsely populated provinces of Northwest Frontier and Balochistan. The National Assembly was not inaugurated initially as President Yahya Khan and the PPP Chairman, Bhutto, conspired to exclude East Pakistanis from the federal government. As efforts at reaching a compromise between the PPP and AL failed, the continued delay in inauguration began to cause increasing unrest in East Pakistan. The then leaders of Pakistan, all from West Pakistan (and PPP), strongly opposed the idea of a government led by anyone from East Pakistan. Bhutto uttered his infamous phrase, '*Idhar hum, udhar tum*' (We rule here, you rule there), thus verbally dividing Pakistan for the first time. The Assembly elected in 1970–1971 was thus never convened.

A Belligerent Pakistan: Operation Searchlight and Operation Barisal

At a conference in February 1971, the then President of Pakistan, General Yahya Khan is alleged to have remarked on the disaffected Bengali majority in East Pakistan, 'Kill three million of them and the rest will eat out of our hands.' The (West) Pakistani military leaders had neither anticipated a prolonged Bengali resistance, nor had they foreseen what later became the inevitable intervention by the Indian military. Mujib was arrested on the night of 25/26 March 1971 (as quoted in Radio Pakistan's news on 29 March 1971) and taken to West Pakistan. Operation Searchlight was launched by the Pakistan Army in the East by General Tikka Khan. This was an overt attempt to kill the intellectual elite and crush Bengali nationalism. This resulted in mass killings as it ensnared the families of those targeted. The genocide launched by the Army led to the rape of half a million women and girls, while millions escaped the fury of the Army by seeking refuge in India. The military displayed stark cruelty, more merciless than the Jallianwala Bagh massacre. Tales of the Pakistani Army asking the Bengalis to lift their lungi to display circumcision or demanding recitation of Muslim prayers, marking the houses of Hindus with 'H', or forcing them to wear a black cloth to identify themselves as Hindus became very common. These systematic acts of violence and bloodshed were aimed at eliminating the core of future resistance. Imagine a Pakistani General asking his troops 'How many Bengalis have you shot today?'

Another one, Operation Barisal, was aimed at exterminating a concentration of activists and sympathisers of independence, utilising naval assets and bombardment. Barisal was situated in the delta of the Padma and Yamuna rivers, allowing larger naval vessels to approach close enough so they could bombard civilian targets onshore.

Exodus of Refugees

Refugees began arriving in huge numbers to India and were housed in tents, locally made shelters or school buildings. The presence of such a huge number of foreigners, who in many places outnumbered the local population, was not sustainable either financially or administratively. For instance, the total number of refugees was almost equal to the population of Assam and Tripura in that year, two of the states most affected by the refugee influx. It also constituted a law-and-order nightmare. Large outbreaks of diseases like cholera due to the unhygienic conditions in crowded camps posed a huge risk to the health of the refugees and the local population. It was impossible to contemplate a permanent resettlement of the refugees within India in the already densely populated areas of West Bengal, Assam or Tripura which bordered East Pakistan. In 1971, an estimated 10 million refugees crossed the border from East Pakistan into India. This movement of people forms the largest single displacement of refugees in the second half of the 20th century. The magnitude of this was staggering.

While visiting Barasat, a city located on the outskirts of Calcutta, West Bengal, Sydney Schanberg, a journalist with the *New York Times*, described the town as a 'swarm' with refugees so thick in the streets that cars can only inch through.' The refugees seemed to be everywhere—sitting on the streets, crouching on doorsteps, sleeping on porches, occupying empty buildings, and cooking in the fields. They attempted to build lean-tos only to have the monsoon rains rip them apart.

Mukti Bahini

On 26 March 1971, Major Ziaur Rahman declared the independence of Bangladesh on behalf of Sheikh Mujibur Rahman. In April, the exiled AL leaders formed a government-in-exile in Baidyanathtala of Meherpur (adjoining the Krishnanagar and Murshidabad areas of West Bengal, India). Some East Pakistan Rifles and Bengali officers in Pakistan's Armed forces joined the rebellion after taking refuge in different parts of India under the leadership of retired Colonel M.A.G. Osmani. With continuing oppression and the Pakistan Army behaving like an invading foreign army, the number of refugees and potential insurgents to take them on kept swelling rapidly. The Mukti

Bahini sought sanctuaries along and close to the Indo-East Pakistan border. They established camps, recruited large numbers of educated youth (mainly Muslims but also including many Hindus who had escaped from the campaign of 'elitocide' that occurred on 25 March 1971). Organised, trained and armed at these camps, they slowly gained operational experience. The Mukti Bahini was trained in approximately 100 reception centres in West Bengal, Bihar, Tripura, and Meghalaya (all regions in India, surrounding Bangladesh) and were given training on tactics and the use of arms and explosives, bolstered by weaponry supplied from India. It was naturally difficult to train a cohesive force properly within such a short period. Mukti Bahini's contribution to victory was strategically decisive in at least four ways. First, their attacks broke Pakistan Army's morale. Second, the Mukti Bahini forced the Pakistanis to weaken their positions by spreading their forces to defend towns and cities thinly over the country. Third, they largely confined the Pakistanis to their bases, disrupting supply lines. Finally, they made the Pakistani army blind—the army was devoid of a critical ingredient of battlefield success, that is, information of what was happening around them.

Response from International Community

World opinion appeared unwilling and unable to call on Pakistan to stop its oppression and genocide in East Pakistan. Nor was help made available to India to cater to the sudden influx of over 10 million refugees or any assistance given to ensure their quick repatriation back to East Pakistan. The US and Western European countries were firmly allied with Pakistan not only due to the North Atlantic Treaty Organisation (NATO) and other agreements and alliances, but also because the US was secretly engaged in an outreach to China with Pakistan's aid. Henry Kissinger's secret trip to Beijing took place in July 1971. Kissinger, Nixon's National Security Advisor, flew to

Beijing from Pakistan. This gave Pakistan added encouragement and support to continue its campaign of crackdown and genocide in East Pakistan. The mood in Pakistan had also turned increasingly jingoistic and militaristic against East Pakistan and India when the Pakistani news media reported the complexity of the situation in the East. However, the reactions from Pakistan's news media pundits were mixed. By the end of September 1971, a propaganda campaign, possibly orchestrated by elements within the Government of Pakistan, resulted in stickers endorsing Crush India becoming a standard feature on the rear windows of vehicles in Rawalpindi, Islamabad and Lahore. This soon spread to the rest of West Pakistan as well. By October, other stickers appeared, proclaiming Hang the Traitor in an apparent reference to Mujib. By the first week of December, the conservative print media outlets in the country had published jihad related materials to boost recruitment into the military.

The Indian Strategy

India had to cater to widely different requirements. These included the following:

* Refugees would need to be repatriated without delay, implying that operations and a war-like situation would need to be wide-ranging, short, and sharp.
* Operations in East and West Pakistan would be entirely different—in the East, the entire country would need to be traversed until the defenders' resolve was broken and a Bangladeshi government rapidly installed, whereas, in the West, operations would be defensive with restricted local offensives.

A multi-pronged strategy, in all probability, evolved around October 1971. International support for India, particularly from the western countries, was not forthcoming. A looming threat from China in the North and a Pakistani Army poised on the West also forced a wait, watch and prepare approach. The Treaty of Friendship with the USSR was a masterstroke. The non-aligned countries did not support India's cause in the United Nations. Under the influence of USA and some western powers, the Middle Eastern countries provided military support to Pakistan. The Indian decision to assist the Mukti Bahini was taken in April. However, they would be available for operations much later. It was, thus, decided to launch the offensive post-monsoon. No one knew the war eventually would last all of a fortnight. As it turned out, things fell into place bit by bit, allowing a two-week blitzkrieg, resulting in the surrender of some 93,000 soldiers of the Pakistani Army and give birth to a new nation—Bangladesh. This then was the gathering storm that presaged the full-scale war in December 1971. Caught up in a self-created hysteria, Pakistan took a cue from the Israelis and attempted pre-emptive strikes on 3 December 1971. Aimed at decimating the prowess of the Indian Air Force, this triggered open hostilities and the war.

Major Pradeep Sharma (Retired) was commissioned into the Madras Sappers. Having served for 11 years, he was posted in Car Nicobar, Poona, Assam, Delhi and Barrackpore, Tripura / Bangladesh. Feeling the strong need to augment his education, he hung his uniform in August 1977. Civvy street and business gave him the chance to travel around the world over a dozen times, besides immersing him in its mores. He lives in Gurgaon with his wife, Neelam.

II
Eastern Theatre

The Burinda Bash

Brigadier Balram Singh Mehta

Following the destruction of Pakistan's 3 (Independent) Armoured Squadron at Garibpur on 21–22 November 1971, the successful hard-fought combat group from the Battle of Burinda[1] opened windows of opportunity for us to capture Dhaka. That this opportunity went unexploited is another story of intriguing possibilities and what ifs awaiting narration.

The lay reader is likely to be astonished by the peppy title of this article and cannot be blamed for his unfamiliarity. This is because, for 50 years now, a flood of brave heart stories about the Western front in the Indo-Pak War of 1971 have invaded the sensitivities of readers across India and the world at large, almost blocking out the war's Eastern front and its stories of exceptional grit, courage, sacrifice and understated achievement. At the end of that war, the general opinion was that, whereas the Western front had yielded a 'no victor no vanquished' status, on the Eastern front, India stunned the world

[1] A hamlet in the Jessore district of Khulna Division, Bangladesh

by delivering in a mere 13 days, a brave new nation, Bangladesh, with over 93,000 Pakistani prisoners of war, and revival of manoeuvre as opposed to attrition-based warfighting. This was a no-holds-barred directive style of command and control as opposed to the vintage, hierarchical style exhibited by us on the Western front. The untrammelled success of the Eastern front had broken Pakistan politically and militarily. However, the 13-day war is a bit of hype and oversell, as the Garibpur battle happened on 21 November 1971 and the one at Burinda a few days later. We did not count it as war since neither nation had formally declared it. Veterans of the Eastern front lost out as the recognition that came their way came decades later, after the pretence of not acknowledging commencement of hostilities before the war's formal declaration was set aside a few years ago. So, here is a war the story beyond the Garibpur carnage of Pakistan's armoured strength that might now command the focused attention of the lay reader. To get the Burinda Bash right, one first needs to understand the background setting.

Jessore district, now part of the Khulna division, once belonged to the ancient kingdom of Banga Janapada, going back to the hoary Vedic period. However, with the vicissitudes of time, the district was eventually transferred, in 1765, to the East India Company along with the rest of Bengal, the British administration being firmly established in Jessore District by 1781.

Jessore district topographically forms the central portion of the delta between the Hoogly, the united Ganges, and the Brahmaputra. It is a vast alluvial plain intersected by rivers and watercourses which, in the southern portion where Burinda hamlet is located, has large marshes. The northern part is heavily populated, prosperous, and has extensive groves of date palms. In the central portion, the population is sparse, the only part suitable for dwellings being the elevated land on the banks of rivers. The principal rivers are the Madhumati (which forms the eastern boundary of the district), with its tributaries the Nabaganga, Chitra and Bhairab, as well as the Kumar, Kabadak (which we crossed to attack Garibpur), Katki, Harihar, Bhadra and Atharabanka. The tide from the southern port city of Khulna travels up to 65 km north to reach Jessore town, which is the centre for sugar manufacturing from date palms. In 1947, Jessore was divided between India and East Pakistan. Except for the Bangaon and Gaighata thanas[2], which merged into India, Jessore district became part of East Pakistan. Bengali soldiers stationed at the Jessore cantonment mutinied against the Pakistan Army on 29 March 1971, a few days after the Pakistani genocide began. Three hundred soldiers were killed, while the Bangla rebels killed 50 West Pakistani soldiers. On 6 December 1971, Jessore became the first district of Bengal to be liberated from Pakistani forces. This was the direct fallout of the Burinda Bash, but more of this a bit later.

Jessore was the location of the Pakistani HQ 9 Infantry Division and its 107 Infantry Brigade; its cantonment housing these formations and the airport protected by permanent defences and a ditch. This key communication hub had three approaches leading to it from the Indian side. Pakistan's competent 107 Infantry Brigade commander, Brigadier Mohd Hayat, was tasked to deny all three approaches by occupying strong, fortified strong points/delaying positions astride each based on an approximate battalion strength. These troops were later expected to fall back after imposing maximum attrition to fight the coordinated battle to defend Jessore city and cantonment. The Burinda approach was the western one, the Jhikargacha approach to Jessore was the south-western one, and the north-western one was the Chowgacha approach. Each, or a major part thereof, was defended by a Pakistani battalion. Accordingly, our allotment of formations was 32 Infantry Brigade for Jhikargacha, 42 Infantry

[2] Police station

Brigade for Chowgacha, and 350 Infantry Brigade and my squadron for the Burinda approach.

Burinda, in Jessore District, is 148 km southwest of Dhaka. In 1971, the banana and bamboo enclosed hamlet of 1,000-odd inhabitants that was scattered with ponds, narrow mud lanes, and dense foliage saw the 15-feet high bunds that protected the hamlet's central water body get defence works integrated into them. The mud-thatched huts were spread over 1,000 m by 800 m in an essentially marshy area. This profile gave it substantial defensive potential. The 107 Infantry Brigade had developed Burinda as a strong point; a Vital Point (VP) occupied by a company plus of Pakistan's 12 PUNJAB[3] to deny the western approach into Jessore city, 8 km away. The balance battalion was deployed around the Burinda VP.

During the tank versus tank battle at Garibpur, on 21 November 1971, 'C' Squadron 45 CAVALRY had destroyed 14 counterattacking Chaffee tanks of Pakistan's 3 (Independent) Armoured Squadron for the loss of two of its PT-76 tanks. As a replacement, the squadron was allotted three T-55 medium 45-Ton tanks as the Army had not catered for any PT-76 war reserves. These tank crews underwent quickfire conversion, training in driving, radio, and gunnery inside East Pakistan. As the drivers and operators gained confidence, the gunners were itching to fire a few rounds of the 100 mm gun. This critical need was met by innovative 'battle zeroing'—aligning the gunner's sight with the axis of the gun barrel—thus circumventing the need to access field firing ranges through convoluted staff procedures. Within 72 hours, the T-55 tank troop was proactively made battle-worthy before Pakistan declared war on 3 December 1971.

Our Garibpur success in tank versus tank battle and the quick conversion and induction of a 45-Ton T-55 medium tank troop into an amphibious 14-ton PT-76 tank regiment had spread like wildfire within the corps zone. The warm reception accorded to tank crews of

---

[3] 12th Battalion, The Punjab Regiment

'C' Squadron 45 CAVALRY placed under command HQ 350 Infantry Brigade for the capture of Burinda added to my troop's sense of pride and achievement. Burinda, a tough nut to crack and well-sited and organised for all-around defence, had taken a heavy toll on us. 1 J&K Rifles, while attempting to take Burinda on the night of 28/29 November, had suffered 3 junior commissioned officers (JCOs) and 16 other ranks (ORs) killed-in-action (KIA) and 50 ORs wounded. Thereafter, the famous Saragarhi Paltan, 4 SIKH[4], attacked Burinda, this time as a combat group on 30 November/1 December, supported by the entire divisional artillery and their mortars and my reinforced squadron. We had our task cut out for sure.

Burinda lay on the shortest of the three axes to Jessore, the division objective in the Corps Phase I, so there was palpable excitement and anticipation. Taking Burinda had become the key to taking Jessore in the minds of the military hierarchy. After an operational briefing from the commander of 350 Infantry Brigade, Brigadier B.S. Sandhu, I joined the 4 SIKH Operations Group while our tank crews married up with the infantry companies. The immediate task set by the commanding officer (CO) was to launch a preliminary operation to occupy an enemy section, thus holding the high ground and dominating a minefield that obstructed our advance.

Two tank troops were tasked to provide fire support and shoot in the infantry company the same evening. A quick-fire plan was prepared, the company launched, and success was reported. The 'D' Squadron's company commander received a big *shabash* as reports of enemy withdrawing came in. The engineers (Sappers) commenced clearing mines for safe lanes for the infantry and tanks. The infantry safe lanes were reported clear. It was when the Sappers were clearing the far more extensive tank lanes when the just-lauded assaulting infantry company commander reported enemy building up for a counterattack. His frantic calls for tank assistance drove the battalion second-in-command (2IC), an ex-cavalry officer, to arbitrarily order

[4] 4th Battalion, The Sikh Regiment

my tanks to negotiate the uncleared minefield. I passed a curt radio message to the troop leader, Risaldar Limbu, to freeze movement and await my orders. The 2IC snarled that I had no right to countermand orders issued by the CO. I had to remind him firmly that the reserve company, which was to have launched through the cleared infantry lanes, hadn't done so. With his aghast adjutant listening in, I advised him that orders for tanks would be passed through me, their designated commander. Unlike deeply ingrained infantry training based on unquestioned compliance, tank commanders flourished in an environment where questioning an order didn't amount to insubordination but contributed to operational efficiency.

Disregarding the command-and-control spat, I ensured, through Risaldar Limbu and a joint on-ground tank-sapper, to check that the tank lane was clear. Induction of tanks speedily followed; the fear of a Pakistani riposte being put to rest. That the infantry CO was offended by my tactically sound action was an issue that sadly surfaced when my CO and the general officer commanding (GOC) arrived to validate the final Burinda attack plan the next day.

The capture of Burinda had become a prestige issue. The Pakistani defences were sited to tackle all enemy approaches with mines, coordinated with interlocked medium machine gun (MMG) fire hinged around a high embankment enclosed water body stretching 400 metres in cross-section. The absence of cover over the last 100 yards made the task of capture even more difficult, as also the ability of troops to advance and finally charge through a barrage of accurate MMG and air burst artillery fire. With most shells exploding in the water body, air strafing and bombing had to be specially tailored given earlier failures. The fire plan was supplemented and now included a dozen air sorties and carpet bombing of the objective to stun the enemy. For the final close support, my troop of the T-55 tanks would shoot in the infantry. The PT-76 Squadron would establish a roadblock in Phase II to prevent enemy withdrawal and thus cause psychological dislocation.

My experience of infantry attack plans was that they followed a standard template of phased attacks by a single company in assault mode with another company in reserve for each phase. This one was no different. Phase I had been launched one hour before, last light, immediately after pre-bombardment. The success of Phase I was tentative. The determined enemy followed soon after with a counterattack. The assaulting 'B' company was reporting heavy casualties. The CO took a command decision and preponed the launch of Phase II, planned for launch later that night. I left the battalion command post, dashing to my tank harbour, 600 metre away, through murderous artillery shelling. The shrill whine of the shells helped determine the likely direction and the point of the explosion. Survival instinct guided me, and my radio operator went to dive for cover. We thus cheated death, including lethal splinter ricochets from two tree bursts. In one lucky escape, I was hit by splinters while cocooned in a shallow ground depression; their energy to injure fortunately was spent before they tore through my black overalls. This experience of escape and evasion from lethal splinters and steel debris is a nightmare that torments me to date. I feel that God sat on my right shoulder.

My operational review noted the precarious situation in which the infantry had landed itself, necessitating preponement. The mine obstacle was carefully described again by the Sapper officer, Lieutenant Purshottam. The tank commanders had assembled for the briefing. My tank crews knew from monitored net radio messages all about the critical situation in which the infantry company had placed itself, necessitating preponement of attack by two hours. It was crucial to brief them again about the extent of the minefield described by Lieutenant Purshottam and carefully follow the outer periphery of the tree line. I would lead the tank column with the engineer officer and a 'C' Company platoon commander travelling on my tank for better coordination to cut off the enemy withdrawal route. Our ability to do this without alerting the enemy was germane to the overall operational success.

The Capture of Burinda

It was near dusk when the Phase II roadblock establishment commenced. With the infantry platoon riding piggyback, the tank column negotiated the marshy area using a bullock cart track through it, with the infantry securing a narrow log bridge. My skilled driver was the first to cross the bridge, with his 14-ton tank, its tracks overhanging by inches across the rickety bridge. Ultimately, all my tanks crossed except the last, Dafadar Ishwar's, which slid off and was later recovered. In the fading, false light before darkness, a rocket-launcher opened fire but was blown up by my gunner, Harish Chandra, with his first round. A sharp firefight followed, which we dominated although the tank behind me appeared to have got hit, a black puff of smoke rising from below the hull, but more on this supposition later. My gunner had spotted a few bunkers and engaged it with high explosive (HE) and MMG fire, forcing an enemy withdrawal. A message from the infantry CO that my tanks hadn't reached his beleaguered 'B' company commander made me get him to speak to his platoon commander and sapper, Lieutenant Purshottam. That put an end to future pesky calls from the CO. Navigating in enemy territory is hazardous in any terrain but negotiating a Bengali village in East Pakistan takes the cake. Thick with lush greenery and water bodies, the main village pond and smaller ponds outside each homestead, there could be rocket launchers or MMG's anywhere. Added to this were the bamboo clusters that lined the narrow winding lanes and mud huts, the infantry guiding us through with repeated reversal of the tanks to crawl along the tenuous lanes. The bamboo whipped back like high-strung bows as tanks pushed past them, hitting the crews and infantrymen who were holding on to safety ropes while the tank savagely rolled and pitched as it moved over water channels, steep bunds, making the tank ride a convulsive experience. One such savage sweepback shattered the cupola hinge and hit my nose, a few teeth falling out. Bleeding and in pain, I focused on reaching the roadblock behind enemy deployment and did ultimately make it. Duggal, the company commander, had done a laudable job despite suffering fresh casualties as the enemy artillery had started firing airbursts. The infantry platoon, riding piggyback, had by now jumped off to secure the roadblock site. The noise of the tank engine, the gun, and the MMG fire was enough for the enemy to withdraw in gathering darkness under cover of murderous airburst fire. I had moved over to the driver's seat, unable to stand on my legs. The combination of a lacerated nose, two displaced teeth, cut lips, blood loss and pain, made me delirious, which my compulsive smoking did not ease. I had barely handed over responsibility to Captain Saighal, the Forward Observation Officer (FOO), as the green flare fired from a (Verey light) pistol announced the success of Phase II. The short catnap revived me as I straightened up to be greeted by Shibe Lal, the operator, to answer an incoming call from CO 4 SIKH.

Unable to get through to the tank troops on the radio, Duggal helped by giving me a Mukti Bahini guide who had accompanied his company. He helped me retrace my steps to track my tanks under the ambient moonlight. As we advanced line ahead, following my tank tracks was the only logical course. Barely a kilometre away, the silhouette of a tank loomed and then another, with no signs of life or activity and with tank guns at unnatural angles. I was within shouting distance, worried, angry, and tense. I had barely taken a few steps off the tank track when the guide held my overcoat firmly from behind, whispering an urgent warning. He was pointing to regularly excavated mounds of earth on one of whom I would have stepped.

It was an anti-tank mine wired with an anti-personnel mine! I had gotten that close to instantaneous death or grievous loss of limb or eyesight. Had the anti-tank mine blasted under the tank, the vehicle would have been destroyed with death or serious crew injury. I thank the Lord that my tank had negotiated 800 metres of this minefield of Density 1 (kill probability 66%). I realised that we had been protected by the Almighty who had sent this life-saving guide too. Indeed, it had been a very close shave!

We kept moving past my two disabled tanks, now back onto my tank track, my worry levels heightened by my rapidly depleting strength due to exhaustion and dehydration, causing dizziness, but walk we did. Added to this was another hulk in the form of a chilly early morning. My men and I were relieved to find out that there were no deaths in the mine-blasted tanks. A serious head concussion had occurred to the troop leader, Chakraborthy, a tall, steely soccer and basketball player, who remained operational with grit and aspirins, and refused evacuation. He had set standards for the regiment to follow. My interaction with my men, despite my joy, made me break out in cold sweat, and unable to stand, I slid down against the tank bogey wheel. One of the tank crew members offered a water bottle, which poured life back into me as I felt the sweat on my brow gradually evaporating and the pulse returning to a normal rhythm. Refusing evacuation, I became strong enough to get up once again and take charge of my responsibilities. Burinda had been taken but at a cost. My losses were two tanks blown up by mines and one damaged by a rocket launcher. Also, one tank driver, Acting Lance Dafadar (ALD) Biswas, had been killed, and four men were wounded—two seriously. The Pakistanis fought bravely from well-coordinated defences, but we outfought them, forcing their withdrawal. The battalion had fought bravely and bore heavy casualties doing so but emerged triumphant, assisted by my tank squadron. The immediate task was to move the serviceable tanks through the minefield to the

'B' Infantry company location and secure it against a counterattack. I instructed the T-55 tanks to position themselves at the mouth of the minefield so that they could dominate the areas ahead and deny the enemy a pot shot at my disabled tanks. My good friend and knight in shining armour, the civilian guide, was still with me to guide me back to my waiting crews. We had barely advanced when a chill went through my heart—an automatic weapon had cocked, and a loud voice had challenged us: '*Tham! Kaun aata hai? Haath upar. Pehchan ke liye aage barh! Aaj ka password?*' (Halt! Who is there? Hands up. Advance for identification. What's today's password?)

Hearing '*load jaldi kareen*' (load quickly) in Punjabi, I yelled at the two dimly silhouetted Sikh soldiers that we were friends. '*Oye, main sadde risale da afsar haan!*' Bereft of the password, we were close to getting shot till the Sikh NCO decided to hold fire and ask us to advance. That is when I let fly with the choicest Punjabi expletives, including his CO's and 2IC's names. '*Ehe bada tej lagdae minu,*' said the startled NCO (this guy is a smart cookie) as he finally stood down and said, '*Sat Sri Akal Saabji*' with a wry grin. This time my move forward was with a Sikh guide escorting us to prevent further mishaps. It was evident that the only safe lane across the minefield was the one my tank tracks had created. A guide was to be positioned on each tank track and ordered to use a torch to illuminate the track and help the driver keep the correct alignment. The tank commander was to sit near the driver's hatch to keep a watch on the track and guide the driver from drifting away by exercising control until the tank had crossed the minefield. Precision driving and tight control comprised the key to safety and success. The ability of the driver was most crucial to the success of the operation. The most experienced driver was to take charge. That was easier said than done because tank crews, particularly drivers, tend to get deeply attached to their vehicles and do not appreciate somebody else taking charge of their tank, especially in difficult situations.

That was a deliberate exercise where ensuring vehicle and men's safety, and not speed, was the overriding necessity, and I set the stage with professional acumen. Dafadar Ramnath's tank was in the lead, followed by Lieutenant Narain's. After some start-up glitches between the driver, track guides, and tank commander, we started the 800-metre-move across the minefield in a tightly controlled manner. I was quietly satisfied with the leading tank safely across and Lieutenant Narain within 100 metres of crossing. My testing times were, however, not over. Saighal had it conveyed to me that my roadblock tank while being re-positioned, had slid into a marsh and needed expert recovery. Assuming the minefield crossing to be well under control, I left Narain in charge, intending to oversee my tank's recovery. While tired, cold, and exhausted, Narain handed over guidance to his NCO to get cosy inside the tank, dozing off cocooned in a blanket.

In his own words, the mine explosion found him flung against the turret roof and in excruciating pain. He was paralysed and found the tank's hull bottom with a two-foot hole ripped by the exploding anti-tank mine. His effort to find a comfortable sleeping posture ironically saved his life as the main axis of the blast escaped him. He was rushed to the Advanced Dressing Station[5], but the tank had been ripped apart with two crew members and a guide injured.

Burinda was a hard nut to crack. Nevertheless, it became a symbol of the Pakistanis' gumption to fight against heavy odds, not witnessed elsewhere in East Pakistan during the 1971 War. 4 SIKH cleared Burinda on 6 December, after suffering 62 casualties—2 JCOs and 12 ORs killed, and 2 JCOs, 44 ORs and 2 NCsE (non-combatants enrolled) wounded. Besides, 1 OR each of 45 CAVALRY and 96 Field Company were killed; 1 officer, 1 JCO and 3 ORs of 45 CAVALRY and 1 OR of 96 Field Company wounded. This loss makes one wonder as to why so much hype was created over Burinda, and towards what

---

[5] First aid is given to casualties here.

end? The answer can be found in this quote: 'It may be worthwhile to remember that two battalions had been tasked for the capture of Burinda. They had made a concerted bid and sustained losses, as had the affiliated troops. That gives us a truthful picture of military incompetence and scant regard for the loss of lives to achieve glory' (Quoted from *Surrender at Dacca* by Lieutenant General J.F.R. Jacob, p.73). This extract by the redoubtable Lieutenant General J.F.R. Jacob, who planned and helped execute the Bangladesh War from its beginning to its victorious end, is an open indictment of the quality of higher-level planning, execution and leadership during the Battle of Burinda and that too from an unimpeachable source.

I find a quote from Shakespeare's famous play, *King Lear*, worth quoting here because it highlights the relevance of Lieutenant General J.F.R. Jacob's sarcasm:

'As flies to wanton boys are we to the Gods;
They kill us for their sport.'

Gloucester speaks these despairing words as he wanders on the heath after being blinded by Cornwall and Regan (4.1.37–38). Gloucester's philosophical musing here offers an outlook of stark despair: he suggests that there is no order—or at least no good order—in the universe. That man is incapable of imposing his moral ideas upon the harsh and inflexible laws of the world. Instead of divine justice, there is only the sport of vicious, inscrutable Gods—the good die along with the wicked, and no reason is offered for the reasons for such sacrifice. These thoughts were floating in my mind while sliding off my tank to stretch out on the sun-drenched battlefield. In the background, I could hear artillery guns blazing away while the planes dropped their payloads over the designated targets, in support of trustworthy devout, infantrymen charging into the jaws of death, with a regimental war cry on their lips, not knowing 'for whom the bells toll'. 9 Infantry Division was now ready to launch their attack for the capture of Jessore. It was to be an unnecessary attack as Jessore was found empty, the enemy having departed for Khulna Port city, 65 km away.

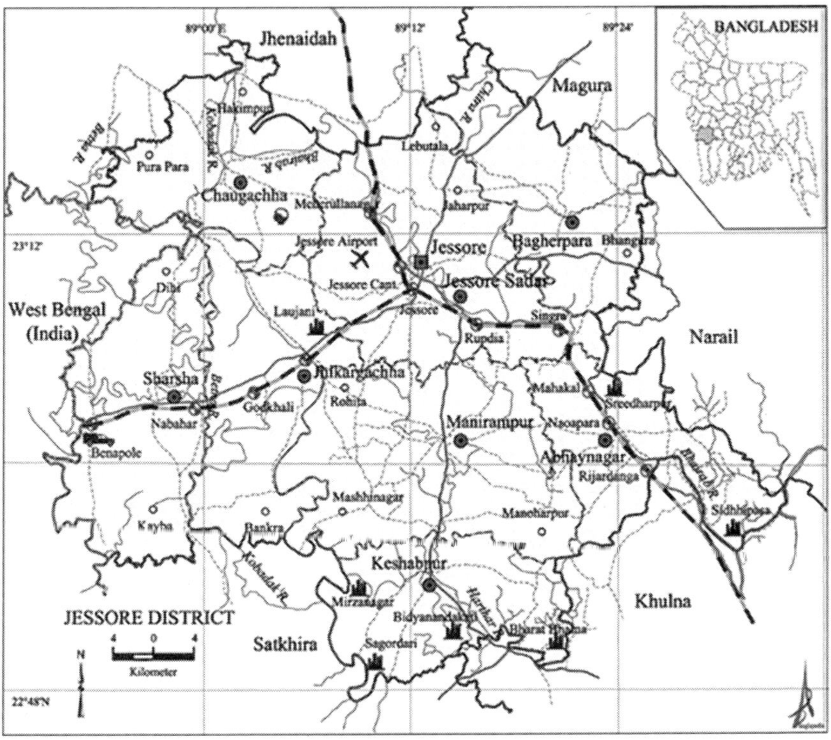

Map of Jessore district

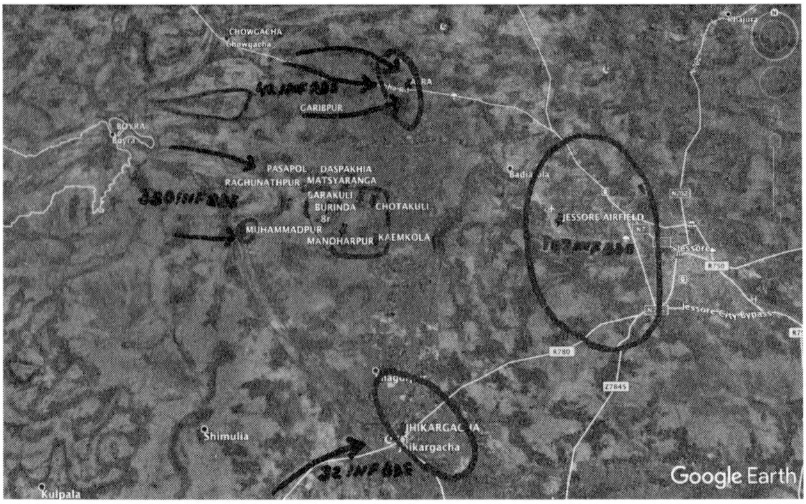

The three approaches to Jessore with the Burinda axis in the centre

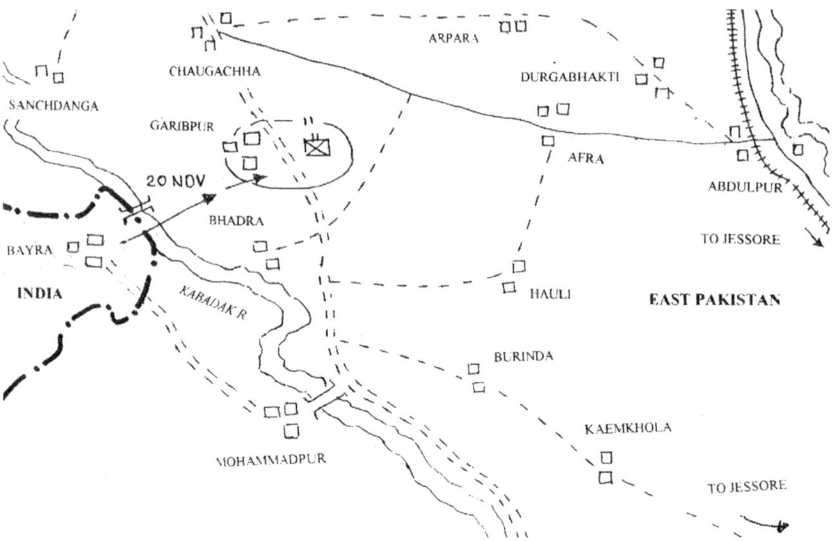

The Garibpur-Burinda linkage

Brigadier Balram Singh Mehta (Retired) was commissioned into 45 CAVALRY in June 1966. During the 1971 Indo-Pak war, he was pitched into command of the squadron amid tank-versus-tank battle as the youngest squadron commander. He has recently authored a book, *The Burning Chaffees*, providing a first-hand account of a tank battle, which has inspired a full-length war movie Pippa by Ronnie Screwvala and Siddharth Roy Kapur, scheduled for release in 2021. Post premature retirement in 1998, he has served with the Government of Gujarat, besides functioning as the vice-chancellor of two universities. He is an advisor to a Gujarat-based NGO looking after martyrs' families and dependents and a consultant to Hare Krishna Exports Private Limited in Surat.

My Most Memorable Learning Experience

Lieutenant General R.S.K. Kapur

This article is a humble attempt to pay my tribute and homage to one of the greatest soldiers and formation commanders of our times, of not only our Army but also of the world's armies. It is straight from the heart and expresses my deep respect and adulation for a person I proudly refer to as a 'Soldier's General'. I had the privilege and honour of being associated with him on two occasions.

First, for a week in February 1971, when he stayed in the guest room of my Regiment HQ at Sapper Camp, North-East Frontier Agency (NEFA). I had just joined the regiment after the degree course and was the only officer present to look after him. The general officer had just taken over IV Corps and had to familiarise himself with the 5 Division Sector. Given the restrictions due to acclimatisation, he decided to camp himself at Sapper Camp, fly daily to the areas of interest, and return by early evening. It was indeed my good fortune to get this opportunity to look after a bold, audacious and highly professional strategist and soldier. This was proven by his immense contributions as brigade commander of the 50 Para Brigade in the liberation of Goa in December 1961. Although 50 Para Brigade was tasked with merely assisting the main thrust of the 17 Infantry Division, its units advanced rapidly across roadblocks, minefields, and four riverine obstacles to be the first to reach Panjim on 19 December 1961. Thereafter, as General Officer Commanding (GOC) 17 Mountain Division, he taught the Chinese Army a lesson of their life during the clashes at Nathu La and Cho La, wherein he defeated the Chinese forces in these clashes and achieved decisive tactical advantage. In response to messages from the Army HQ to cease firing, his firebrand statement was, 'Message not received. Let them have it.' It was followed by salvos of artillery fire on the Chinese. These clashes displayed his grit and determination as a soldier to win battles, come what may.

It was a godsent opportunity and an honour for me to be blessed with his company for an entire week. Though nervous when I received him at the helipad, I truly felt I was on cloud nine in the company of a great human being who had such a positive and cheerful vibe. I did not feel overwhelmed or intimidated by his towering personality because of his immense humility and his quality of being gentle with subordinates to make them feel at ease and so that they could open up and chat with him. I vividly remember the first evening when I asked him what drink I could offer him. He told our mess waiter, Bhagirath, that I was a guest in his room and that he should serve me a drink as well. Though I was a teetotaller then, I had my first whisky that evening. His simplicity was evident when he asked me which city I belonged to, and I replied that I was an Allahabadi. He promptly asked me if he could also call himself an Allahabadi, since his wife had done her Bachelors in Education from Allahabad! The week just whizzed past and left behind some very pleasant and satisfying memories, giving me an insight into the human side of this exceptional military leader.

The second time our paths crossed was for nearly six months at the operational HQ of IV Corps at Teliamora, Tripura, from April to December 1971, where all the planning and preparations were undertaken for the operations of the 1971 War for the liberation of Bangladesh. I was the company commander of 67 Field Company which had the singular honour to construct the corps field HQ. The site selected was barren, an undulating area with no local resources. My task included construction of basha accommodation for offices and residences, an air-conditioned operations room of appropriate size and model, a partially air-conditioned signal centre, Alfa and Bravo Officers' Messes, Corps Commander's pre-war den, a field hospital with an air-conditioned operation theatre and ICU, and finally a helidrome with nearly eight to ten helipads. All these had to be completed in a couple of months. The accommodation provided had electricity supply round-the-clock and running water supply from overhead water tanks with a well-marked, sign-posted road network as the means of access. It was my first war experience, hence the most challenging yet professionally satisfying. The experience was exhilarating because I was also exposed to the human face of the corps commander that often hid behind the military facade. Every evening he would take a walk around the campus to see the progress of its construction and its quality assessment, with me often in attendance and sometimes accompanied by the chief engineer of the corps as well. On one such occasion, he asked me what factors I had considered while designing his hut, like the sun's direction, wind, etc. Being a Dapodi[6] engineer, I had no other choice but to respond as a soldier—'Sir, all those are peacetime criteria for designing accommodation, but this is the operational hut of the Corps Commander IV Corps to liberate Bangladesh, so your hut

[6] Engineers in the Indian Army join from two distinct streams: technical graduates from civilian engineering colleges and engineers trained in-house at the College of Military Engineering (CME), Dapodi. Those from the latter are called Dapodi Engineers. While initially, CME did not award BE or BTech degrees, now these Dapodi Engineers are awarded a BTech degree from the Jawaharlal Nehru University, New Delhi.

must always face the enemy.' He approved the idea with a great laugh and a good hug-and-shake for me. I shall never forget that moment.

The most memorable compliment I have received in the forty years of service was from the general. One fine morning, the Command HQ sent a message that the Army Commander would be visiting our HQ after two days. It came out of the blue and wasn't expected for some time as we hadn't been there for long. During the evening walk that day, the general mentioned to me that all aspects of the HQ were perfect for receiving and conducting the Army Commander but how he wished that he could have had lunch with all the officers in a proper mess rather than the two of them eating in his caravan. I assured the general that his desire was my command and the mess would be functional before the visit. He was very apologetic and felt guilty for pushing me. He insisted that I reconsider and suggested that they would lunch at his caravan complex. I worked tirelessly through those two days, and on the morning of the visit, when he saw the mess ready and in place, he asked his Military Attaché (MA) to call his son. The surprised look of the MA prompted him to clarify that he wanted him to call me. His tight hug and 'Well done, son!' said it all.

I am choked with nostalgic emotions reminiscing about the greatest general I have ever served with. His passion for soldiering was evident because whenever there was an important battle fought, he would spend the next evening with us in the Bravo Mess to share his thoughts about it, whether complimentary or one of anguish, when units did not perform up to his expectations. He was on top of the world on one such occasion since an infantry battalion had achieved a great victory after having not done so well the previous night. He insisted on reposing his confidence in the battalion, much against the advice of a few staff officers. A decision to the contrary would have destroyed the morale and image of a very good battalion.

That he was a big-hearted general was also evident when, about the second-in-command (2IC) of the battalion who had to spend the night in the no man's land during that battle, he said, 'How I wish I was a Maharaja and I could weigh the officer in gold.' That he recommended my name for a Sena Medal was a great compliment for a young sapper officer.

My association with him taught me some essential character qualities for being a perfect general officer in our great Army:

* The first and foremost was to be a good human being and a gentleman—he was perfection personified.
* He was upright, forthright and most importantly, had the courage of conviction to stand up to seniors, whether politicians or in uniform, for the righteousness of a cause.
* The general officer was humility personified.
* He was passionate about soldiering and had genuine compassion for all ranks. In October 1971, the general noticed that I was seriously sunburnt due to severe exposure to the summer sun of the Northeast and was also totally bushed with fatigue. He rang up my commanding officer and directed that I be sent on temporary duty to the Command HQ for a well-deserved rest and recoup. I have not come across a general who took such personal interest in the welfare and well-being of a young officer.

On a lighter note, all of us are aware of the great victory achieved by our Armed forces had achieved due to the brilliant and very precise planning of the operations at HQ IV Corps. However, what has remained top secret until now, I need to declassify now—'The comfortable and conducive working environment provided to the corps commander and his staff at HQ IV Corps at Teliamura was by my very own, indomitable and second to none, all ranks of 67 Field Company, 234 Army Engineer Regiment.'

The performance of 67 Field Company at HQ IV Corps earned us the honour and privilege of being selected to provide close engineer support to Kilo Force Brigade in its task to advance to and capture

Chittagong. The task involved mine clearance and other tasks in close support of the battalions and the brigade. A major task was to keep the main lines of communication open for the move of the formation, especially the guns and heavy equipment. It was made difficult with the enemy having demolished all the bridges along the main axis, with the road at a much higher level than the surrounding area. To achieve this task, we operated a ferry across the river at Feni, which was later replaced by an equipment bridge and constructed several improvised crossings by utilising the railway tracks, sleepers and other resources available at the Pakistani railway stations. As a result, the brigade successfully accomplished its operational objective of capturing Chittagong and we were thereafter deployed there at the naval base.

I was indeed blessed to have been given such a great operational learning experience, that too at such an early stage of my career and most notably under the bold, audacious and exemplary leadership of the finest general of our Army—General Sagat Singh. No words of mine will ever be adequate to express my gratitude to him for teaching me the essential character qualities required by an army officer. Therefore, with immense pride, I salute the finest soldier, leader, officer, and gentleman.

Lieutenant General R.S.K. Kapur (Retired) is one of the most decorated officers of the Corps of Engineers who was commissioned into the Corps of Engineers in June 1966. He is a veteran of two wars—Liberation of Bangladesh 1971 and the Kargil War in 1999. Since childhood, he has excelled himself having been the school captain in his school, the best Army cadet at the NDA and first in the order of merit amongst sappers officers at the Indian Military Academy, where he also received the Chief of the Army Staff's Banner. He is a graduate in Civil Engineering from CME and has a master's degree in Defence Studies from the Defence Services Staff College, Wellington and in Computer Science from the University of Alabama, USA. He has also attended the prestigious Higher Command and NDC courses. Being a very fine sportsman, he has represented the NDA, IMA and CME in football, hockey and cricket and has been awarded the Colours in Football at IMA and CME.

Snippets from the First Mission

Major General Virender Budhwar

The urge to assist the plight-stricken refugees from across the border was tremendous in the population around Calcutta. Senator Edward Kennedy had come from the US to apprise himself on the condition of the 10 million or so refugees from across the border. These hapless people had crossed over to India to save themselves and their families from the sheer onslaught of terror and mayhem unleashed on them in their own homeland. Some of us who were tasked to deploy close to the border were given orders which were direct and without any innuendos—'Scale new heights and start operations pronto', meaning, put the enemy in distress by escalating violence. This would assist in eventually bringing about a capitulation of the enemy forces. A tall directive, but something had to be done to alleviate the suffering of the people of East Pakistan.

I hate to stand out in a crowd, hence the urge to maintain a low profile. This is especially so while working in an alien environment. It was necessary to maintain stealth, especially while conducting nocturnal clandestine operations. The first mission was a challenge, to say the least. It was to be undertaken by the Mukti Bahini with about two weeks of military training opposite the Silchar sector. The mission involved infiltration across a swift-flowing river— highly in spate, travel five kilometres or so on foot, lay demolition charges on an existing bridge, destroy it and, finally, exfiltrate. Mind you, the fun and adventure of it was that the mission was daunting. It had its tactical merits in that if the bridge was demolished it would probably block road movement on the lateral road running inside enemy territory. This lateral was used to move men and material to posts on the border and possible switching of troops for reinforcement and mounted patrols. The deployment in the enemy area was not known, or perhaps at that time, there was no definite intelligence of their deployment. Perhaps the enemy was busy doing whatever they were to subjugate their brethren, especially by murdering the intelligentsia, pillage and committing atrocities against their female population. Early escalation of violence was required to bring both fear and caution in the minds of Yahya Khan's troopers. A word about the overall mission itself—the aim was to disrupt the areas in the vicinity of the border from various points of ingress into enemy territory.

The terrain beyond the river line was paddy fields and the crop was about a foot tall at that time. The target area lay in a large bowl with groves of trees and bushes and human habitation on its periphery. To maintain surprise, the movement had to be slow. It was along narrow bundhs between small fields. Occasionally an odd body from the infiltrating group slipped and fell into the water-logged paddy. This broke the eerie silence but the element of surprise was not lost. At each stage, patrol members were cautioned to maintain stealth. At about half a kilometre from the target, the troops were deployed in a patrol base. The villages on the periphery came alive for some reason. A few torches and lanterns could be seen. Dogs started barking and intermittent fire opened all around. There was shouting, which seemed to be the means of communication between the villagers. It was soon realised that the firing was in fact due to firecrackers being set off to scare stray animals.

All this while the entire patrol laid low and observant. A recce party from the patrol discerned that there was no enemy on the target. As the commotion amongst the villagers was dying down, suddenly a person with a weak torch was seen approaching towards the southern side of the target. The assault group was approaching the target with caution from the north at that juncture.

The target itself turned out to be a two-span bridge instead of a single span, about 30 metres in length under which there was stagnant water. A fire assault team of three people with light machine guns (LMGs) moved towards the target followed by a five-member demolition team. The assault team was briefed to fire two or three bursts from the LMGs. This would be enough to eliminate or scare away whoever was approaching the bridge. The entire operation was rehearsed many times over. Despite the briefing and rehearsal, instead of two or three bursts, the assault group fired an entire magazine till a stoppage occurred in the LMGs. No one was probably hit, but one person seemed to have discharged a shotgun and then two or three people were seen running away from the bridge towards the south. The demolition team had carried a prepared charge for a single span. This was quickly placed in the middle of the span and tamped with sandbags. During the approach march, unfortunately, the safety matches had become completely damp. The team could not light the safety fuse to initiate the explosive charge. The rest of the troops in the patrol base was getting ready to leave the area expecting the charge to blow up soon. Nothing happened for ten long minutes and then the demolition team was seen returning. The team leader informed us of the disappointing failure to initiate the demolition as the fuse could not be lit. It was fortunate that there was a cigar smoker around—there was one who had carried a cigar and a gas lighter in his pocket. A Ronson lighter was a prized possession those days. Incidentally, it was purchased from the Chor Bazar in Calcutta near Chowringhee.

After having come all that way it would have been disastrous for the confidence of the Mukti Bahini members of the patrol if the mission was aborted at this stage. It was decided to use the gas lighter to initiate the charge which had been left behind on the bridge. The target was approached on the double and the fuse was lit. Soon there was a flash and a loud boom that caused shock and awe. The area around became silent for a while, but soon after it erupted making people shout, and others cry, while the dogs began to howl.

Nearly 15 minutes later, vehicle lights could be seen approaching from a distance. Meanwhile, the patrol had drifted away from the area. It turned to twilight just short of the river where a boat was expected to be waiting. Reaching the river was a priority as there was cover available on its banks. The patrol reached the rendezvous near the crossing point one hour later than the initial plan and disappointingly there was no boat there. It was best to take cover. Radio silence that had been maintained until now had to be broken. The concerned authorities were contacted who informed that a boat would be available within half an hour to enable the crossing. While awaiting the arrival of the boat the better-trained members of the patrol were deployed. Fortunately a boat arrived soon enough.

The river crossing was swift but tense as it had turned to daylight and there was no one available to provide covering fire. Good cheer and euphoria only sunk in when the patrol reached the safety of their own land. The cigar was then lit with the same gas lighter and the pleasure was enormous. This was the first mission carried out by the Mukti Bahini which was an unqualified success. This gave them the confidence necessary to march on, causing disruption, creating caution and fear in the minds of the enemy troops. Reports indicated that the opposing side did not know what on earth was going on and who was doing it for quite some time.

We had upped the ante and the violence generated continued till the war ended with the surrender of 93,000 Pakistani troops. The ultimate victory was won by the Indian armed forces but the brave Mukti Bahini surely contributed to it.

Major General Virender Budhwar, AVSM, VSM (Retired) was commissioned in 16 KUMAON and commanded the same battalion in Sri Lanka during the Indian Peace Keeping Force (IPKF) operations. He attended the Canadian Forces Staff College and was the Deputy Military Advisor in the Indian High Commission in London, UK. He has served in various sectors in India and held staff and instructional appointments. He also commanded a division in Ladakh, was Chief of Staff of a corps in the desert and was the Director General Resettlement before superannuating.

1971
An Eventful Year

Brigadier Sukhdev Singh

Upon completing the degree course at the College of Military Engineering, Khadki, Pune and promotion to a captain, I rejoined my parent unit, 58 Engineer Regiment, and took over as the Commander of 73 Field Company in January 1971 at Lucknow.

In March 1971, the regiment moved to Purnia in Bihar, by road from Lucknow to render aid to the civil authority in the run-up to the 1971 elections. Two months later, upon return to Lucknow in May, we were scheduled to be relieved by the 9 Engineer Regiment so that we could move to our new location in Misa, in Assam. My course mate and friend, (late) Captain R.N. Gupta, came with an advance party of the 9 Engineer Regiment. It was nice being able to spend a fortnight together, little realising what the future held in store for the balance of the year, or that this would be the last time we would get to spend more than a few hours together.

The influx of refugees from erstwhile East Pakistan had become a veritable flood, and the refugee camps housing them were proliferating. In July, I was detailed to report at a Mukti Fauj Training camp located near village Jarain on-road Jowai–Dawki in Meghalaya. Another officer and a few sappers were part of this training team.

I reported to 5/5 Gorkha Rifles[7] (Frontier Force) (GR (FF)) at Shillong, along with my detachment. We were subsequently transported by road to the camp, which was located in a thick bamboo forest about a kilometre off the Jowai–Dawki road and about ten kilometres from the India–East Pakistan border. The Camp Adjutant was a course mate, Richard Khare, of 5/5 GR (FF). The camp closed in the last week of September, and we returned to Misa for a fortnight. This was a first and a brand-new experience for all of us wherein we were training Bengalis/East Pakistanis to fight the Pakistan Army for the liberation of their motherland. Each course had a strength of about 50 odd people, and the training concluded in three weeks, with a passing-out parade. Weapon training and fieldcraft training was carried out by instructors from the infantry, whereas my job was to impart field engineering training with a special emphasis on the use of explosives.

In the first week of October, orders were received for the regiment to move to Kanchrapara near Kolkata in anticipation of the impending operation that had been codenamed Operation Cactus Lily. 58 Engineer Regiment was initially in support of 9 Infantry Division but was subsequently moved to Barrackpore, in integral transport, in support of 4 Mountain Division.

In the third week of October, I was, however, ordered to move to Krishnagar along with 73 Field Company to provide engineer support to HQ 2 Corps, which was under raising at Krishnagar. Apart from the routine engineer support to the Corps Headquarters, 73 Field Company constructed an Advanced Landing Ground (ALG) for the fixed-wing air operation flight and established the Corps Bridge Point, which received bridging equipment from various locations in the country. It was very likely that in the contemplated area of

---

7 5th Battalion, The Fifth Regiment, Gorkha Rifles

operations, construction of the new or damaged bridges would be required. 4 Mountain Division was allotted two regiments (rather than the usual authorisation of a single Engineer Regiment). 58 Engineer Regiment was placed for close support to the three brigades, and 63 Engineer Regiment was placed for the line of communication tasks with a special emphasis on bridging tasks. The longest composite (Bailey Pontoon and Folding Boat Equipment) bridge, over River Madhumati, measuring 1,388 feet, was constructed, utilising the bridging equipment that had been assembled at the Corps Bridge Point at Krishnagar.

In mid-November, 58 Engineer Regiment moved to Krishnagar and my company re-joined them in the assembly area. My company was allotted to the 41 Mountain Brigade of 4 Mountain Division. We moved for operations on 2 December 1971 and were tasked to provide engineer support on the road axis Darsana–Aundla Bari–Jhenida–Kushtia–Hardinge Bridge on the Ganges. The objective where the operation was planned for eventually, however, was terminated. Thereafter, we returned to Police Lines, located in Kushtia, prior to returning to India on completion of the operation. 1971 was indeed a busy year, moving from Pune, Delhi (on leave), Lucknow, Purnea, Misa, the Mukti Fauj Training Camp, Misa, Kanchrapara, Barrackpore, Krishnagar, East Pakistan / Bangladesh and finally, back to India.

We suffered a personal tragedy on the very first day of the war of 1971—my brother-in-law, Major S.P.S. Waraich, a forward company commander with 15 PUNJAB[8], went missing in action during the first enemy attack on the evening of 3 December at Hussainiwala, Ferozepur. My father came to know immediately but decided to not inform me during the operation, but instead requested my Commanding Officer (CO) to send me on leave on completion of the operation. I arrived in Delhi in the last week of December. Major S.P.S. Waraich, 15 PUNJAB, figures as the first name in the

---

[8] 15th Battalion, The Punjab Regiment

list of 54 missing prisoners of war (POWs) of the 1971 war whose whereabouts and well-being are to this date unknown.

I started the year in Delhi and ended the year in Delhi, but a lot happened in between.

The Jaintiapur Episode

The training imparted to the Mukti Fauj consisted mostly of telling them about the use and safety while handling grenades and explosives. The trainees who had been selected were young boys who were trained over a short period of three weeks, after which there was a passing-out parade during which they sang their anthem 'Sonar Bangla'. These boys were then taken to Shillong, where they were issued weapons and were sent to launch pads along the border for induction into East Pakistan.

We were about 10 km from the International Border, in the hills just adjoining the northernmost plains of East Pakistan. From our elevated position along the border, we could look into a fair distance of some tens of kilometres into East Pakistan on a clear day. One prominent white building, which drew our attention, was in a village named Jaintiapur on the border, located on the forward spur running from India into East Pakistan. It was rumoured that this building was a *rajbari* (the Jaintiapur Palace), the residence of the erstwhile rulers of the capital of the kingdom of Jaintia, which comprised of the Khasi Hills and the plains of Jaintia. Jaintiapur was in a sort of an enclave bounded by a river that ran from Dawki in India, encircled Jaintiapur and meandered back into India. It was linked to Sylhet by the main road, which had a bridge on the river encircling the town.

Our camp was under the operational command of the General Officer Commanding (GOC) 101 Communication Zone. During one of his visits to the area, the GOC visualised the vulnerability of Jaintiapur. It was, therefore, decided that Mukti Fauj would be used to roll down into Jaintiapur using the spur from a hilltop named Mahadev Tilla. The Engineers would, thereafter, blow the only bridge on the road that connected Jaintiapur to Sylhet, leaving the enclave in control of the Mukti Bahini. The task was allotted to second-in-command (2IC), 5/5 GR (FF).

The troops of the Mukti Bahini were led by a captain who had defected from East Pakistan Rifles. Two radio operators were to be provided to the Mukti Bahini Captain by 5/5 GR (FF) for communication with the control HQ. My 2IC, Lieutenant J.S. Judge, was tasked to blow the bridge. He was to be provided with BSF Personnel to carry the explosive required for demolition. The training started earnestly under 5/5 GR, and the selected Mukti Bahini was adequately motivated to capture Jaintiapur. When the D-Day finally arrived, all concerned moved to Mahadev Tilla during the night with the H-hour set to be at first light. Lieutenant Judge, along with BSF personnel and the explosives, moved to the launch pad at Muktapur, on the border close to Jaintiapur. At first light, in mid-September, the attack was launched from Mahadev Tilla. There was concentrated small arms fire from both sides. Considering the volume of fire, I felt a bit depressed, thinking of the casualties on my trainees. There were sounds of mortar fire as well.

The first communication we received from the Gorkha radio operators attached to the attacking party was, 'Captain Sahib mar gayo!' Apparently, a 2-inch mortar shell had landed nearby and a splinter had knocked the captain unconscious. The Mukti Bahini was, therefore, leaderless but having been launched, the assault continued, nevertheless. The Pakistanis, being outnumbered, gave way and left Jaintiapur in vehicles. Lieutenant Judge had, meanwhile, started as planned from Muktapur and proceeded towards the bridge with the BSF personnel carrying the explosive on their heads. We assumed that the operation was a success and Jaintiapur enclave would fully be in our control once the bridge was blown. The retreating Pakistani vehicles could be seen in the far distance, and we thought we had seen the last of them.

To our surprise and consternation, the vehicles soon stopped and turned around. The white building location was possibly their company or the battalion HQ. Two more vehicles joined them and the convoy, with reinforcements, started the return journey of about 4 km to Jaintiapur. We had lost communication with the Gorkha radio operators and could not ascertain the latest situation. Upon capturing Jaintiapur, the Mukti Bahini decided to celebrate by looting the Jaintiapur bazaar. Without a leader, they failed to hold the bridge or take up the all-round defence that was necessary for such a situation. When they saw the Pakistanis returning, they immediately retreated into the Indian territory.

The Pakistanis now held the bridge once again while Lieutenant Judge, along with the BSF and the explosives, kept advancing towards the bridge, oblivious of the fact that the bridge was now held by a Pakistani MMG Detachment. When the Pakistanis saw Lieutenant Judge at a distance, they fired upon the demolition party. The bullets went overhead owing to the distance. The BSF dumped the explosive and ran back. Lieutenant Judge went into the dead ground in a nala and kept moving but had little sense of direction as, by then, the day had ended and darkness had fallen.

Meanwhile, the Mukti Bahini returned, carrying the spoils of war. Despite my apprehension and foreboding, the Mukti Bahini had had only one casualty; a bullet wound in the stomach. The casualty was carried back by his colleagues.

The end result in sitrep form was that Jaintiapur went back in the hands of the Pakistani Army, 2 GORKHA operators on radio silence and missing, one captain of the Mukti Bahini/East Pakistan Rifles injured and presumed dead, location unknown; and Lieutenant Judge of 73 Field Company, 58 Engineer Regiment, missing in action. The captain and the Gorkha radio operator duo were located on our side of the border on the spur leading down from Mahadev Tilla once they established contact with us in darkness. That left only one person in a quandary, yours truly, Captain Sukhdev Singh.

I was worried and fully expecting the news that Lieutenant J.S. Judge had been captured inside East Pakistan in September. He could possibly be produced before the world and in the UN as proof of India's complicity. What bothered me most was what would I say to my CO if this happened! We waited for two days, anticipating the worst. However, good tidings awaited us on the third day. The BSF post on the border about 15 km from Muktapur (location from where Lieutenant Judge was launched) reported that he had managed to reach the border. He re-joined us the same evening. I was most relieved and welcomed him back with a warm hug. This was indeed a fiasco but benevolent to the participants.

I vaguely remember someone saying that GOC 101 Communication Zone had promised the Army Commander lunch at Jaintiapur Palace on a particular date. As the sole basis of recalling a failed adventure, hearsay runs the peril of being dangerous 'fake news'.

Richard Khare was the Camp Adjutant. He may be able to throw more light on the incident.

The Kushtia Episode

My experience during the war was confined to movement as part of Brigade HQ of 41 Mountain Brigade. I was initially the Commander and later the 2IC of 73 Field Company of 58 Engineer Regiment. The three platoons, which comprise a field company, were in support of the three infantry battalions of the brigade, namely 5 GUARDS[9], 9 DOGRA[10] and 5/1 GR[11]. The platoons saw the action first-hand and were intimately married with the infantry, whereas the Company

[9] 5th Battalion, Brigade of the Guards
[10] 9th Battalion, The Dogra Regiment
[11] 5th Battalion, The First Regiment, Gorkha Rifles

HQ came on the scene later, as a part of the Brigade HQ.

We moved on the orders of the Deputy Assistant Adjutant and Quarter Master General (DAA&QMG), as, in 1971, the Deputy Brigade Commanders were not yet authorised to a Brigade HQ. This was because the Brigade Major was located ahead, with the Brigade Commander as part of a Tactical HQ, which usually moved ahead of the main Brigade HQ whenever an offensive action was to be executed. The axis of advance of the 41 Mountain Brigade was Darshana–Aundlabari–Jhenida–Kushtia–Hardinge Bridge. We advanced successfully, and after overcoming enemy opposition at Darsana and Aundlabari, we captured an enemy Brigade HQ at Jhenida on 9/10 December.

Jhenida was a medium-sized town that, during peacetime, housed the East Pakistan Army Cadet College. During the war, however, it was occupied by a Pakistan Army Brigade HQ with many buildings containing rear elements and heavy luggage of the infantry battalions, which had been either defeated or bypassed, by the advancing Indian Army. Our advance to Jhenida was so swift that the Pakistan Brigade HQ, commander and staff, barely managed to escape towards Kushtia in the nick of time.

Our next objective was Kushtia, about 40 km away and linked by a good Class 9 road. 41 Mountain Brigade had a troop of PT-76 tanks, ex 45 CAVALRY, commanded by 2 Lieutenant Chandravarkar, in support. This troop of PT-76 tanks had been with the brigade since the commencement of the operation and had performed commendably in all the battles that the brigade had been engaged in so far. 41 Mountain Brigade advanced towards Kushtia but was not tasked with the capture of Kushtia. The task for the capture of Kushtia was allotted, instead, to the 7 Infantry Brigade with a troop of 45 CAVALRY in support.

My Company HQ, as part of HQ 41 Mountain Brigade, was located astride the main road, about 2 km short of Kushtia. A canal extended along the entire length of the city on the line of approach to Kushtia. The bridge on the main road was fit, but other multiple approach bridges were very narrow, making it difficult for tanks and heavy vehicles to cross safely.

The Brigade Commander, Brigadier Zail Singh, wanted to enter Kushtia on a wide front, but the GOC, emboldened after the success at Jhenida, felt that there was no opposition in Kushtia. Besides, the state of minor bridges on secondary entry points tilted the decision in favour of a single approach on the main road into town. My Company Commander, Major J.S. Gill (Late Lieutenant Colonel J.S. Gill), told me that the GOC, along with the Commander of the 7 Infantry Brigade, had landed by helicopter at the Kushtia stadium. The Pakistanis had been there but played possum, thereby giving the impression that Kushtia was unoccupied. If true, this could also have been the reason for entering the town along a single axis on the main road from Jhenida. The plan was for Lieutenant Chandravarkar, in a PT-76 tank, to lead an infantry battalion, 22 RAJPUT[12], in vehicles along the main road into Kushtia. The road was elevated, owing to the terrain in erstwhile East Pakistan. As it entered, there was a level crossing and to the rear, about a kilometre short of Kushtia, was a bridge over a canal.

When Lieutenant Chandravarkar reached the level crossing, he found it closed. He was deciding whether to open it or smash through it when an RCL[13] fired from close range, disabling his tank and killing the officer and possibly the tank crew. Simultaneously, the bridge over the canal was blown owing to a prepared demolition, unknown to us. Mortar fire was brought along the road thereby, causing damage and casualties to 22 RAJPUT mortar vehicles and personnel.

The attack was a failure. The entire 4 Mountain Division then concentrated on this axis. After a delay of three to four days, the

---

12 22nd Battalion, The Rajput Regiment

13 Recoilless gun fitted onto a jeep and used by infantry and mechanised infantry for defence against tanks. They are shoot-and-scoot because of the considerable backblast, flash and smoke.

Indian Army entered Kushtia. The approach to the next objective, Hardinge Bridge on the Ganges, was uneventful as the Pakistan Army had withdrawn across to the far side of the bridge. One span of the Harding Bridge had been damaged by the IAF; hence, only the personnel could cross by rope across the gap in the bridge created by the bomb. On the home side of Harding Bridge, we found the artillery mortars which had been firing on us during previous battles. All vehicles, which had escaped our roadblocks, some with radio sets, were also lined up on the home bank.

The Brigade HQ, thereafter, returned to Kushtia, where the war ended for me, on 15 December 1971. Balram Mehta of 45 CAVALRY was with the regiment. From 45 CAVALRY sources, he would likely have had a better version of the Kushtia episode and Lieutenant Chandravarkar's demise. I had been a kilometre away from the bridge on the main road and would have given my impression based on my observation and as per data fed to me as well as what I experienced in the subsequent days when the whole division concentrated on this axis.

I have included it in my war experience as a two-part lesson—never underestimate your enemy and do not violate the basic standard operating procedures (SOPs). Had we entered Kushtia from multiple fronts, it would have been a success story, similar to the capture of the enemy Brigade HQ at Jhenida.

Fog of War: A Raid by the Enemy on a Brigade HQ

On the night of 7/8 December 1971, I did see enemy action first-hand in the form of a Pakistan Raiding Party with 41 Mountain Brigade HQ as their target. Darsana was captured on 4 December and Aundlabari on 6 December. The Brigade Tactical HQ had moved ahead for the next battle, and the remainder of the Brigade HQ, comprising of the Adjutant and Quartermaster (A&Q) branches under the

DAA&QMG, along with the 'B' echelon of the infantry battalions, supporting arms and services (Signals, Engineers, Electronics and Mechanical Engineers [EME], Ordinance, Medical), moved into and around village Aundlabari, at the last light on 7 December.

The artillery in support of the brigade was not a part of the Brigade HQ. They harboured in their wagon lines, which moved forward on orders of respective command and control elements as the battle progressed. All harbour procedures were completed, and we settled down for the night in an area that was predominately a bamboo grove with houses scattered infrequently. It was around midnight when I was woken up by my Company Subedar, Subedar Beant Singh. He woke me up and stated, '*Sahib, appa under attack haan*' (Sir, we are under attack). My Company Subedar had 27 years of service and was a veteran of both the Indo-Pak wars in 1947 and 1965, whereas I was under fire, for the first time, with barely five years of service.

I heard the sharp crack of MMG fire, but the bullets were well above our head. Thereafter, a mortar shell landed nearby with a splinter hitting a bulldozer blade with a loud, sharp noise. I could smell the cordite in addition to an intermittent sharp crescendo of MMG bullets hitting the bamboos above our heads.

My Subedar informed me that his reading of the situation was that a Pakistani jeep with a mounted MMG was circling the brigade harbour and firing intermittently, whereas the mortar was firing from a fixed location. Having no idea of what I should do, I asked him to arrange an armed escort to accompany me to the Brigade HQ to consult with the DAA&QMG. In the harbour, the Brigade HQ used to be in the centre with the elements of supporting arms and services on the inner perimeter and the 'B' echelons of the three infantry battalions manning defences on the outer perimeter.

It was pitch dark, but my escort and I reached the Brigade HQ, only to find that it had been vacated and I was on my own! I was not aware of any other officer amongst the 'B' echelons of the infantry battalions or supporting arms and services. Hence, I returned to my own location.

Meanwhile, owing to the MMG fire coming from different directions, the troops vacated inwards, away from the direction of fire, resulting in troops of various units getting mixed up in the interior of the harbour. Some of my troops reached infantry battalions 'B' echelons, and some reached my area too.

The enemy mortar appeared some distance away, and the MMG-mounted jeep was circling our location but maintaining a fair distance from us. We could either wait for them to go away on their own or take some action. My war-experienced Company Subedar had no solution. Hence, I decided to investigate for myself, to ascertain the strength of the enemy raiding us. I do not remember exactly why, but I decided to take a patrol in the direction of the mortar fire to locate the exact location of the enemy mortar position.

We had reached about 200 yards from the village when we heard a soft, '*Tham, kaun ata hai?*' (Halt, who is coming?) We went to the ground and replied, '*Dost. Hum Brigade HQ se aa rahen hain. Aap kaun hain?* (We are from Brigade HQ. Who are you?) He replied, '*Hum Arty Regiment ke wagon line hain. Quartermaster (QM) Sahib hamein chhod kar aur ammunition lene gaye hain.*' (We are the wagon line of the supporting Arty Regiment. The QM has left us here and has gone to get more ammunition.)

We got up and moved forward to find the religious JCO, the unit's pandit ji, along with about 4 Other Ranks (ORs), very scared but maintaining fire discipline in not firing in the direction of the enemy. In front of them were barrels full of petrol and diesel, and behind them, a large stack of artillery shells required for the next day's battle.

When the mortar started firing, and the MMG fired from a distance, Pandit ji told the ORs not to fire because that would give away their position and would assist the enemy in ranging onto their position. If even one shell hit the fuel or the ammunition, they would be finished. Since it was dark, the enemy could not know their exact location; hence, he maintained his distance. The mortar shells landing in our area were overshooting this location, whereas the intended target of the raiding party was the Arty Regiment Wagon Line. We were too few to take any offensive action against the mortar position and were wary of the MMG-mounted jeep, which kept changing location while firing from a distance. Since Pandit ji's strategy had been successful, we decided to follow it and wait and watch. After some time, we heard the mortar vehicle starting and then it receded into the distance, followed by the MMG-mounted jeep soon after. The situation became clear when I spoke to Pandit ji. The regiment's Quartermaster had reconnoitred the location in the forenoon and had brought a lot of ammunition and fuel in the evening while leaving Pandit ji with a few ORs, and then had gone back to get some more.

The location was seen by a Pakistani recce party, and they planned a raid for the same night. Brigade HQ moved in, on the other side of the village at last light and had no idea of the presence of the artillery wagon line, the intended target of the raiding party, being in close proximity. Had the raiding party known the presence of a few hundred of us, comprising the Brigade HQ with attachments and detachments (atts and dets), we may not have been a witness to a raid and the subsequent chaos that followed.

I returned to my Company HQ location and had a restless night. At first light, all concerned were sent to their respective units. Despite the MMG and the inaccurate mortar fire, we were lucky in that we had no casualties except some bamboo groves being damaged and a bulldozer blade slightly nicked by a lone wayward shell that fell in our vicinity. Hats off to Pandit ji and the fire discipline of the Regiment of Artillery. Thanks to a wagon line of the artillery, whose location was initially not known to the Brigade HQ, I experienced live small arms and mortar fire from close range, and can now boast, in the words of my company subedar, '*Appa under attack haan*'. In the ultimate analysis, a raiding team, consisting of two vehicles, an MMG, a three-inch mortar and six to eight enemy soldiers, had around 300 armed personnel of the Indian Army on tenterhooks for two hours. A classic example of 'The Fog of War'.

The Exuberance of the Youth who Helped to Dispose of a 1,000-pound Unexploded Bomb (UXB) in Quick Time

The operations were over, and I was relaxing in the Police Lines at Kushtia. We had chased the Pakistanis across the Ganges at the Hardinge Bridge and had thereafter returned to Kushtia.

It was 17 December, and we were awaiting orders for return to India. The platoons were of my field company were dispersed in support of the infantry battalions and still co-located with them. The manpower available to me were 15 ORs from the Company HQ and operators of the Earth Moving Plant, which had been attached with the company for the duration of the operation.

At around 10 a.m., my Company Commander, Major J.S. Gill, informed me that we were required to dispose of a UXB lying at the Kushtia Railway Station. I informed him that we were not equipped, and this was a task for a bomb disposal unit. He curtly informed me that he was well aware of the tasks of the bomb disposal unit, but there were no such units available. To add urgency to the situation, a train with prisoners of war from Dacca was expected to pass through the train station by 5 p.m., which was within a few hours; hence, it would best be to get on with the job at the earliest.

I quickly referred to the bomb disposal procedure as contained in the 'Sappers Field Engineering Bible', termed Engineer Reconnaissance Pocket Book (ERPB). This Bible stated that a UXB should be preferably detonated in situ. In case it must be moved, a deep enough trench should be dug at a suitable distance. Thereafter the bomb should be pulled along the ground using ropes, while the troops engaged in the disposal task stay well inside the cover of the trench. Armed with this knowledge, my team of 15 and I proceeded to Kushtia Railway Station.

The UXB was easy to locate and was found in a jiffy. It was lying between the rails at barely 50 metres from the station building. There was nobody at the railway station except us. With no tools, dismantling the railway line was not an option. It would be impossible to drag the UXB from the spot we had found it in. The trench disposal method could, therefore, not be applied, nor was there time to try such methods; it would be 5 p.m. soon. I studied the UXB from a reasonably close distance. It seemed to be a 1,000 lb bomb dropped by the IAF. The outer body of the bomb was intact, but upon hitting the ground, the fuse seemingly had got bent, preventing the firing pin from striking the percussion cap and letting the bomb do its intended job. I assumed that even if I moved the UXB, there was little chance that the firing pin would be activated.

I looked around and observed that the area around the station was elevated with respect to the Madhumati river, which flowed close by, within a 100 metres distance. I did a recce of the area and decided on the location where I would detonate the UXB. Had I detonated the bomb above the ground, the station building would have gotten badly damaged. The bomb detonation would be safest if done underwater as this would tamp down the explosion and reduce the shrapnel that could result. Too bad for any fish!

I checked the depth at the chosen location; it was about ten feet. My other reason for an underwater explosion was the hope that we would get some fish for the unit's langar. I had never seen or heard a 1,000 lb explosion from close by; hence, I could only relate it with a few gun cotton slabs that one was more familiar with. The plan was to lift the UXB, carry it over the decided route to the river for detonation. Being aware of the danger involved, I asked all married personnel and the only sons in the group of 15 Sappers to step aside. Out of the 15, four were ineligible, leaving 11 ORs and myself to carry the bomb. The load per person was 90 lb which was heavy but manageable. A Bailey panel weighs 560 lb, and even as officers, six of us have carried umpteen panels during the Young Officers' (YOs) course in the bridging classes.

Poles and ropes were arranged, and the dirty dozen carried the 1,000 lb UXB to the riverbank where it was prepared for detonation. I personally attached the explosive, primer, detonator and the extra length of the fuse to the UXB and lit the fuse. We rolled the UXB into the water. I had measured the fuse to allow us three minutes to move far enough from the UXB. I waited and observed the UXB settle in the water. Some bubbles on the water surface gave an indication that the fuse was still burning.

Thereafter we ran back, as fast as our legs could carry us, towards the railway station and sat under cover, below a goods wagon on an adjacent track. We were now about 50 feet above the level of the UXB and about 100 metres horizontal distance. We waited apprehensively for the explosion, and when it came, it was far worse than what we had imagined. It was a tremendous explosion, the railway wagon working as our overhead protection shook as if in a major earthquake. Electric poles in and around the railway station were partly uprooted and tilted. A huge crack emerged on the Kushtia Railway Building too! We were rewarded with a huge crater about 50 feet across and 10 feet deep. Most depressing was the fact that there was no fish.

The UXB level at the point of detonation was well below the level of the railway station. The pressure wave of an explosion supposedly travels at some 45 degrees from the point of explosion. The entire embankment on which the station stood came in the path of the shock wave, causing extensive damage, short of flattening the building. The sound of the explosion and the subsequent damage it caused was scary. I resolved never again to attempt to kill fish using a 1,000 lb UXB!

The next day we received further requests for disposing UXBs around Kushtia. Remembering our previous day's experience, we politely refused, leaving it to the bomb disposal units to do the needful whenever they arrived. The POW on the train, when it passed that evening, would probably wonder as to how the Kushtia Railway Station was in such a war-ravaged State. What we did had been utterly foolish. Had the UXB exploded during handling, all 12 of us would have been history. It was the exuberance of the youth which had made us oblivious to the danger of what we were attempting while dreaming of the bonus of free fish for the unit's langar!

Brigadier Sukhdev Singh (Retired) was commissioned into the Corps of Engineers on 15 June 1966. He served with 58 Engineer Regiment during the 1971 operation and later commanded 235 Engineer Regiment in Nagrota. He has served as the Chief Engineer of the Airforce with the SWAC (South-western Air Command) and later as the Chief Engineer of Project Himank in Leh. In his career of 36 years, he has served as DAA & QMG of an infantry brigade, the Brigade Major (BM) of an Engineer Brigade, and DS in Junior Command wing in the College of Combat.

Letters to My Wife

Brigadier Shimi Kanbargimath

When my wife, Girija, and I decided to write the biography of my late father, Lieutenant Colonel S.S. Kanbargimath, we started our search for all the old documents. What a treasure trove of letters, diaries, and documents we found—all of them meticulously preserved by my wife and me for the last 50 odd years! Among them, serendipitously, and much to our delight, out tumbled a bundle of letters that I had written to Girija when I moved from Belgaum to take part in the 1971 war for the liberation of East Pakistan, which later became Bangladesh. My letter of 14 November 1971 was the first one of the series of letters that I wrote to my wife as we moved to Eastern Command and thereafter into East Pakistan. Five decades ago, letter writing was the only popular mode of being in touch. We, in the infantry, especially had a special attachment to the red inland letters issued by the Army Postal Unit.

I was serving with the Commando Wing as an Instructor, just married to Girija, and we were in the midst of our excitement in setting up our first home with our first child on the way! Barely after a few months of bliss, though, I got my orders and began to pack. The war clouds had started to gather over East Pakistan, and by September/ October 1971, we were certain that war was imminent. Our task was to train and lead the Mukti Bahini (freedom fighters of Bangladesh) for commando tasks once the war started. By November 1971, the Commando Wing was ordered to move to Headquarters, Eastern Command, for further instructions. Letters now would be our only means of being in touch. The first letter is dated 14 November 1971. Our paths parted from the Belgaum Railway Station. This is how the letter reads.

Dearest Girija[14]

Here I am sticking to the promise that I made to you last night. The train journey so far has been comfortable. I shall keep writing to you. I have bought a dozen inland postage letters and am waiting to change over to broad gauge here. Be cheerful, and I am sure God will have everything working right for us.

16 November

We have reached Nagpur. It's a longish wait here as we have to change trains tomorrow, 17 November, at 4 p.m., for Calcutta. We went out for dinner and thought of seeing a movie but decided against it. After a post-dinner stroll near the station, we got into our compartments and are currently preparing ourselves for a good night's sleep and our onward journey to Calcutta. I am now lying down to read *Love Story* by Erich Segal.[15]

It is 17 November today, and I continue with the letter as I wait for our breakfast to arrive. Khatri and Kanwar are also writing letters home, and Dogra (all commando instructors) is with the morning local newspaper.

---

[14] For convenience, I have used Dearest Girija only once. Also, my wife has prevented me from sharing the mushy expressions in these letters! Thus, only details regarding my movement have been narrated here.

[15] I could not complete the letter.

19 November

We have arrived at Calcutta and in HQ Eastern Command. There are hectic activities, officers running all over with files. Colonel Das Gupta has gone over to meet the general for a briefing. My team of commando instructors and I have been instructed to fly to Guwahati on 20 November.

20 November

I am writing to you from the Dum Dum airport. I am getting ready to board our flight—it is a packet aircraft—to Guwahati. The wait here is comfortable. The airport is nice, and I am feeling excited at the prospect of joining the units deployed for operations.

25 November

I reached my destination after an interesting road journey from Guwahati to the border town, Tura. I could not write earlier as I was busy getting my briefing and settling down. I hope you have received my letters and the telegram that I sent yesterday from the local post office. The morale here is high, and everyone seems relaxed and getting ready to take off for the long-awaited war. I am with 95 Brigade, which a flamboyant commander, Brigadier Kler, is commanding. I am looking forward to exciting times.

30 November

It was such a relief when your telegram was read out to me over the telephone as I am now at a place where there is a civil post office. I hope this letter reaches you quickly. I am eagerly waiting for a letter from you. There is not much news to give at the moment.

I am sure you all are tuning in to the AIR news. There is heavy firing going on all over the border. As usual, the Pakistanis are exaggerating the casualties on our forces to boost their morale. They are hard-pressed in all sectors, and they know they are fighting a losing war. The Mukti Bahinis are playing merry hell into them now—their action has confined the Pakistani troops to their heavily fortified defences. It's such a pity, though, that we are losing men in this damned, undeclared war. How I wish war is declared soon so that action can start and the ordeal is over. I am taking the liberty to inform you where I am located. If you look at the map, I am on the northern border of Bangladesh, you will know where I am. It is a border town called Tura in Meghalaya.

(We refer to East Pakistan as Bangladesh now. We have started greeting all the locals with 'Joi Bangladesh'! Pray for us.)

7 December

I am writing from Bakshiganj. The war started on 3 December. On the evening of 3 December, I was told to report to the commanding officer of 1 Marathas, Lieutenant Colonel Brar. He told me to take 30 Mukti Bahini men from a nearby camp and briefed me to establish a roadblock to facilitate the attack on Bakshiganj. Along with my junior commissioned officer (JCO) and a non-commissioned officer (NCO), I moved in with the Mukti Bahini men for our task. We established the block, but it seemed to be away from the road from where the Pakistanis started withdrawing the same night. I heard the rumbling of vehicles, and I tried to get in touch with Commanding Officer 1 Maratha Light Infantry (CO 1 MLI). I thought our artillery guns had a very lucrative target to engage, but alas, I could not establish contact. Our wait was in vain. The next morning the force leader got us blankets and arranged some lungis for us as he wanted us to look like the locals. Bakshiganj is a built-up area, and our forces had to clear these defences to advance. There was not much opposition here as the Pakistani troops decided to withdraw to the depth areas. Everything is okay with me, and we are moving in fast. I have joined up with the Brigade HQs and am moving along with them. Sherpur was bypassed and cleared. The attack on Jamalpur is being planned. I have been tasked to lay a roadblock once again. I am so happy when your letter dated 25 November was handed over to me.

22 December

The enemy suffered heavy losses at Jamalpur and started withdrawing towards Dhaka. After the successful battle of Jamalpur, the Brigade linked up with the troops of 2 Parachute Regiment (PARA) airdropped at Tangail on 10/11 December. The Mukti Bahini was detached from me here, and the advance from hereon was fast and furious. After 2 PARA operations in Tangail, there were frantic preparations for the final thrust on Dhaka. Good sense prevailed on General Niazi, and on 16 December, the surrender was announced. Brigadier Kler was keen to get into Dhaka. The Brigade Education Officer, Captain Balbir Singh, and I decided to go in to look for accommodation for our stay. Somehow, I got left out, and a couple of hours later, we got the sad news that he had been killed by the Pakistan troops who were still holding on to their posts inside Dhaka. I had lost a good brother and an officer. His sudden loss also made me think of what a narrow escape I'd had. I was reminded of the saying, '*Goli-goli pe likha hai marne waale ka naam*'. We entered Dhaka and stayed at the President's Palace as Brigadier Kler, the brigade commander, wanted to do so for the first night (we later moved to the cantonment area). I hope you have received my letter written on the President's crested paper which I posted on 17 December.[16]

On 17 December, the surrender of the Pakistan Armed forces had taken place in the parade ground. On 18 December, our Chief, General Sam Manekshaw, had addressed all of us at Dhaka. There had been political turmoil, and the people had been waiting eagerly for the arrival of Mujibur Rehman. I had not ventured out to the market area as the shops had not opened then. The place had been a mess as West Pakistan was least interested in the development of this part of their country. On 21 December, the Bangladesh officials in exile had arrived.

[16] Unfortunately, this letter is missing from the bundle. In that letter, I had described our night in the President's Place. It had been a very comfortable night—food had been delivered from a five-star hotel, and we had the choicest whisky to drink as well as a comfortable bed to sleep on. We had shifted to the Pakistan Officer Mess accommodation in the cantonment area next day.

All had been praying for Mujib's safety and had been eagerly awaiting his arrival. There had been a great deal of apprehension about the future of Bangladesh without Sheikh Mujibur Rehman. I had been glad to know that my wife had been doing well and had asked her to send a photograph of the baby bump as soon as she could have.

24 December from Dhaka

There is a great deal of uncertainty about our move out. Our stay is going to be longish—I suppose till such time that the Bangladesh government feels confident of managing their affairs. I have been exploring the place, and I went to the Dhaka International Hotel for coffee. A funny incident occurred when I accompanied my friend, a Sikh officer from the brigade HQ, to the military hospital (staffed by Pakistani doctors) for treatment of his tooth. When he was on the chair getting examined by the dentist, a Pakistani nurse came up and asked me whether it was safe for her to attend to him! Later I learned that they were told in their school and home to keep away from Sikh men. I have made a few local friends here. I have been invited to attend a birthday and a Christmas party at Ghosh's place. Mr Ghosh and his wife, an Irish lady, are a very hospitable couple. I have been advised not to shop on my own as the lady will help me later.

26 December from Dhaka

I met a few friends. Captain Anand (Commando Instructor) is also in Dhaka. We both tried to book a call to Eastern Command to inquire about our move back, but there was no answer. Christmas was a quiet and a homely affair at Ghosh's place. The locals are still reeling under the effect of subjugation by West Pakistan but now have great hopes for a better future in their liberated land. As for the Pakistanis, I hope that this humiliating defeat, surrender, and the treatment that we have given to their prisoners will put some sense into their heads.

The above was the last letter to my wife. We made the best use of our time waiting for orders to move back. I managed an airlift to Chittagong, the city famous for leather goods. With the help of my local friends bought some of the famous Dhaka saris. In January 1972, we moved back to Belgaum, and on 13 June, our son was born. In the meantime, all my letters were compiled and published in the local magazine by my father who had settled in Dharwad. They were titled *My Son's Letters from the Battlefield*. I had carried a Kodak box camera, bought from our CSD canteen in Belgaum, and had carried a few extra film reels with it too. The results were fairly good. I am uploading a few of them with this write-up.

The Bangladesh War changed the course of history and the geography of the continent. This year, when we are celebrating its golden jubilee, I feel happy that in addition to the opportunity to participate in the war, I have also been able to capture a part of history through my letters and photographs from the battlefield.

Late Captain Balbir and the author having lunch with the Mukti Bahini

I am the boss now–address by a member of the Mukti Bahini

The author with Brigadier Kler & General Nagra in Dacca

Surrender of Pakistani troops

General Manekshaw's visit after the surrender of Pakistani troops

Jubilant Bangladeshi friends

The author with Captain Anand and GLO IAF

Brigadier Kanbargimath (Retired) was commissioned into the Dogra Regiment in 1966 and he joined his battalion in Nagaland. He later served as Instructor, Commando Wing, Belgaum, and took part in the War of 1971. After a stint at IMA, Dehradun, he commanded 2 DOGRA[17], a battalion commanded by his father. Thereafter he served in Junior Leaders Wing, Belgaum, and later commanded 112 Mountain Brigade in North Sikkim. He retired from the College of Combat Junior Command Wing and is happily settled in Bangalore.

[17] 2nd Battalion, The Dogra Regiment

The Kilo Flight

A Chronicled Personal Account

Air Commodore Arun Karandikar

Kilo Flight was a clandestine unit formed with a few Pakistan Air Force pilots who escaped from East Pakistan during the refugee influx into India after the genocide inflicted on the local populace from 1970 onwards.

I was posted to No. 43 Squadron in January 1971 after the Command Conversion Course. In early May, Flying Officer K.S. Rajan, Flight Lieutenant P.L. Chopra (Navigator), Flight Lieutenant Biswas (Flight Signaller) and I were selected by the commanding officer, Wing Commander K.C. (Koka) Sharma, for a detachment to fly for Eastern Command. As per him, we could pass off as Bengalis! I wasn't convinced at all.

For about 15 days, we airlifted bridging and other equipment, Army and Mukti Bahini personnel wearing civilian clothes and lungi, to generally unused landing grounds like Ambari, Coochbehar, and Balurghat on the border, and Agartala and Bagdogra. We were told to keep quiet about what we did or saw. These places were also in proximity to the training camps where the Indian Army trained the Mukti Bahini. It entailed a lot of flying in the notorious pre-monsoon weather of that region, including a massive airlift of refugees from June onwards.

A variety of transport aircraft undertook the airlift to relocate the lakhs of people streaming into India. Two C-130s of the USAF supplemented the force. They mostly lifted people out of Agartala, the most convenient entry point, herded them into the aircraft, seated them on the floor, and then them herded out. The aircraft was cleaned and disinfected after every sortie.

I knew nothing about Kilo Flight until I was detailed to join them on 1 December 1971 from No. 43 Squadron (Ibexes), flying into Dimapur where they were based with Squadron Leader S.K. Chaudhary, a senior pilot and Qualified Flying Instructor. The raison d'etre of creating this unit was to give its pilots a sense of participation in the war to liberate East Pakistan from the Pakistani rulers. The aircraft I was allotted was the HJ882. It had nosed over the previous day during a full-power run by a technician, and both propeller tips got bent! They just changed the propellers and declared the aircraft serviceable with a lower maximum RPM![18]

The aircraft was like a personal possession till 16 December. There were 9 Pakistan Air Force (PAF) pilots; the senior-most was Squadron Leader Sultan Mahmud, who later became the Chief of Air Staff and was a helicopter pilot. I remember Flight Lieutenant Alam, who had flown the F-86 and another Flight Lieutenant Alam, a C-130 pilot, a Captain Shahabuddin from a regional airline and one Sharafuddin. Sultan Mahmud and the fighter pilot, Badrul Alam, were trained on an Allouette helicopter by Squadron Leader C.M. Singla, the rest on the Otter by Squadron Leader Ghoshal. Both aircrafts were fitted with 30-mm rocket pods and a machine gun firing sideways in the rear, the door being removed on the left side, operated by an airman crew member. There was talk of equipping a

[18] Revolutions per minute

Dakota similarly, but it was never done. Nor was any pilot trained to fly a Dakota at that time. Their tales of the unique privileges enjoyed by military officers in Pakistan was the cause of some envy!

Group Captain Chandan Singh, Vir Chakra (VrC), then Station Commander Jorhat, was the Task Force Commander—a dynamic go-getter, an AN-12 pioneer and a VrC awardee for his role on AN 12s in the 1965 war with Pakistan.

When Air 2, Western Air Command, sent me, a newly commissioned Pilot Officer, he was the one who put me on an AN-12 squadron to train and fly as a co-pilot. Till then, these aircraft were flown by experienced, relatively senior pilots. I logged about 12 p.m. in 2 years there, and that jump-started my flying career. There was a sense of impending war as the monsoon receded, particularly around Diwali, but nothing happened. We had assumed visibly aggressive postures on both our eastern and western borders, waiting for Pakistan to make the first move. There had been undeclared attacks on Pakistani forces in some sectors, in late November, supposedly by Mukti Bahini, but with significant Indian Army involvement.

On 2 December 1971, we moved from Dimapur to Kailashahar airfield—a small 3,000 feet strip, usable only in daytime and unmanned. A low-level sortie, about 300 feet above ground level, an ultra-low run over the strip to drive away cattle, as we did daily at Lilabari, a short circuit and a short field landing! Flying without restrictions of any kind was enjoyable! There was an Air Observation Post (AOP) Auster already on the small apron. Captain Kripalani, ex 22 NDA, and Captain Grewal were the pilots. They had been directing artillery fire of the field guns supporting the initial raids in end-November, behind enemy lines, to secure some tactical advantage for the attack on Shamshernagar, just across the border. The space in the terminal was limited—the Bangladeshis and Squadron Leader S.K. Chaudhary occupied the available office space, and there were only two toilets other than the one with the Aerodrome Officer's room occupied by

Group Captain Chandan Singh. The Bangladeshi airmen had tents. We managed a transistor radio from the aerodrome officer on which we could listen to the news broadcasts. There was an army field telephone. My bed was the ubiquitous holdall of those days, rolled open to sleep on wherever there was space in the building. In the morning, I rolled it up and put it in the aircraft. My flying suit was a 24-hour attire!

The balloon went up on 3 December 1971 with Pakistan attacking our airfields in the western theatre. To give the Bangladeshi pilots the privilege of firing the first shots in East Pakistan, Chandan Singh sent the Allouette with Sultan Mahmud and Alam around midnight to attack the oil tanks at Chittagong Port, and the Otter with the other Alam and Sharafuddin to attack the fuel depot at Narayanganj. Their rockets set the tanks on fire at both places. However, both were uncertain of their position while returning. The Alouette was recovered at Teliamura near Agartala with petromax lamps and the Otter at Kumbhigram on gooseneck flares. Luckily both places had air traffic controllers and homers. I flew into Kumbhigram in the wee hours of that night with essential spares for the Otter. Other than that, my task was to undertake sorties between Kailashahar, Kumbhigram and Dimapur on an as-required basis. One sortie to drop a few troops at Shamshernagar, just across the border on 5 December, resulted in Pakistan artillery targeting the airfield, as informed by Captain Kripalani, who saw the explosions. All sorties were flown at 300–500 feet above obstruction level (AOL).

Till 6 December, when we got official word that there was no enemy air force threat present. Then onwards, we flew as we pleased but above 5,000 feet over enemy territory to stay clear of ground fire. All the flying was on verbal instructions from Chandan Singh; only flying hours were filled in Form 700.[19]

[19] A prescribed form of the Air Force

Special Helicopter Borne Operations (SHBO)

On 5 December, while we were sitting around during the evening meal, Chandan Singh mentioned his idea of using helicopters for quick induction of troops. Lieutenant General Sagat Singh, the dynamic and bold general officer commanding IV Corps, was his close friend. Like other formation commanders, he wanted to be the first to reach Dacca!

Their first objective was to contain the Pakistani garrison at Sylhet. So, the first operation was to heli-lift the 4/5 GR[20] of 59 Mountain Brigade, with a SHBO. No. 110 Helicopter Unit (HU) Mi-4s flew into Kailashahar on 7 December from Teliamura where they had first assembled from dispersed locations. They initially inducted these troops in two waves of three vics[21] each to a football field south of Sylhet. The CO, Squadron Leader C.S. Sandhu, led the first wave and Flight Lieutenant P.K. Vaid the second. The first-ever night-SHBO was planned on 8 December from Kailashahar. It was great to have some familiar guys to chat with the chopper guys around, all excited about the event and first-ever night SHBO. But I had to find a new spot to roll out my holdall to sleep!

Flying the Dakota all Alone

On 7 December, Chandan Singh summoned me to undertake an urgent flight to Kumbhigram for some essential stores for the next SHBO. To my surprise, he asked if I was confident to fly the Dakota alone! Apparently, Squadron Leader Chaudhary was not available. That was quintessentially Chandan Singh, I cannot imagine any other commander taking such a decision, even in wartime. It was an eerie feeling to be all alone in a cockpit meant for four. I had two East Pakistan airmen to look after the load. There was a great flow of

[20] 4th Battalion, The 5th Regiment, Gorkha Rifles

[21] A formation devised for military aircrafts with three or more crafts flying in close formation with the leader at the apex and the rest of the flight en echelon to the left and the right, the whole resembling the letter 'V'.

adrenaline the first time! I had to execute all that the co-pilot would typically do, like reach out across the right-hand seat to operate the gills, operate the flap lever and raise and lower the undercarriage (wheels). The only complicated part was the undercarriage—it required me to take the right foot off the rudder immediately after take-off, kick off the lock of the latch lever, leave the throttles, pull up the latch lever with the right hand, then reach out and raise the gear operating handle. We barely cleared the trees after take-off on that short runway. At about 85 to 90 miles per hour, an engine failure could cause serious problems if the foot was not on the rudder or the wheels were down! The sequence was reversed for lowering the wheels, but it was not critical like on take-off. All the flying was manual, the autopilot was primitive and normally unusable, but the Dakota could be trimmed to fly a very steady heading and altitude. The ground crew at Kumbhigram were shocked to see the right seat empty when I taxied in. The next night, I repeated the same trip. It gets much lonelier at night with nothing to see; the few towns that had lights were blacked out, and Assam was generally a black hole in those days. It gave an eerie feeling to see vacant cockpit seats of co-pilot, navigator and signaller bathed in ultraviolet light. There was radio silence, too, as no one else was flying at night in that area. Quite an experience! At least we had clear skies; the moon rose around 8 p.m. and progressively later as the days went by.

I flew six such solo sorties. On one flight to Silchar and back, Captain Shahabuddin of Bangladesh, who had Pilatus Porter experience, asked to accompany me. He was allowed to do so.

Operations After 9 December

On 8 December, the SHBO was completed ex-Kailashahar by 110 HU, including a first-ever night operation. I did my last solo flight late at night to Kumbhigram, returning early morning, and then flew with Chandan Singh to Jorhat. On the return, the squadron detailed Flying Officer Nanu Narayan to fly with me. The helicopters flew to Agartala that morning for operations ex-Agartala.

Over 8 and 9 December, we airlifted the Kilo Flight to Agartala and did a couple of flights to Kumbhigram. Our accommodation, again shared with the helicopter pilots, was whatever space was available in the terminal building; the men had tents! The next SHBO by 110 HU was to lift troops of 57 Mountain Division (4 GUARDS[22], 10 BIHAR[23] and 18 RAJPUT[24] and their artillery and engineers) across the Meghna River near Brahmanbaria, to Narsingdi and Bhairab Bazaar. Sagat Singh, Chandan Singh, CO & Flight Commander 110 HU flew in an Allouette to reconnaissance the area for suitable helipads. They were fired upon but realised it only when the co-pilot, Flying Officer G.P.S. Sidhu, got a bullet in his leg. There were many bullet holes seen on the chopper after landing back. Subsequently, the entire helicopter lift of 57 Division went off without a hitch or casualty. Mi-4s of 111 and 105 HU also took part. The operations were both by day and night over the next four days.

At Agartala, there were numerous casualty evacuation sorties by Dakota and Packet aircraft during the day. Hundreds of casualties would arrive, with stretchers laid out along the tarmac area. It was distressing to see a large number of mine-blast injuries. Their physical state would be assessed, and their transfer to various hospitals organised by the medics. It was surprising to see no civilian welfare effort, unlike the western front, except the Red Cross, to provide any assistance while they lay there. Some of us aircrew used to go around with water and orange juice. When not busy with Kilo Flight commitments, I was tasked with a couple of casualty evacuation trips with sitting casualties, as the aircraft was not modified with stretchers. From Agartala, we mainly had commitments to

---

[22] 4th Battalion, Brigade of the Guards

[23] 10th Battalion, The Bihar Regiment

[24] 18th Battalion, The Rajput Regiment

Kailashahar, Dimapur and Kumbhigram for logistic support of the Mi-4s, and Allouette and dropped some leaflets en route too on a couple of flights. We got news of the Para Brigade being dropped at Tangail, north of Dacca, on the evening of 11 December. That resulted in 2 Para Battalion (Colonel Pannu) getting ahead of IV Corps to enter Dacca first!

On 15 December, I was directed to fly at dawn to Kailashahar to airlift troops to Agartala. I am not too sure of the battalion/ companies that were airlifted. Probably de-inducted elements of 81 Mountain Brigade, likely 4 KUMAON[25] from their physical appearance. One Dakota from my squadron joined us and flew three sorties during the day before returning with casualties from Agartala. Flying virtually nonstop through the day and till near midnight, we completed the task. I carried out 15 landings in all, seven at night. At Kailashahar, the short airstrip had only six goosenecks on each side for night landing. At Agartala, the available flares were laid out along only one edge of the runway to mark its length. Depth perception and perspective assessment were very difficult. Except for the lights at Teliamura, there was no other lighting which made it easier to spot.

Surrender Ceremony at Dacca

On 16 December, I flew to Jorhat to pick up Chandan Singh and return to Agartala. There was a buzz about a ceasefire/surrender. There had been an airstrike on the Government House at Dacca when a high-level meeting was on. On the way, he confirmed that there would be a surrender ceremony at the Race Course in Dacca and that I could go in one of the Mi-4s to witness the same. I went with Flight Lieutenant Jayaraman and Flying Officer B.L.K. Reddy. It was an amazing experience to fly over fully manned anti-aircraft guns, see the Pakistani troops formed up on parade with all their weapons, and get cheered as we alighted and carried on the shoulders of the local public as we

---

[25] 4th Battalion, The Kumaon Regiment

got out of available vehicles, to the venue. I was standing at the table moments before the historic picture was taken, as I gave my place to Squadron Leader Aujla, the Senior Administrative Officer Jorhat, the Sikh officer in the picture, who had come along with Chandan Singh. I met some army course mates, Pradeep Sharma of the Engineers who came in on a PT-76 tank with the leading elements, and Ashok Choudry, aide-de-camp (ADC) to General Krishna Rao of 8 Mountain Division, who flew in on a Mi-4. It was evening when we arrived, and we had to leave in a hurry after the ceremony for the return trip to get airborne before nightfall. It was an exhilarating experience for all to see Lieutenant General Niazi signing the instrument of surrender and Lieutenant General J.S. Aurora counter-signing. I flew back to Jorhat that night with Chandan Singh, missing the celebrations at Agartala with the chopper boys.

The war had ended! I had flown a total of 49 sorties, five as a single pilot on the Dakota in 14 days, including 15 on one day! Throughout, we never thought of rest or food; we just did what was required and sustained ourselves with what was at hand. Though we faced no enemy bullets, it was a great experience for a fledgeling pilot to undertake these flights on short runways with less than basic facilities and almost no lighting at night.

On 20 December, I flew with Chandan Singh to Dimapur for the formal handing over the Allouette to Sultan Mahmud and the winding down of Kilo Flight. As a piece of memorabilia, I got my Bangladeshi flag inscribed on 16 December 1971, signed by him (see photograph below). His request for rockets on the Allouette, to settle some personal scores, was firmly turned down by Chandan Singh. We went to Agartala overflying the Dacca runway and Dimapur again before returning to Jorhat late that night. I also flew to Dacca during the subsequent days for various reasons after the runway had been somewhat repaired.

Kilo Flight was now history!

Group Captain Chandan Singh was awarded the Maha Vir Chakra.
Squadron Leader C.M. Singla & Squadron Leader S.K. Chaudhary were each awarded the Vir Chakra.
Squadron Leader C.S. Sandhu, CO 110 HU and Flight Lieutenant P.K. Vaid, Flight Commander were each awarded the Vir Chakra.
Most of the Bangladeshi pilots also received gallantry awards from their government.

Air Commodore Arun Karandikar, VM, VSM, (Retired) is an alumnus of the 28th NDA Course and a bronze medallist. He was commissioned into the Indian Air Force with the 97th Pilots' Course. He was part of the first batch of pilots trained on the Boeing 737-200 inducted for VIP operations. He was listed in the *Limca Book of Records* 1996 for maximum hours in military flying.

The Battlefield Blues

Brigadier Balram Singh Mehta

Chance, luck, or randomness plays an important role not only in life but also on the battlefield. Reflect on your own life from the time you left home for education, from college to a career, from being single to nurturing a family, from Captain to Colonel, or from the first hole of golf to the eighteenth, and you will agree that success or failure sometimes arises neither from remarkable skill nor from great incompetence, but fortuitous circumstances, from a serendipity of sorts.

On the afternoon of 20 November 1971, the C Squadron, 45 CAVALRY[26], received orders to cross the Kabodak river flowing alongside the International Border between India and erstwhile East Pakistan and advance a few kilometres to establish a firm base. The Squadron Commander Major Narag, (Chiefy), gave short and crisp orders. To add excitement and zing to the proceedings, Chiefy, in a rare moment of inspiration, gave names of important towns of Pakistan—Rawalpindi, Karachi, Lahore to the tactical bounds

---

[26] 45th Cavalry Regiment

selected by him. These were dutifully jotted down by the troop leaders but consigned to memory by Chiefy. The briefing was to end with the usual *'koi shuk ya sawal'*, when the newly promoted junior commissioned officer (JCO) troop leader raised a genuine doubt, 'Who will give the orders to open fire?' The question, asked in all innocence, jolted each one into the harsh reality that this was not another formation-level exercise but the start of a war. The tank commanders and crews suddenly realised that they would now have to exercise their training and discretion and no longer wait for orders to shoot. The transition is easy for trained soldiers but can be traumatic for the more sensitive. The hesitation or reluctance to 'shoot to kill' however melts away after the first few rounds have been fired.

Two companies of 14 PUNJAB[27] (Nabha Akal) were to ride piggyback on our PT-76 tanks while the rest were to footslog to the given rendezvous. The tank column led by troop leader Lieutenant Teji Sidhu commenced the advance around 4 p.m. on 20 November. From the International Border (IB) till the first bound, the advance was deliberate and entailed basic troop level drills of leapfrog and one leg on the ground. The riverine terrain and bamboo clusters demanded vigilance and caution as a movement of suspected Mujahids around the villages was noticeable. With dusk descending, it became imperative to speed up the advance. Chiefy accordingly gave orders to Teji Sidhu to change course and now advance towards code word 'Lahore' instead of 'Rawalpindi'. Teji was quick to respond and moved in the direction ordered after checking his map. It was not long before bedlam broke out on the squadron radio net. Chiefy was on the air to correct Teji that he was heading for 'Karachi' instead of 'Lahore'. Teji gave fresh orders for change of direction to his tank commanders, only to be berated that he was now heading for 'Rawalpindi'. Much of what was exchanged as radio messages cannot be put down in writing. It would suffice to say that memory

---

[27] 14th Battalion, The Punjab Regiment

can sometimes lead you astray when advancing into enemy territory. The advance was soon resumed by referring to the cardinal points of the prismatic compass. By dusk, we were in the vicinity of our given rendezvous when the Commanding Officer (CO) 14 PUNJAB, Colonel R.K. Singh, gave orders to halt the advance and deploy in darkness.

Before midnight, the marching columns arrived followed by the 'F' echelon of the infantry battalion. The general atmosphere was one of a formation-level exercise without umpires. The 14 PUNJAB riding piggyback had slithered off 'C' Squadron tanks to dig weapon pits and take up a hasty defence while tanks deployed around infantry company localities.

During the night movement of vehicles on the road, Chaugacha-Jessore was observed from a distance of 2–3 kilometres. The presence of tanks was suspected, but could not be confirmed as all observations were based on the sound of engines and vehicle lights were seen. The troops remained alert but there was no alarm. Past midnight, a full moon appeared over the horizon. In the moonlight, the silhouette of soldiers digging trenches could be seen followed by the sound of a pickaxe or shovel striking a rock or the metallic sound of empty water *pakkhals* (water container) or defence stores being unloaded. From the trench close by, one overheard the tragic watery grave of nine brave-hearts of the Battalion when their boat carrying fully armed soldiers capsized while crossing the Kabodak river. One could not help but admire the strength and tenacity of this Battalion's personnel, who despite a tragedy stood determined to fulfil their soldierly duty.

On 21 November 1971, we were greeted with dense fog that limited visibility to 20 metres. The tanks were adjusted pre-dawn, fire arcs were coordinated and engines switched off when a runner arrived with a message from the Brigade HQ to detach two troops under the squadron 21C of 'C' Squadron to a different location. Teji and I walked back towards Chiefy's tank. He read the message and reacted in the typical cavalry tradition: important orders for attachment and detachment of troops must come from the commandant directly. His quick riposte, 'no move till further orders; return to your tanks.' By the time we returned to accept a cup of piping hot tea from Ris Chakraborty, Lieutenant General A.A.K. Niazi was ready to launch his biggest attack of the 1971 war in East Pakistan to teach India and the Mukti Bahini a military lesson. For this attack, he had marshalled two infantry battalions, supported by 3[I] Armoured Squadron with 14 Chaffee tanks and the normal complement of other arms and services under Brigadier Mohammad Hayat, Commander 107 Infantry Brigade.

Chiefy, like a full-back of the NDA football team playing the Durand Cup final in 1953, was now called upon to play his destined role. His team consisted of talented and well-trained troop leaders and tank commanders and crews from Other Indian Classes (OIC). The OIC virtually represented all classes of personnel who were listed as non-martial by the British, and therefore denied the honour to enrol as combatants till 1947.

After Independence, the government corrected this anomaly by raising this sub-unit under the OIC category. This OIC Squadron now formed the forward line in the battle zone not only of the combat group deployed but of the entire Army and country. The dice was about to roll, and chance, luck, kismet, would determine the fate of not just the soldiers deployed along the borders but also that of 10 million refugees deprived of home, hearth, human dignity, and justice.

Dawn comes early in the East. On 21 November, the winter sky was enveloped with dense fog and a thick blanket of cumulus nimbus clouds. An eerie silence permeated the morning gloom with not a bird chirping or flying in the skies above. It was as if the entire battle zone had frozen into inactivity. Each tank crew and section deployed on the ground was encased in a cocoon surrounded by dense fog and limited visibility, creating a feeling of isolation. The tank crew formed small groups of early morning tea tasters enjoying this elixir of life and nursing the warmth of the enameled tea mugs to ward off the bitter cold when suddenly the sound of gunfire triggered every one into action. A heavy barrage of artillery shells was all over us as we quickly mounted our tanks and switched on our radio sets to hear: 'Enemy tanks advancing! Fire, fire!'

Looking through the gun-sights you could only register the flash of the Chaffee tank as it fired from behind the shield of dense fog. The tanks came belching fire, tearing through the screen of fog to be greeted by the PT-76 Squadron. Every flash from the enemy guns was picked up by our tank crews, and soon each one was claiming '*ek tank barbad kar diya*' over the radio net. Bedlam had broken loose. The full-back footballer of yore moved his tank up and fired the standard high explosive (HE) round preloaded in the gun chamber, followed by the Armour Piercing (AP) shot that ricocheted off the Chaffee. Finally, the High Explosive Anti-Tank (HEAT) projectile set the Chaffee ablaze. Chiefy was all excited, and his shaabash to the crew got carried over the squadron net: '*Maro, Maro, Shaabash.*'

Like all tank commanders, Chiefy too had his head and torso exposed and the tank cupola open.

'Reference last kill, right, 2 o'clock, tank.'

A random medium-machine-gun burst caught Chiefy in the chest while the gunner waited with his thumb on the firing switch and the enemy Chaffee within the crosshairs of his gunsight when he felt warm blood splash all over him. Distracted, he looked up and saw Chiefy collapse and slump over. The crew, ready to engage the enemy tank, were shocked and stupefied by this grave tragedy. As the tank-versus-tank battle raged outside, the gunner, L.D. Dineshwar Nath, now drenched in blood with the squadron commander's head resting on his lap, passed the most unfortunate radio message in his Assamese accent with a heavy, grieving heart: '*Saab ab aur nahin hai!*'

The message shocked and numbed the minds of all tank crews. Momentarily, it appeared as if the squadron had been overwhelmed by this tragedy, till the squadron second-in-command's voice came on air to announce: 'Delta 40 for all station Delta, I have assumed command.'

The battle continued till the enemy's 3 (I) Armoured Squadron was destroyed and two battalions badly mauled. Hours later, the tank crews would extricate Chiefy's body from the tank and line up on both sides of a dirt track to bid their final farewell to their beloved squadron commander. In a different setting, we would have been singing 'He's a jolly good fellow, and so say all of us', but that day all we felt was a deep pain inside us at this loss. In a fitting tribute, crew members fired a 21-pistol salute to a fallen comrade as the vehicle carrying his body left for the Regimental Headquarters while the rays of the setting sun spread over the battlefield. The enemy artillery fired a salvo as if to pay tribute to this fallen brave.

Chiefy had made the supreme sacrifice. He lived and died as a soldier, bringing honour and glory to his family and unit. Chiefy's decision to delay the move of two troops was critical to the outcome of the Garibpur battle. Chance, kismet, luck had played its hand, and the rest is history.

It is exceptional and rare in tank warfare for one squadron to destroy an enemy squadron of 14 tanks at the cost of a single loss. Niazi, who had planned and orchestrated this battle, had a few days earlier boasted to foreign correspondents: 'We have never lost. Look in the history books. I challenge you to find in history anything but victories. We have never lost, and the Indians have never won. I can easily take them on, three to one.' Besides the loss of a complete armoured squadron, two battalions and the Reconnaissance & Support Company of Pakistan were badly mauled and prisoners captured. In the air battle over the same battlefield on 22 November, our Gnats downed three Sabre jets and captured two pilots. As this battle took place before the open declaration of war, it significantly impacted Pakistani military leadership. It influenced the power play and diplomacy between nations such as the USA, USSR, China, and deliberations at the United Nations.

The Battle of Garibpur fought on 21 November 1971 represents a significant and radical change in the political and military mindset of the country. India, which was humbled in 1962 and had fought an unfinished war in 1965, prepared itself for 1971. Garibpur acted as the viagra to infuse our defence forces and the citizens with a new spirit of being second to none. As a country, we were about to shed the 'historical baggage' of our past to soon emerge as an assertive regional power capable of projecting its cultural identity, human values, and military might.

On 24 November, Indira Gandhi made a historic statement in the Parliament on the Battle of Garibpur, informing that it resulted in the destruction of Pakistan's 13 Chaffees Tanks and three Sabre jets and the capture of their two pilots, sending shock waves across world capitals. This early victory served as a trumpet call across the globe, virtually announcing the birth of a new nation, Bangladesh, and India emerging as a regional power.

A word about the tank PT-76: the Russians called it the Palavushi Tanka-76. The Indian troops referred to it as 'Pippa'–a tin-can afloat on water. With light armour no thicker than a steel helmet, a small calibre 76 mm gun, a three-man crew, and an amphibious tank shaped like a matchbox with water-jet propellers, it did not win favour within the Armoured Corps Inducted in the 1965 war by the 7 CAVALRY, PT-76 were soon after allotted to the 63 CAVALRY, after being discarded by these illustrious regiments to re-equip their independent squadrons. The balance tanks were relegated to the new raising of 45 CAVALRY and 69 Armoured Regiment. These regiments grew up as poor country-cousins of the mainstream Risala, forming a part of various armoured divisions and independent armoured brigades.

PT-76 regiments played out their destined role in the riverine terrain of East Pakistan. They became a symbol of military pride, having played a significant role in what the Indian Prime Minister Narendra Modi, in a speech on 8 April 2017 at the Manekshaw Centre in New Delhi, called the 'biggest battle for human dignity and humanitarian cause fought in the previous century'. The 45 CAVALRY takes pride in that it led the Eastern Army supported by other arms and services to create a new country—Bangladesh. The 'Pippa' won the only tank battle in the eastern theatre and the only tank battle that our 'Kharga' strike corps (II Corps) has seen as yet. It was India's finest hour and the most significant victory achieved by the Army by humbling the pride of the Pakistan Armed forces, when 93,000 of its personnel laid down arms in surrender on 16 December 1971 at Dacca (now Dhaka).

The Solitary Sapper

Major Pradeep Sharma

My first and only war ended in 1971. What happened therein is a little hazy. While I vividly recall small bits of action, I find it tough to recall the names of people, places, and even the exact sequence of events. More so, because there is an almost total absence of access to recorded unit history and other available data, and very little material could be located through repeated internet searches. Nevertheless, bits and pieces were collected from a variety of sources and put together for penning the narrative below.

Almost ten million refugees walked across from then East Pakistan into India as Pakistan Army's infamous Operation Searchlight (among others), and a devastating cyclone caused perhaps two million deaths there. A new country was born, and possibly the world's largest surrender of military men took place. All this happened in less than one year. Yet, the lack of reliable historical records is suppressed, possibly due to Pakistan's alliance and collusion with the West. Besides, there is a disdain for history and general indifference to what happens in this part of the world.

After my post-degree course at the College of Military Engineering (CME) Poona, I was posted to the 3 Engineer Regiment just after New Year's Day in 1971. The Regimental Headquarters (RHQ) was at Tamalpur, a short drive from Rangiya (Assam), where 23 Mountain Division headquarters were located, 3 Engineer Regiment being the Divisional Engineers. Major General 'Rocky' Hira was the General Officer Commanding (GOC) 23 Division. Our regiment was housed in bamboo bashas. Life was going on in a typical, lazy way with a peacetime routine and training with occasional flood relief duties. Little did we realise how eventful and momentous 1971 was going to be.

A new Commanding Officer (CO), Lieutenant Colonel (later Major General) Joginder Singh, took command of the regiment in July, three to four months prior to the balloon going up. There were some questions of 'crossing sheets of water', 'when the monsoon waters in paddy fields would dry up', and the like, asked of us by the middle of the year. Our regiment was ordered to move to Tripura in July–August. It took five special trains carrying all ranks with equipment and stores for a rail journey from Rangiya to Dharmanagar. The Divisional HQ and Regimental HQ were located around Kakraban, a small village near Radhakishorepur in southwest Tripura. I was assigned to the Regimental HQ as the field engineer/adjutant. Once we reached Kakraban, operational works were the main activity for a couple of months.

Huge cash payments that ran into lakhs of rupees were being given almost daily to refugees and other muster roll labourers employed for track construction. Drawing cash from the treasury, which was a two-hour drive away, handing it over in bulk to individual sub-units/sites, and depositing back the undisbursed amounts before the close of cash hours was a major assignment and headache over several weeks.

The CO was on a daily early-out-late-return routine from recces and visits to field companies every day. The three field companies of the regiments (58, 60 and 375 Field Company) were attached to and located with the three brigades of 23 Division (83, 181 and 301 Mountain Brigades). Within a couple of days of the war, operational areas and objectives stretched from Comilla to Chittagong, over some 150 km aerial distance or 200 km by road.

50 Field Park Company was at the Dharmanagar railhead (a four-hour drive from the Regimental HQ, around 180 km away). With all sub-units widely dispersed and scattered over some 100 km, the Regimental HQ had barely ten all ranks available as its total strength. We were housed in dug-in tents in Kakraban, not far from the Divisional HQ. The border and Comilla Cantonment (in what was then East Pakistan) were barely 10 km away.

The first skirmish in which we took part was in the Belonia Bulge on 15 November 1971. Coincidentally, I turned 25 on the same day. The actual war, called Operation Cactus Lily, commenced 18 days later, on 3 December. A somewhat humorous exchange took place on the D-1 radio net after Parasuram (the Division's objective in the Belonia Bulge) was captured on the night of 15/16 November 1971.

Major General Hira excitedly told the Colonel (General Staff) of the Division, Colonel Rawat (Gunners), clearly on the radio net:

Hira: 'Rawat, we got P.'
Rawat: 'Sorry, Sir, I don't understand.'
Hira: 'Dammit, we captured P.'
Rawat: 'Sorry, Sir, I don't follow.'
Hira: 'We captured Papa.'
Rawat: 'Sorry, Sir, I am unable to get that.'
Hira: 'We captured; I spell Papa Alpha Papa Alpha!'

The only real excitement in November for me was a low-level, high-speed sortie flying in an Alouette chopper painted with Bangladesh colours with the Commanding Officer (CO) and Flight Lieutenant Singla (one of the trainers of Kilo Flight, which became the Bangladesh Air Force). With only two seats in the chopper, my legs were dangling outside the canopy with an MMG slung between the legs. The task was to assess the condition of the roads and count the number of bays of decking needed on Bailey bridges on the roads that were likely to be used after the war commenced.

Lieutenant Colonel Joginder casually asked me on 2 December, 'How do you like the war?' Truthfully, I answered, 'Not much seems to happen. It is far more exciting and action-filled in the movies!'

Little did I know that I would be in the thick of the action within a day or two of this.

Late on 4 December afternoon, Lieutenant Colonel Joginder told me to get ready for an immediate move. From what transpired over the next few days, the aim was to provide engineer support to 1 Independent Armoured Squadron (7th Light Cavalry) attached to the Division. My CO had volunteered to go as 'engineers in support' but was turned down as too old—a youngster being required for the task. PT-76s from the tank Squadron had assaulted the Lalmai hill feature near the Comilla cantonment. Surprised by an unexpected minefield, several of the squadron's PT-76 tanks got blown up, and the squadron was left with barely six to seven serviceable tanks to be an effective spearhead for the advance of 23 Division. The Squadron Commander had, therefore, insisted on adequate close engineer support before continuing any further advance. A lot of information gathered over subsequent days allowed me to grasp what had happened.

Asking my *thambi* (batman/*sahayak* in a Madras Sapper unit) to get my Field Service Marching Order (FSMO) ready, I went in vain looking for maps and instructions—anything at all—to prepare for the task for which I had been detailed. Nothing whatsoever of the sort was available. 'Reach Division HQ helipad at the soonest possible' was the sum of instructions. The helipad was not too far from our location and I foot-slogged to it as soon as I could.

Within an hour of receiving orders, kitted out in FSMO, with a Sten gun and prodder in hand, I cut a solitary figure at the helipad. A Mi-4 helicopter landed there soon after. From inside the chopper came a shout, 'Where are the Engineers?' The crew asked me to jump in, the rotors having never been switched off. As I climbed in, the pilot shouted, 'Where are the others? Are you the only guy they sent us to drop off?' Recognising the voice of my 28 NDA course and Kilo Squadron mate, Bani Kant Sarma, I tried calling him down from the perch above. We were meeting after years, but there was no time even to exchange any pleasantries—Bani Kant had to drop the Sappers (meaning me!) and be back at his base before the last light. Sadly, that was also the last time I saw him.

In about half an hour, just before the last light, I was dropped off by the Mi-4 at an improvised helipad amidst paddy fields at an unknown place. I had no idea of where I was. Within a minute of my alighting, the helicopter whose rotors had never stopped, took off back to its base.

It became almost fully dark shortly afterwards. Two soldiers approached (who later identified themselves as being from the Squadron) and asked where the Engineers were in chaste Punjabi. All I could reply was, 'Tell me what needs doing.' The duo took me a short distance away and, pointing in a vague general direction, told me that a few of their tanks had got blown 'there' by mines, and some survivors on those tanks had gathered near a damaged tank and needed rescuing and guiding back out of the minefield.

With no compass, no map, no landmark and a vague direction to proceed into a minefield, in complete darkness, I moved forward. The lack of information and clarity was rapidly increasing by the hour! Faced with a situation I had never visualised before, all that occurred to me was to proceed in the manner one had been trained in. Clearing a minefield is done after a detailed recce of the edge and/or extent of the minefield, types of mines laid, plus an appreciation of the likelihood of the enemy on the other side of the minefield firing upon anyone attempting to clear mines. The only way to locate a plastic mine (as of 1971 and probably even now) was to prod the ground. Imagine a thickish metal needle pushed into the ground in a grid every few inches (so that no mine is missed out). Whenever resistance to the prodder is felt, the person prodding checks if the object that stops the prodder from going into the ground is a stone, a mine or whatever. That is how one was trained in the 1960s. It was a very slow and deliberate activity that was to be done diligently, a few inches at a time, moving ahead only after making the path safe from any mines. This is a task where being careless is a near guarantee of instant death or serious injury.

Clearing a safe lane in a minefield is also normally done by well-trained and closely-knit teams of around six to eight people, wherein two to three prod the ground ahead of two persons who, in turn, mark either edge of the cleared lane with a broad white tape staked to the ground every few paces. Teams are rested every hour or two to ensure fatigue and tension does not endanger their safety. Doing a perfect job of clearing and marking a lane is absolutely vital. After all, one must not forget that one walks back into the safe lane once it has been cleared! Of course, tanks/flails/lane clearing explosive hoses can be used, but none of these was available or deployable in this situation. In the present case, this was to be done at night in virtually zero visibility!

Having read about and being aware of the consequences of stepping on or driving over mines, I was, of course, fully aware of the risks of injury or death that lay ahead. The only surety was the presence of mines since several tanks had been blown up. The simplest option would be to ask for reinforcement in the form of an adequate number of trained Sappers to do the mine clearance and await their arrival. However, that would mean halting the advance of the Squadron (which itself was the spearhead of the brigade, 23

Division and IV Corps in advance to the objective, Chandpur, the inland port on River Meghna). Also, abandoning casualties awaiting rescue from inside the minefield to their fate was not something contemplated or acceptable.

What flashed through my mind was that I was foolhardy, unthinking, and stupid. However, I had been trained to think only of accomplishing the mission or task allotted, just following orders and carrying on to the best of one's ability. Thus, I decided to proceed single-handed with 'whatever one possessed'—just a prodder in this case—and the will to rescue those stranded (and possibly wounded inside the minefield) and assist in the advance with the least delay.

Telling the Squadron representatives to hold on to my backpack and Sten gun, I started to prod and began to move in whatever I could make of the direction as had been pointed out by the duo.

I had forgotten to wear my watch and all idea of time is as recalled from hazy memory. After possibly an hour or more, it seemed pointless to keep bending over, prodding and proceeding in an indeterminate direction. I had covered probably 25 metres and not encountered or located a single mine. It would be hours before advancing even a few hundred metres. Making headway and that too without any person or tape to mark the path checked and found free of (anti-personnel and anti-tank) mines was equally futile. So, I wondered if anything worthwhile would be achieved by continuing further prodding through the night.

Realising the futility of the task in hand, considering the time, tools and resources available, it seemed that just walking in the generally indicated direction was the only course open, even if it was dangerous, hazardous and fraught with the risk of loss of a limb or life as it may be. I knew that my decision could easily become worse, with no assurance of success or survival. What egged me on was the hope that maybe it would get better.

By putting one's head closer to the ground, some slightly

taller objects seemed to be vaguely apparent against the night sky. They were some distance away in roughly the direction I had been proceeding on earlier. Abandoning prodding entirely, I started walking in that general direction, albeit hesitantly. After an hour or two, I must have made some noise because I heard a shout, '*Oye kaun haiga? India kay Pakistan?*' in the same chaste Punjabi Doaba accent as the two cavalrymen who had met me some hours back! After assuring them that I was indeed 'India', I told them to get off the tanks they were perched on top of and walk behind me while carrying any of those injured with them. I walked in the general direction I had taken to reach them. I had yet to report the arrival of the sappers to the Squadron Commander, though. I hoped that the duo who met me earlier had done the needful already.

Just before first light next morning, we somehow managed to get back to the two cavaliers who were still waiting for us. I put on my backpack, picked my Sten gun and was escorted to Major Inderjit Singh (the Squadron Commander), sitting on a culvert with bloodshot eyes, worry writ large on his face.

'Where are the Engineers?' was his first and only question. When I told him that the available sappers comprised just me, he asked, 'And what the hell will you do by yourself?' I answered, 'Whatever needs to be done by the Sappers'. By then, he had apparently received more than his share of radio messages asking the Squadron's remaining tanks to start leading the advance of the 301 Brigade towards Chandpur. Major Inderjit apparently decided that as the sapper answerable for the safety of his remaining squadron of tanks, I would be positioned on the leading tank. I would stay alert, and hawk-eyed might have been his reasoning for this!

The PT-76 has limited space outside the cupola. The three-man crew inside is also cramped. A rope is tied around the cupola to allow any accompanying infantry soldiers to stand and hang on to the moving tank. That is what I held on to for my dear life as the tanks advanced.

I don't know if I was expected to discern mines while hanging outside the cupola of a PT-76 tank or whether it was reckoned, in the fitness of things, for the Sapper(s) to be the first casualty in case of any untoward happening! So, there I was, hanging on to a rope outside the cupola of the lead tank, commanded by their Squadron second-in-command (2IC), whose name I learnt later to be Freddie Singh Deo. There were just six tanks, and we were moving in stages, waiting for the infantry on foot to catch up between short moves.

An extract from the book by Major General Hira will broadly paint the prevalent situation that night/day when I met Inderjit.

> *'He seemed somewhat depressed despite having assaulted the enemy positions earlier in the day and scattering them in the process. On query, he informed me that he had already lost one-third of his squadron during the first day's fighting and that there was a lot more fighting ahead. I told him of the success, and the enemy's reverses caused by the bold action of his squadron and comforted him. He had enough tanks, I added, to support the divisional offensive. The following day, he was a different person, and there was just no holding him back.'*

Perhaps I can justifiably claim to be part of what transpired that night and, in some small way, the reason for Inderjit being a different person the following day!

Getting back to my story of hanging on to a moving tank, doing so off a rope strung around the cupola of a tank is scary. The slightest negligence (or falling asleep) would make one fall off, with a good chance of getting run over by the tank tracks. Hearing bullets from a machine gun bouncing off the cupola is the scary icing on the cake! In such a situation, nothing is possible for survival except to try and move a bit towards the rear of the tank and hope that there will be no bullet flying around with the name of the hanging Sapper on it—me.

The next day, we were nearing a town in the area Hajiganj-Mudafarganj. The lead tank, with me on the outside of it, approached a river with a Hamilton girder type bridge. I soon found it to be a road-cum-rail bridge with timber decking allowing wheeled vehicular movement on what essentially was a railway bridge. My hair stood on end when a medium machine gun burst from the far bank bounced off the cupola of the tank I was hanging outside of.

Surprisingly, after the first machine gun burst, no more bullets flew. Then, Freddie fired the main gun suddenly without warning in the direction from which the MMG burst had come. In the process, I became deaf in the right ear for some time. He then stopped the tank, opened the hatch and asked me to check and confirm if the bridge was safe to cross.

I dismounted from the tank, discarded my backpack, Sten gun and the prodder. Warily, I walked forward to check, dreading walking into another MMG burst while unarmed in the open. Reaching the bridge safely, I found to my dismay, what looked like a black safety fuse poking out from some loose soil in the middle on the near abutment. One could also see piers (five to six brick masonry piers) that appeared to have been prepared for a deliberate demolition with boreholes connected by an orange-coloured detonating cord. It was a bridge that, to all appearances, had been prepared for deliberate demolition 'in the face of the enemy'. Such preparations for the demolition of a bridge take many weeks of effort. Securing and saving this bridge was vital. Its destruction would delay the advance for hours or days until equipment for a substitute bridge could be brought forward from the rear.

Constant radio messages asking the tanks to secure the far side of the bridge so that the infantry could also cross and resume their advance was promptly, regularly and loudly relayed to me. A bit nonplussed, I was wondering what to do. The bridge, to all appearances, had been thoroughly and painstakingly prepared for a deliberate demolition. The far bank had been 'held' till just a few minutes back by at least a machine gunner who had fired on us. He, or any other person, could as well have set off the demolition charge while firing a machine gun burst.

There were no sappers besides your truly. That too, without digging tools or implements, or even any real-world experience of dealing with such a situation beyond the Young Officers (YOs) course at CME in 1966. So, borrowing a mess tin from the tank crew, I started removing the loose soil from the abutment, hoping against hope that the fuse had just been planted to delay us while we (I) thoroughly checked out the bridge—something that would need an hour or two at least.

I scooped out more loose soil and went further into the ground. To my horror, I saw the fuse going lower and lower into the ground, even beyond two to three feet. It did not now seem to be delaying tactics. I kept digging as fast as I could and finally encountered gun cotton slabs with primers and detonators inserted. By now, I was sweating, less due to the physical work that had just transpired and more due to the worry and fear as this did not appear to be a decoy safety fuse planted solely and merely to interrupt us.

It was impossible to understand why the bridge (at least its abutment) had not been blown up by the same enemy troops who had fired with automatics onto our tanks. All it would have taken is simply a matchstick, a cigarette, or the pressing of a plunger on a generator. My fear now was that this was a booby trap with some kind of a release switch below the explosives. This is usually done to blow up the bridge along with any sappers trying to defuse a prepared demolition. I kept removing all kinds of explosive materials with shaky hands, including the explosive slabs, artillery shells and bags of God knows what explosive materials. Meanwhile, there were constant reminders from Freddie and the crew to hurry up so that the advance could resume. Reaching carefully and gingerly under the last and lowest explosive material, I was relieved to find nothing that suggested a booby trap.

Guess I was very lucky that day at having found nothing untoward. I quickly removed the detonators and primers and chucked them into the river, and proceeded to fill up the excavation as best as possible. Finally, I walked across the bridge and motioned the tanks to cross. Thankfully, no other booby traps or other such lethal stuff were encountered. All in all, it had been a very tense and tiring few hours—but with a happy ending!

Around dusk, the advancing tanks, with a small amount of infantry and elements of the leading Brigade HQ, reached an embankment leading off to the right of the road to the river port of Chandpur, the objective of 23 Division. As we later found out, this was a microwave repeater station of sorts that was abandoned except for a caretaker who showed his face when he was reassured that we were not planning to shoot any locals offhand.

Being without any food for over a day (except *shakarparas* scrounged off the tank crew) and no rest or respite from hanging off a rope outside the PT-76, I could not help but feel that it would be great if one could get a bit of rest, something to eat and maybe a wash around the area. I found a caravan, a nicer civvy version of what we had seen many Shaktiman trucks converted into. The wonder of wonders! In it, I found a foam mattress on which I could lie down. I had found it, and the 'finders keepers' policy held true. I decided to lie there till hunger pangs and a desire to wash took over. With barely any visibility in the almost total darkness, in search for some food and water, I felt what seemed to be a generator control panel right beside the caravan. The generator roared to life on pressing one of several switches. Putting it off at once, I thought of getting permission to start it and get some electricity at least. Walking across to the Brigade Commander, I asked, 'Sir, how would you like the sappers to provide you light?' His answer was an incredulous 'Can you do that?' So, the generator came on, and after checking a few switches, lights along the road on an embankment leading to the microwave station came on. Soon we had bright lights illuminating the area all around us. Looking inside the now lit-up caravan, I found a huge sack filled with American and European tinned food (intended most likely for the firangi occupant of the caravan who had long since decamped). The tank crew and I had a terrific feast. There was even a small electric geyser in the bathroom built into the caravan. Unpacking my backpack, I found a towel and a white kurta-pyjama which my thoughtful *thambi* had packed for wearing at night. After a hot bath on a full stomach, I went to sleep on a soft, comfortable bed, clad in a white kurta. Worried that the fuel in the generator would run out, I switched off the generator and slept. Switching it off also meant that we would have some light before our advance recommenced at first light.

Three or four hours later, the Pakistanis hit us. Starting with small firearms, then moving on to Light Machine Guns (LMGs), then Medium Machine Guns (MMGs), and finally, the whizz of incoming mortar rounds woke up everyone. There was some hurried shouting about whether the sound of tank engines would draw RCL fire[28] as the four or five tanks could be vulnerable sitting ducks parked along a straight narrow road leading off the highway. Finally, it was decided to start and rev up the tank engines. Lucky again. The Pakistanis ran off upon hearing the tank engines without causing us any damage.

By now, the speed of advance accelerated remarkably with no resistance and, that too, along a highway. I was asked to get back to my unit. A couple of days later, driving down in a jeep to convey some instructions, I was stopped at the 375 Field Company location. Even as we tried to hurry off after conveying instructions, Major Kewal Anand (Officer Commanding 375) forced us to wait, saying that it was a 375 tradition that any person passing through during operations had to have at least a cup of tea before leaving, delaying us for about ten minutes. As we were leaving, we heard loud sounds

[28] A 106-mm recoilless gun fitted onto a jeep and used by infantry and mechanised infantry for defence against tanks. They are shoot-and-scoot because of the considerable backblast, flash and smoke.

of firing. Unknown to us, while we waited for the unplanned 'tea break', a platoon from 375 had left with its stores loaded to the gills on two one-tonners, which was all the transport that was available at that point.

Overloaded vehicles were a given. 23 was a mountain division, now operating in the plains with no extra vehicles. The two vehicles were ambushed by the Pakistanis a kilometre ahead (we would have been the victims if not for the 'tea break'). We sadly lost as many as 11 sappers from the regiment, and 5 were wounded. Along with B.K. Oberoi (2IC, 375), we evacuated the wounded, including Havildar George, in a cycle rickshaw with a field dressing improvised out of a lungi. George had been hit by an MMG burst in the abdomen with horrifying results of his innards scattered in a recently harvested paddy field. It was truly a miracle to see him a few months later when he came back to the unit, albeit in a low medical category.

The next day, walking along a road to Chandpur, the Corps Commander, Lieutenant General Sagat Singh, landed in a chopper and hailed us. His order was, 'Chandpur has fallen. Turn around and head for Dhaka!' This is how orders were given and received in those good old days.

The final adventure was on 16 December when (then) Major Nirmal Mitra, the 2IC of our regiment and I were footslogging along a road towards Narayanganj en route to Dhaka. Somewhere near Chandina (if memory serves), a grey jeep stopped beside us. Major Mitra recognised the occupant. It was Major General Shubeg Singh (in civvies with a patka) who was with the Mukti Fauj. Once introduced as part of the 23 Division/3 Engineer Regiment, he told us, 'There will be a ceasefire in Dhaka this evening; hop in if you want to be there.' So, hop in we did, and the late afternoon saw us at the Racecourse, among the very small strength of the Indian Army 'contingent'. We were hopelessly outnumbered not just by the Pakistan Army troops but also by a huge crowd of locals.

Within a short while, a few choppers carrying officers from HQ Eastern Command, led by the Army Commander, Lieutenant General J.S. Aurora, landed nearby, and the surrender (of some 93,000 troops, the largest since World War II) was signed, minus any pomp, show or significant gestures.

Just before the actual signing, I was approached by an 'old' lady who introduced herself as a Time magazine correspondent. She asked me, 'Captain, why did you guys win this war?' Surprised, I told her to ask any of the generals present. She refused to take that as an answer and instead brought Major General Gandharv Nagra in tow. General Nagra wanted to know why I was not answering a lady and whatever happened to the Army's chivalry! I told him I had nothing worth saying, but the lady said she would still want an answer. Meanwhile, General Nagra had made the officers present (me among them) to fall into threes to the right as we faced the table laid out for signing the surrender documents. We were on the 'wrong side' and did not appear behind the generals who signed the documents in the famous photographs.

As the surrender document was signed and Lieutenant General Niazi's sidearm was handed over to Lieutenant General Aurora, locals started taking off their chappals, brandishing them to the chant of 'Bastard, Niazi'. Aurora and Sagat Singh quickly asked all of us standing in threes to form a cordon of sorts around them and Niazi, and they were whisked off before something uglier happened.

The lady correspondent again came and asked me for a quote on why we won the war. All I could think of (and what I said to her) was, 'We guys were bad, but they (the Pakistanis) were worse'. I don't know if this had made sense to her or if it has appeared in the Time, but at that time, to me, it has seemed to be a concise and accurate description of what happened in the Bangladesh War.

Was I dumb, foolhardy, inexperienced, just doing the job assigned, courageous or plain lucky? I would say a bit of each for sure. Would

I do the same again? Maybe, but hopefully with some improvement in information and intelligence.

The main lesson that the war had taught me was that war would usually be a period of confusion and lack of information. Resources will be stretched, if available at all. 'When in doubt, do' will need to be translated into 'Stop worrying, overthinking and instead start doing whatever you are trained for and able to do.'

The War in the East
Through the Eyes of a Pigeon

Lieutenant General Arvind Sharma

In the War of 1971, which led to the creation of Bangladesh, I was holding the appointment of General Staff Officer 3 Intelligence (GSO3 (Int)) in Headquarters 81 Mountain Brigade, which was located at Chakabama, in Nagaland (in radiotelephony parlance, my appointment is referred to as 'Pigeon'). It was a part of the 8 Mountain Division, responsible for counterinsurgency operations in Nagaland and Manipur, directly under HQ Eastern Command.

It was in the morning of 9 July 1971 when the intercom in my office squawked. The Brigade Commander, Brigadier R.C.V. Apte, told me to get his jonga[29] immediately as he had to go to the helipad where the General Officer Commanding (GOC) was landing in a few minutes. We managed to reach the helipad as the helicopter was landing. As soon as the GOC, Major General K.V. Krishna Rao, disembarked, he and the Commander walked off away from the helicopter. They were engaged in a pow wow for about ten minutes,

---

[29] A Nissan designed vehicle used by the Indian Army. Jonga was an acronym for Jabalpur Ordnance aNd Guncarriage Assembly.

after which the GOC boarded the helicopter and flew off. As we got into the jonga, the Commander asked me, 'You want to go on some leave and meet your fiancee?' I was stumped as, just three weeks back, I had returned from casual leave after getting engaged. Without waiting for my response, he said, 'We are going to war, you can go for a few days leave now if you want. After this, there will be no leave for anyone.' Thus, the brigade got the warning order to start preparing for war.

The battalions of the brigade were 3 PUNJAB[30], 4 KUMAON[31] and 10 MAHAR[32]. The units being on the counterinsurgency grid, they had to reorganise, hand over counterinsurgency duties to the paramilitary forces and the local police; thereafter, move to an area called Bokajan, which was near Guwahati, for a four-week training. After training, the brigade moved into the Cachar–Tripura area, by road and rail, between 14 and 20 October.

While the battalions were carrying out their training, the GOC and the brigade commanders were doing reconnaissance of the likely operational areas. On a number of occasions, the Commander accompanied the GOC for the reconnaissance (I used to accompany my Commander, whereas Ashok Choudhary (5053/J), aide-de-camp (ADC) to GOC 8 Mountain Division, used to accompany the GOC). During one of the reconnaissance, our Signal Officer, Captain Jagannath, spoke out, 'We are going around with weapons, in jongas, why are we wearing civvies? You think the enemy cannot make out we are faujis?' Before anyone of us could say anything, General Krishna Rao turned around and said, 'Yes, young man, they can make out that we are faujis, but they don't know at what level the reconnaissance is being done'. First lesson for us youngsters! Quite a few reconnaissance sorties were done in Mi- 4 helicopters by the GOC and my Brigade Commander, where Ashok and I used to tag along. On a few occasions, we were flown by Flight Lieutenant

---

30 3rd Battalion, The Punjab Regiment

31 4th Battalion, The Kumaon Regiment

32 10th Battalion, The Mahar Regiment

Banikant Sharma (5179/K) of 105 Helicopter Unit (incidentally, one helicopter of this unit was always based at Chakabama, in support of 8 Mountain Division; I, therefore, knew most of the officers of this unit).

Battalions of the brigade were deployed in the Y-Sector towards the end of October, covering road axes coming into the Cachar area of Dharmanagar–Kailashahar, from the Sylhet district of East Pakistan. The border outposts, held by the Border Security Force (BSF), were placed under the operational control of the brigade. The brigade was providing artillery support to the Mukti Bahini operations, besides administrative backing. 8 East Bengal Rifles Battalion was placed under the brigade's command; the Commanding Officer (CO) of this battalion then was Major Zia-ur-Rehman. He went on to become the Chief of Army Staff and then the President of Bangladesh. I did meet him quite often there, but none of us knew then that a leader of that stature walked amongst us.

As part of the operation plan of 8 Mountain Division, 81 Mountain Brigade was to advance on the axes of Kailashahar–Shamshernagar–Munshi Bazar–Maulvi Bazar–Sherpur/Sadipur Ferries–Sylhet. The attack to capture the area south of Shamshernagar was launched on the night of 29/30 November by 10 MAHAR and 3 PUNJAB. Initially, the enemy put up stiff resistance but was overwhelmed by the ferocity of our attack(s). The enemy artillery was very effective and resorted to shelling at every locality that they lost. The Commander, with his rover group[33], always moved immediately behind the leading battalions. Thus, we also shared many an experience of enemy artillery fire, and at times, small arms fire. The battalions did suffer a number of officers and men killed and wounded during this attack.

On the afternoon of 2 December, two Pakistani aircraft strafed our positions around Shamshernagar; fortunately there were no

[33] The rover group of a brigade commander refers to his communications vehicle and Signals detachment that accompany him. The Signals officer is sometimes referred to as Sparrow.

casualties. On 4 December, Air Commodore Chandan Singh landed in a helicopter at the Shamshernagar airfield and met the Brigade Commander. He told him that the Pakistani Airforce had been wiped out, and we need not worry about an air threat.

3 PUNJAB captured Munshi Bazar on 6 December, suffering quite a few casualties. A couple of hours later, towards dusk, a company commander of the unit raised an alarm that he could see about 200 enemies forming up to attack his location. Fortunately, by the time guns were ready to fire, they realised that it was the local villagers who had gathered and were coming towards our troops to escape the wrath of the Pakistan Army!

On 8 December, an airstrike was planned at Maulvi Bazar. After necessary approvals, the airstrike was scheduled at about 2 p.m. The forward air controller (an Air Force officer), who had moved up and joined the Commander's rover group, decided to place himself at a small mound for better observation. I also accompanied him as we were fairly close to the road. A few minutes before the aircraft reached the contact point, the forward air controller realised that his stomach was not behaving, and it was an emergency for him. He dashed off behind a bush, about 20 metres away, leaving the radio set with me. Soon the pilot called up, and I had to respond. With the officer yelling out instructions from where he was squatting, I was giving instructions to the pilots! We had a successful airstrike on the target. (This experience helped me in the Part D[34] examination in October 1972, which had a full question on the planning and execution of an airstrike!)

The attack on Maulvi Bazar was launched on the night of 8/9 December by 10 MAHAR and 4 KUMAON. Heavy shelling preceded the attack; one of the shells perhaps hit an ammunition dump, resulting in a thunderous explosion. When 10 MAHAR reached the objective, they found no enemy but rather found a lot of untouched,

---

[34] Tests young officers for basic assimilation over the years. Testing for tactics, military law, current affairs, administration, and morale. Earlier, officers were not promoted to the rank of a major if this exam was not cleared.

cooked food lying in the tourist lodge, which was perhaps the officers' mess of HQ 313 Infantry Brigade. The next morning, they found nameplates of the brigade commander and his staff hanging outside the rooms, confirming the identity of the brigade. I became the proud owner of a nameplate on which was emblazoned in brass—Captain Zafar Iqbal. He was my contemporary in the enemy brigade HQ! This nameplate did cause some confusion later. Posted at NDA in 1976, I put it in the veranda of my house; when Rajinder Singh (4672/H, 3 GR) came to my house, he saw the nameplate and was about to go away thinking it is the wrong house, till I came out and stopped him.

The advance to Sylhet was resumed on 10 December by 3 PUNJAB. No resistance was met at the Sherpur ferry but the enemy had damaged the ferry site and destroyed all other means of crossing. The troops managed to cross the Manu River in local boats, but the ferry needed repairs and the engineers had to construct rafts to cross vehicles. When we reached about 500 metres short of the Manu River, we found the road blocked as all vehicles were trying to get as close to the river as possible. I had to get down and walk ahead of the Commander's jeep, clearing traffic for him to move. What a sight it was, with more than 50 vehicles clogging the narrow single lane road; it presented a lucrative target to enemy aircraft, as even one pass would have caused immense damage! Fortunately, the enemy aircraft had been shot out of the skies earlier. The leading elements of 3 PUNJAB contacted the Sadipur ferry, where again no enemy was encountered as he had withdrawn to Sylhet to give a fight there.

3 PUNJAB, eventually, was in contact with the enemy by midday of 13 December when orders were received that the rover group of the brigade and 10 MAHAR were to move to Agartala to act as the corps reserve for operations against Dhaka. This was to be followed by the Brigade HQ, 4 KUMAON, and 93 Mountain Regiment less one battery. The next morning, the rover group of the Brigade

Commander, CO 10 MAHAR, and CO 93 Mountain Regiment drove down and reached the Corps HQ at Teliamura by late evening. Lieutenant General Sagat Singh, GOC 4 Corps, briefed them on their task, which was a helicopter lift ex-Agartala to a place in the vicinity of Dhaka and the capture of a vital area to be indicated later. On the evening of 15 December, the Brigade Commander told me that I should hitch a ride on a helicopter with one of my Airforce friends the next morning to find out the location of the leading elements of 57 Mountain Division as it would help us in planning for the next task.

In the early morning of 16 December, I proceeded to the Agartala airfield in search of a pilot who would help me in my task. Fortunately, I found Banikant Sharma, preparing to take off to the forward line of troops of 57 Mountain Division. (It appeared that God had sent his messiah for me to accomplish my task.) We took off at about 6:30 a.m. After flying for about 15–20 minutes, the helicopter descended and landed in a stadium. On landing, Banikant told me that he had gotten orders to pick up a few casualties during the flight. He would be back in about 30 minutes, and then we would embark on my task. I got down from the helicopter and found myself in a sports stadium. I could see some troops in olive green (OG) uniforms on the other side of the stadium. I walked up the stairs, where spectators are normally seated, and sat down. After some time, a junior commissioned officer (JCO) walked up to me. He was the B Echelon JCO of a RAJ RIF (Rajputana Rifles) battalion (regrettably, I cannot recall details, as it happened almost five decades ago). I had landed in the stadium at about 7 a.m. and after a cup of tea, arranged by the JCO, I waited. The wait was rather long (almost seven hours, sitting alone in a stadium with nothing to read and nothing to do!) Finally, at about 2 p.m., the helicopter landed; as I was walking towards it, I could see Banikant signalling to me to hurry up.

Onboard the helicopter, he told me that they had to ferry about 20 casualties, and we had to return to Agartala as they were low on fuel;

my mission was thus aborted. While flying back towards Agartala, we noticed 4–5 helicopters flying in the opposite direction. The next day we learnt that those helicopters were taking the big wigs for signing the 'Instrument of Surrender' at Dhaka! 81 Mountain Brigade fought the war in East Pakistan, successfully completing allotted tasks, killing and capturing Pakistani army soldiers, losing our comrades in battle, but when the surrender took place, ironically, we found ourselves back on Indian soil, in Agartala, lonely as a garrison left out of battle!

On 19 December, towards the evening, the Brigade Commander told me that he wanted to go to Dhaka the next morning to meet the Corps Commander. Once again, 105 Helicopter Unit came to my rescue, and they took the Brigade Commander and me to Dhaka on 20 December. We landed at Dhaka, amongst a lot of joy and merriment that was taking place; loud cries of 'Joy Bangla' and the firing of shots in the air by jubilant Mukti Bahini cadres was heard. It was a sight that remains etched in my memory. We went to the Corps HQ, which was then in the location of Eastern Command HQ of Pakistan Army, in a commandeered jeep and saw a number of their officers roaming in the corridors there, sans their belts and weapons! After returning from Dhaka, the Commander ordered a move back to Nagaland. Civil transport, and trains were requisitioned and move back commenced. We were back in Chakabama to herald the New Year 1972!

Lieutenant General Arvind Sharma (Retired) was commissioned into 2/4 GR[35]. During his service of more than four decades, he has served in J&K, Ladakh, Sikkim and the Northeast. He was an instructor at the National Defence Academy and the Defence Services Staff College, Wellington, and the Defence Attaché at Kathmandu, Nepal. He has served in counterinsurgency operations in Nagaland, Manipur, J&K and Punjab. He commanded the division in Manipur, a Corps in Ladakh and was the army commander of the Eastern Command prior to superannuation.

[35] 2nd Battalion, The Fourth Regiment, Gorkha Rifles

A Nation is Born

Brigadier Trigunesh Mukherjee

After Mujibur Rehman's election being unacceptable to West Pakistan, often news came about crackdowns in erstwhile East Pakistan. By April 1971, it seemed that we would be required to be involved in some operations there. Being a G3[36] at a brigade headquarters (HQ) had its information advantages. Since we were part of the division that had not been deployed, it was very likely that our division would be one of the first to be tasked.

83 Mountain Brigade, like other brigades, was tasked to organise training for the Mukti Bahini cadres. As there was some fluidity in the circumstances, therefore, people were moved overnight in covered vehicles from the border areas to our location. The units of the brigade did a fantastic job in finding suitable areas in the jungles and in setting up camps with hardly any notice. Later, transport, equipment, instructors and logistic support were pooled from various formations.

[36] Staff Officer Grade 3 Intelligence

Getting maps was a very difficult task and we could get only a few copies of the relevant maps, even after sending a person to the Survey of India, Dehradun. We needed to get maps of many areas because it was not clear, at this stage, which area would finally be our ingress point. Remember, photocopying hadn't come in at that time. Battalions, of course, had to have maps, and essential personnel in the HQ. At the HQ, therefore, we decided to have only table working maps—for the Commander, Brigade Major (BM) and G3 (the DQ[37] was very annoyed).

Detachments from our battalions supported operations launched by the Mukti Bahini from our side of the border. The volunteers in the Mukti Bahini were a mixed lot. The younger lot was very spirited and took to training very well. A percentage of people seemed to be there because they had nowhere else to go. However, the intensive training made even the latter ready for operations.

Around this time, I asked the Commander who was from my unit, though he had commanded a different battalion, to let me return to the battalion. I said, 'Sir, this may be the only chance to be in war with the battalion.' He said that he would think about it. After a day, he said that though he understood my urge to join my battalion, he didn't want to upset the HQ functioning, adding, 'We definitely will have to go to war, but I am not so sure about how much the western front, especially the valley, will be involved'. The urge to be with my unit was understandable, but I think I experienced and learned a lot over a longer period.

Finally, in August, we got orders to move. The Commander's party (as a G3, managing the details was my job) left early from Tamulpur and stopped at Shillong. The Commander was hoping that the HQ of 101 Communication Zone would assist us with more information and perhaps some maps. So, we had planned to stay for two days. The stay turned out to be very fruitful and it was

[37] DQ is short for DAAQMG, that is Deputy Assistant Adjutant and Quartermaster General, another type of staff officer in a brigade.

very comfortable at the Holiday Home (turned out to be our last comfortable stay till we reached Chittagong) before we moved onto Tripura.

Our location was Shantirbazaar, close to Sabrum. The 23 Mountain Division HQ was at Udaipur, slightly north of us. The Mukti Bahini (MB) Sector Commander, Major Rafiq (ex-Pakistan Army, who had managed to get out of the cantonment) linked up with us. They had already established camps, with training areas and firing ranges. Some of the weapons they had been able to bring but mostly our army had to support them.

Rafiq was a professional and he had a few others from the erstwhile Pakistan Army as well, but he also had quite a few young volunteer officers who were keen to do very well and did not shy away from hard work. Plans were quite flexible at this stage, therefore, as the G3, I was almost constantly looking for covered routes to different areas since points of ingress had not been finalised. This also helped to keep the enemy guessing, denying him possibilities of reinforcing some locations.

I think all units and HQ were quite prepared for sudden changes; this led us to be pretty open to ideas and variations. One sensitive issue was to decide on how much to share with the MB forces till the operations were launched. It was important to keep in mind that quite a few had people across the border, and many of their relatives were collaborating with the Pakistan Army. It was not easy for them to mentally accept that.

Our HQ camp had troops from 4/5 Gorkha Rifles[38] (GR), and the intelligence section boys were excellent. They were kept very busy (sometimes we had to lend a hand too) as plans changed frequently, therefore, enlargements and sand models had to be remade quite often. The International Border wasn't clearly demarcated in this area. Once, while on a recce, our sparrow[39] (Lieutenant P.K.K.

---

[38] 4th Battalion, The Fifth Regiment, Gorkha Rifles

Menon) and I almost drove straight into an erstwhile Pakistani border outpost (BOP). He compared the speed of my reversing the jeep out of harm's way with an incident at Kanha sanctuary when their vehicle had been charged by a bison!

South Tripura has a small bulge of the neighbouring country coming in and a narrow piece of Tripura jutting in like a tusk into East Pakistan (Belonia is at the tip; this area is referred to as the Belonia Bulge). The final plans that evolved had been for our brigade were to straighten out this bulge. 2 RAJPUT[40] and 3 DOGRA[41] were assigned this task. The third battalion leaned from the direction of Belonia and was in reserve. These operations commenced on 6 November. The battalions progressed very well, and by morning, they had linked up around Parshuram. However, though the enemy had pulled back, it was not certain that there were no stay-behind parties to harass us.

The two battalions had to slowly check every village. The railway line came up to Belonia, and the Pakistan Army had used the railway to pull out troops and equipment. As the enemy had vacated the area opposite Belonia, the Commander went in to see it for himself. The Junior Commissioned Officer (JCO), who was located there, indicated that there was sporadic medium machine gun (MMG) fire, but its location couldn't be determined; perhaps the MMG post was on a tree. The JCO had a detachment of 106 RCL[42] there. Having been the RCL Platoon Commander in my unit, I suggested that I should go forward and give it a shot. Before Brigadier Sandhu could react, I was off with the detachment, sitting at the gunner's seat. We went forward and took up position and listened carefully to the MMG fire. Then I decided to fire at the tree that seemed to be holding the MMG post. It was quite thrilling to be able to actually fire the RCL in that situation. We stayed on for a while, didn't really know what happened, but the MMG went silent.

---

[39] The Signals officer is sometimes referred to as Sparrow.

[40] 2nd Battalion, The Rajput Regiment

[41] 3rd Battalion, The Dogra Regiment

[42] Recoilless

In hindsight, it was foolish of me to take off like that, but one does foolish things when one is young. When I returned, the Commander only said, 'This is not your job, but I am glad you acted in this way.' Since war had not yet been declared, the Pakistan Air Force could strike at will and pull up vertically at the border so that they would not violate our air space. Our brigade had been allotted two L40s[43] but they weren't much of a deterrent. However, the MMG of one infantry battalion damaged an enemy aircraft which was excellent for the morale.

Education for a lot of us was how to handle the prisoners of war (POWs). Processes become visible beyond a brigade level, so we were really learning on the job and remembering all our teachings. Casualty evacuation was more streamlined except we learnt how to handle enemy casualties. We actually saw the Geneva Convention being followed. To speed up operations, we were allotted another battalion for one offensive (Nileki). That night, for three hours or so, our radio communications went awry partially due to jamming and partially it just happened.

I learnt a big lesson about how critical communications are for any operation. *Dighis* (or ponds) usually had high bunds and since the area around was like a tabletop, any defences on the bunds dominated the area. Chauddagram (on the Dhaka–Chittagong highway) defences were based on a couple of *dighis*. The bunkers were built into the bunds.

One attempt to attack it during daylight ground to a halt and the unit suffered some casualties. They needed the night to regroup. At the Tactical HQ that night, the artillery regiment's Commanding Officer (CO) and one of the other COs suggested to the Commander that the attacking unit should continue the next day.

The CO said, 'Not during the day, we will go after last light.'

---

[43] An anti-aircraft gun used by Air Defence units to engage the enemy aircraft.

Egged on by the other lieutenant colonels, the Commander asked, 'Are you refusing to attack?' The CO calmly said, 'I will attack, Sir, but after last light.' Being in the proximity (G3's privilege!) I heard the two COs suggesting to the Commander that the CO should be sacked. Fortunately, the Commander did not immediately act. After the COs had left, I utilised my unit affiliation to say, 'Sir, you will be very wrong if you listen to these COs.' The prompt reply was, 'Who the hell do you think you are, telling me what to do?' I said, 'Sir, please think calmly—it was an error on your part to push them into attacking during daylight hours when recce had indicated fairly strongly against it and there were dominating defences protected by minefields. They still went and suffered casualties. Now that they have a good idea of the defences, please let the CO follow his plan. He surely wants his unit to succeed more than you do.' I was chased out of his room and thought that it was time for me to get sacked, but a successful attack was launched the next night. Much later, in Chittagong, Brigadier Sandhu thanked me for not letting him make the sacking decision. This made me think even more highly of him as a mature senior officer.

A few incidents worth mentioning:

* We had been very stretched as the operations developed. One day, from the Tactical HQ in a border outpost (BOP), the sparrow and I took off to lay a line to 2 RAJPUT, leaving the Commander alone with the Radio Operator and our driver. There was no manpower but having learnt the lesson of the criticality of communication, Menon and I thought we would quickly link up with the battalion and return. While walking we thought it was not correct to have left the Commander on his own, but we had not still reached the unit. Menon and I decided that he would carry on with one drum of cable and I would return. Thinking back, one realised it was amusing how two officers were walking around without any confirmation that the enemy had been cleared. Later, we shared a big laugh about our stupidity. When Menon reached the battalion

HQ, the CO was surprised and told him, 'The enemy has not been fully cleared and you are loafing around on your own?'. However, our communication was through. Menon was mentioned in 'Despatches' but his work and contribution deserved more.

* We had established our advance to an HQ inside a BOP that had a fair amount of space. The BM was a very intelligent and sharp person but simply did not know how to rest. One morning, when he went inside a basha, to freshen up, we locked him in because we were really apprehensive that he may just fall asleep when he was really needed. I ran across to the Commander and told him—fortunately, he also agreed that the BM definitely needed to rest. The BM, of course, screamed at us but we had to ensure he rested, which he did. All food etc. went through the window.

* One day at, the same BOP (we stayed there for a few days) when the DQ visited us he told the BM, 'See, now I have a proper map so I had no problem getting here.' The BM obviously knew of the scarcity so he wondered how I had organised a set for the DQ. He picked up the DQ's map, and after one glance, came running out of the operations room to me. 'You idiot, you must tell me when you play such pranks! I would have burst out laughing when I saw the DQ's map.' I had to confess that since the DQ was always wanting a set I had thought that I should give him a nicely marked map, even though it covered the area about 200 km north of us. The DQ had been happy though.

* It was still November. One day quite a few staff officers from the Division HQ came to visit us. While they were still around, the Pakistan Air Force came in to attack troops on the ground. The Commander and I were observing the air attacks from the top of two bunkers. The Commander asked, 'Do you see anything different?' I used the binoculars to see better, but the Commander said, 'Not there—look behind.' Not one person from the higher HQ was around. The brigade made steady progress and cleared the bulge, and we were west of the tusk across a river. Our field company had rebuilt the bridge that had been destroyed by the

enemy when they had pulled out. I think the place was Parikot. The village huts had been converted to spacious and strong bunkers but the roofs had been left so that it looked like a village. This was after 3 December and now we could see our Air Force going in for attacks. The Pakistan Air Force was neutralised, and they had moved out a number of aircrafts to erstwhile West Pakistan. The brigade was on its way to Laksham and then to Chandpur to provide a bridgehead for another brigade to cross the Meghna river. Out of the blue we received information that the Corps Commander would brief our Commander during a helicopter recce the next morning. The Commander took off from the ad hoc helipad with the 4 Corps Commander and the Division Commander. The BM was left wondering what, and which, area he should prepare for and what to tell the units. The Division HQ had no information to share. The Commander returned around 4 p.m., pretty close to the last light.

Our brigade had to turn south and capture Feni before moving towards Chittagong. The only way to move the units quickly was to get hold of a civil transport. 2IC DOGRA was made responsible and I was his sidekick (because I could speak the language). We left as darkness fell and decided to try along the Laksham–Noakhali road, as also the Dhaka–Chittagong Highway, south of Chauddagram. Needless to say, we had absolutely no information about what was available or where they could be found (trucks, buses anything). We were fortunate to find a few vehicles at the first stop. People were extremely helpful, and since they knew the area, it was not difficult to send the vehicles to the HQ.

As we were driving along at speed, with parking lights, visibility was rather poor. We suddenly saw a few lanterns waving frantically and coming towards the road. Frankly, we had no idea what was in store but we slowed down. We realised that they were villagers. I stopped the vehicle but kept the engine running. When they came close, I hailed them in Bengali. They came closer and said that the bridge about 40 metres in front of us had been blown by the Pakistan

Army. Both, Major Jaswant and I thanked our stars and the villagers who then guided us cross country back to the road. Three or four towns gave us all the vehicles we needed. We could thus return to the HQ by early morning.

Just before the assault was launched on Feni, we got information that the biggish town had been vacated. Not taking any chances, the units moved with deliberation and captured Feni. For the artillery, there was a bonanza because the enemy had left behind quite a few guns. After cannibalisation, we had a battery of enemy 105 field guns with adequate ammunition to be used in our attack on Chittagong. The Mukti Bahini and locals confirmed that most of the enemy had pulled back towards Chittagong. The brigade moved astride the highway (Dhaka–Chittagong) and concentrated, for the attack on Chittagong, around Zoraganj. The plan was to utilise the hill tracts and outflank Chittagong with one battalion; the other two battalions would operate astride the highway. We had to ensure the battalion outflanking was always within range for artillery support. By the morning of 16 December, blocks established by the outflanking battalion were in position; the other battalions had also established themselves for the advance.

The artillery regiment had been deployed and the field company had created task forces to deal with obstacles, especially the destroyed bridges. Late in the evening, the sparrow told me that a flash message was coming in. The BM was not with us in the Tactical HQ, so we were wondering who would open it. I went to the Commander and he said, 'You may never get a chance to open a flash message, so go ahead and open it.' The message was about surrendering the next day, that all hostilities to stop at midnight and that the Chittagong brigade commander was travelling to our location to discuss plans for the next day. There was much jubilation among the few of us at the Tactical HQ.

The immediate requirement was to tell the battalion, whose

blocks were already in position, to not shoot any vehicles coming along the highway from the south. Murphy's Law—we got through to all the battalions, but the battalion was not in touch with the block closest to the highway.

The sparrow and I spent a harrowing half an hour trying to reach the officer on the unit net, climbing a hill, getting on to the highway and changing locations. Ultimately, we contacted the officer who said, 'Busy! About to take a shot at a vehicle with a red light flashing.' Somehow, we managed to get him to not take the shot otherwise it would have been an unsavoury incident.

Brigadier Taskinuddin arrived at our Tactical HQ around midnight to meet our Commander. They sat on two chairs across a table (I was in attendance–G3's job) and exchanged pleasantries. Suddenly our Commander stood up and saluted the enemy Commander and said, 'Sir, you were my Platoon Commander at the IMA.' Talk of coincidences! Then the modus operandi for the next day was firmed up. Brigadier Taskinuddin promised to send vehicles to a place where the bridge had been destroyed so that we could proceed further.

Major Rafiq, the Mukti Bahini Sector Commander came to the HQ late at night and said to me, 'Please don't refuse what I am about to give you.' I was naturally taken aback. He said, 'I know you don't drink, but when you do, you like Black Dog, so here's a bottle. Also, this is the Bangladesh flag. We had made two, one for the circuit house and one for the commissioner's office—he will have to make his own.' I was overwhelmed by this show of affection. At that time the Bangladesh flag had the map of Bangladesh in yellow / gold inside the red round.

Early in the morning of 17 December, we moved to Faujdarhaat Cadet College. While the Engineers worked on building a passage, we crossed the nala and got into the Pakistani Army jeeps that had been sent. Bigger vehicles were also sent to transport one of our battalions into Chittagong to protect the Bihari colonies. Since they had collaborated wholeheartedly with the Pakistani Army and had perpetrated crimes and atrocities, they would be the first target of the Mukti Bahini and locals. In fact, they were hated even more than the Pakistani Army. Brigadier Sandhu did not want further bloodshed on his watch.

At the Faujdarhaat Cadet College, the bulk of the Chittagong garrison was lined up with their arms and equipment. Our Commander met the senior-most officer and indicated that one of our battalions would soon arrive to formally take over all the arms and equipment, and they would be transported to camps. After that Brigadier Sandhu was keen to get to Chittagong and ensure a quick return to normalcy. In our hurry, we didn't realise that the sparrow (Lieutenant Menon) had been left behind at the Cadet College. For a couple of hours, he was the only Indian at Faujdarhaat with the Pakistan Army all set to formally surrender. I would never hear the last of that and Menon had every right to be annoyed with me for not ensuring that he was with us.

Entering Chittagong was a momentous occasion with jubilant crowds carrying flags of India and Bangladesh, flowers, garlands, and welcoming us all through. The Commander asked the Commissioner to arrange a meeting at the circuit house which was on a hillock in the centre of the town. The Pakistan Army did not have the time to clean up the torture chamber (inside the circuit house) and it presented a terrible sight.

At the meeting of Chittagong officials, the Commander crisply indicated the following:

∗ 'This is your city and you have two days to get your act together. During this period some of our columns will be moving around the city. Thereafter, my troops will not be in the city.'

∗ 'After two days, the city must function normally, including markets and services.'

∗ 'No violence will be tolerated.'

∗ 'All arms and ammunition recovered from non-army personnel is to be deposited with the nearest Indian Army unit.'

While the meeting was on, some of us were outside on the lawns and felt like exhibits. People were keen to just see us, shake our hands, garland us and joyfully welcome us. It was truly an incredible experience for all of us. One young man asked me, 'How come you are not carrying any weapons?' I simply said, 'We had come for you and now that we are with you, we don't need weapons, do we?' There was a roar of approval, which made us happy.

The Commander told the COs that no unclaimed civil cars and vehicles were to be used by us. There was more than enough fuel left behind by the Pakistan Army so we could use that. There were no restrictions on moving around in our vehicles. At the cantonment helipad (pretty large) we had scores of unclaimed vehicles. They were later handed over to the Bangladesh Force HQ.

There were a number of felicitation ceremonies for our brigade and later for VIPs like the GOC 23 Mountain Division (Major General Rocky Hira) and the Army Commander (Lieutenant General Arora) when they visited. All were organised very well and indicated genuine happiness. Initially, the HQ officers stayed in a building which had been abandoned. Fortunately, there were some other vacant buildings close by to house the offices and our boys. We waited till the cantonment was absolutely clear before moving in.

We went around inspecting the destruction caused by our air force and fighters from INS *Vikrant*. The docks, along the Karnaphuli river, displayed a model of accurate bombing; so much destruction but not a single crane had been hit since they would be needed to work the port.

A lot of people came to us at the HQ with really sad stories and requests about their close ones. Being the only Bengali-speaking officer, I was tasked to listen and give them some replies. Most complaints ran: 'My father was picked up on 23 October and taken to the cantonment; we have no information after that. Will you please check the cantonment?', or 'Have you found any mass burial grounds?', or worse, 'My sister and three friends were taken away from the market and we don't know if they are alive.' It was very difficult to stay calm. I had to repeat the requests to the Commander, which made it doubly painful. By now, others had come in to handle the civil administration and to look after the movement of the surrendered forces back to prisoners of war camps in India. Our units provided help as and when required.

Our war correspondent arrived on the intervening night of 20/21; the *Time* and *Newsweek* correspondents moved with the troops through all the actions. The last of our authentic war correspondents possibly were Melville De Mello, Victor Langer and Situ Mullick. Much later in 1987 I had the opportunity of interviewing Melville de Mello and I will never forget his words, 'If you don't love the Army, you can never be a war correspondent.'

Units went back to their daily routine of training, games, etc. Our moving around town for good food (Chittagong used to be world-famous for the cooking, and on ships, the bulk of the cooks/chefs were from either Chittagong or Goa), playing tennis, etc., were restricted to the evenings and for Sundays. We spent time well. Finally, in March, we started our move back to our permanent locations. It was a very happy send-off by the people, again with flags of both countries and a lot of cheering. On 12 March 1972, we were on our way back.

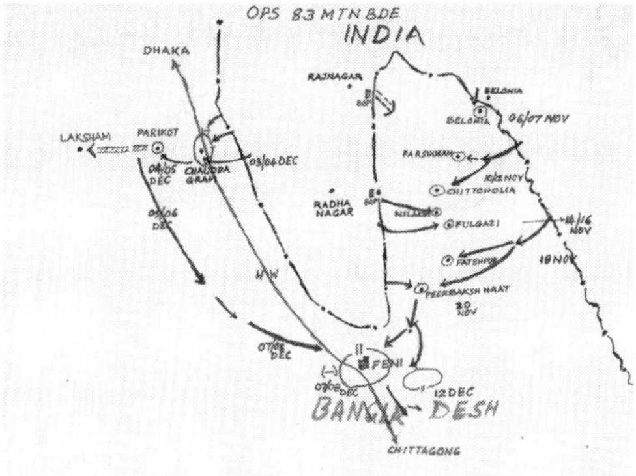

South Tripura has a small bulge named Belonia Bulge

Commanders at Chittagong : L to R Lt Col Ajit Chopra 3 DOGRA, Lt Col D.R. Dutt 2 RAJPUT, Brig Bhupi Sandhu 83 Mtn Bde, Lt Gen, J.S. Arora Army Commander, Maj Gen R.D. Hira 23 Mtn Div, Lt Col M.S. Virk 57 Mtn Regt, Lt Col O.P. Bisla 8 BIHAR

Enemy gun positions at Parikot with overhead cover

Taking a break at Peerbaksh Haat railway station. Maj Anoop S. Gahlaut (centre) was awarded the MVC posthumously

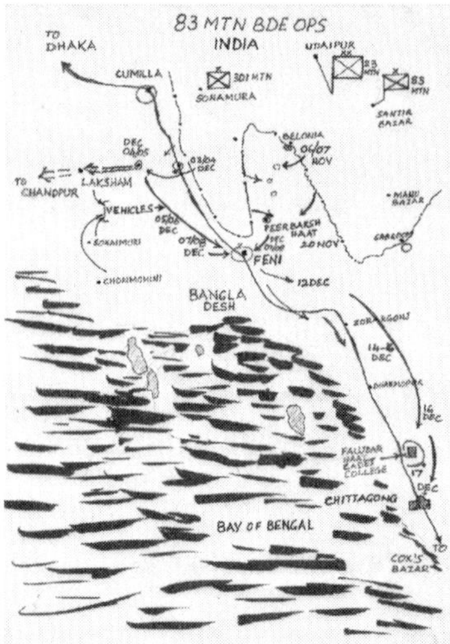

Our brigade had to turn South and capture Feni

Pucca houses were reinforced by Pakistan Army as defences

Sappers quickly construct a bypass next to a bridge blown up by the Pakistan Army over Parikot river

The Greek ship *Avlos* was suspected to have carried weapons and ammunition from Karachi. First, the missile boat approached it through the river and attacked it with explosives. Thereafter, an aircraft from INS *Vikrant* split it in half.

Brigadier Trigunesh Mukherjee, AVSM (Retired) is an alumnus of the National Defence Academy (NDA), Indian Military Academy (IMA) and the Defence Services Staff College (DSSC). He has been a faculty member of the Army War College and the College of Defence Management and was the Commandant of Counter-Insurgency and the Jungle Warfare School. He has seen action during the 1971 operations in Bangladesh and various other insurgency areas. Since 1998, when he left the Army, he has been facilitating learning programmes for the corporate sector and academic institutions. He is the co-founder of Exper Executive Education and Inme Learning. He has authored the book *Inside the Indian Army* and published numerous articles in various magazines and journals on defence, education, travel and management.

Airman or Tankman?

Brigadier Balram Singh Mehta

Having participated in the Tank vs Tank Battle at Garibpur on 21 November 1971 under Headquarters 42 Infantry, the 'C' Squadron 45 CAVALRY was subsequently entrusted by the Headquarters 350 Infantry to assist 4 SIKH in the capture of Burinda on the night of 4/5 December. Jessore was occupied by 9 Infantry Division on 7 December. To keep the momentum, the Squadron was placed under HQ 32 Infantry Brigade to outflank the enemy by undertaking a wide hook across a 40-kilometre stretch of riverine terrain to cut the Jessore-Khulna road at Ramnagar. By 10 December, faulty planning and differences in perception at Division, Corps, and Command level, elements of 9 Infantry Division were found strung out on the Jessore-Khulna highway.

The terrain configuration and defences taken up by elements of the Pakistani Headquarters 107 Brigade and stiff resistance by the well-entrenched enemy brought the 9 Infantry Division's advance virtually to a halt. The PT-76 squadron was ordered to conduct another wide outflanking move to get behind the enemy defences at Siramani. The movement across the waterlogged paddy fields with high embankments, village tracks sinking into village ponds, and driving over deeply rutted bullock cart tracks where the tank would belly before the driver realised why his engine was stalling, or moving over bamboo culverts, not knowing when it would collapse due to the weight of the tank, was a nightmare. The driver was the worst-off, driving at night using the infrared night vision device. A hazy, blinkered field of view made worse by the unnatural greenish yellow light to decipher the lay of the ground ahead while advancing over enemy territory was every tank driver's nightmare. Infantry, riding piggyback on the tank, had to suffer the effects of the rolling, pitching and yawing of the tanks, besides inhaling the diesel fumes and swallowing dust. Many fell victim to the low hanging branches and thorny bushes tearing away pieces of flesh and fabric. The radio operators were constantly at risk of tank antennas striking power lines to see sparks overhead or may be smoke rising from their radio sets. The tank commander and troop leader had the added responsibility to dismount and guide the tanks across vulnerable areas with their feet, boots and socks wet, shivering in the cold winter night. Every obstacle, bypass or change in direction demanded foot reconnaissance to keep the momentum of advance. Reversing the tanks or navigating it through the village, sometimes towing the tank out of the marshes and bogs, added to the stress and anxiety besides sapping your stamina and resolve.

After our last outflank, the squadron had deployed at Naopara a few kilometres short of Siramani. Due to terrain configuration, elements of Armour were deployed to shoot in the infantry while my squadron awaited fresh orders. For the 9 Infantry Division, the battle of manoeuvre had now become a slogging match demanding greater sacrifice of precious infantry lives, as battalion after battalion was launched to overcome the stiff resistance of enemy occupying the Siramani defences. While waiting for fresh plans of advance, I was accosted by a Bengali 'Deserter' of the Pakistani Defence Forces. A middle-aged, short-statured, dark, stocky cyclist, frantically waving a paper in the air caught my attention. On getting off his bicycle, he saluted to announce that he was an ex-sergeant of the Pakistani Air Force.

'Can I do something for you?' I asked.

'No, Sir. You are already doing everything for us. Give me a chance to serve you.' With that, he handed over the paper he had been waving earlier. It was a charge sheet in which his name, rank, and the offence of inciting mutiny was mentioned.

'So were you cashiered or dismissed from service?'

'Neither. I have been declared an absconder—to face court martial, if caught.'

'Do you belong to this village?'

'Sir, I belong to Naopara, I was born here.'

'How can I help you?'

'Give me a chance to join you and fight for my country.' He appeared determined and resolved.

'But we will not carry your bicycle,' I told him, more in jest.

He burst out laughing, 'No problem sir.' He yelled across in Bengali for two boys who appeared and carried his cycle away, adding: 'Tell them, I will stay with the tank regiment until the war ends.'

Though initially sceptical of his claims and talents, in time, I realised that he was a devoted patriot and proved to be of great help. Being an ex-Air Force serviceman, he understood and willingly accepted the discipline imposed on him. He soon merged with the tank crew and even learnt to load the gun and help the crew with odd tasks. His knowledge of the local terrain and cross-questioning of locals to verify and sometimes extract information proved invaluable. This devoted airman, true to his word, stayed with us until the end of the war to share with us the dangers and experiences, without making any claims or demands. On one occasion, he even suffered minor burn injuries from the tank exhaust. On another occasion, finding the .30 medium machine gun (MMG) unmanned, he fired at the retreating enemy infantry. He was with the tank column on the day the surrender ceremony took place at Khulna. We congratulated him on the victory of the allied Army and tears rolled down his cheeks. Yes, it had been a victory and he was grateful to all of us for having reposed trust and faith in him and provided him the honour to fight, not for the injustice done to him but for the honour and independence of his country. He did not want any certificate or citation for his contribution towards the war effort. The memory of the association and the pleasure of having served with 'C' Squadron 45 CAVALRY would sustain him through the years ahead. We left behind a reliable and dependable friend in him, an excellent guide, and a fine 'airman-turned-tankman' of the allied Army.

III
Western Theatre

A Battle After the Ceasefire
The Case of Pul Kanjri

Colonel Tarlochan Singh Kalra

Pul Kanjri is a legendary site on a high ground located near the Attari–Wagah border in Amritsar. It is a relatively dominant feature in the entire area and was held as the Indian Border Security Force (BSF) Company Headquarters for administrative purposes before the start of the War of 1971.

On the evening of 3 December 1971, Pakistan attacked the border outposts (BOPs) with massive shelling. On the directions of the higher headquarters, all units deployed on the border started consolidating their defences and made them more compact and effective. In a similar requirement, Lieutenant Colonel S.C. Puri, the Commanding Officer (CO) of 2 SIKH[43], assigned Major Koak to lead a patrol to the Pul Kanjri forward outpost, retrieve the BSF strength deployed and under attack, and get them to the main defences on the DCB. Major Koak conducted this tedious task with great elan

[43] 2nd Battalion, The Sikh Regiment

and courage. He was successful in not only leading and guiding the BOPs to repulse an attack by the Pakistanis on this post but also caused casualties on the assaulting enemy troops. Despite very heavy shelling and continuous automatic enemy fire, Major Koak successfully retrieved about two section strengths of BSF personnel safely, along with the heads of two Pakistani soldiers killed during their assault on the BSF post. He, thus, accomplished this task with tremendous grit and determination with no casualty on our side. Major N.S. Koak was awarded Sena Medal for this very bold and courageous action and its timely, successful accomplishment.

With continuous pressure built by the Pakistani forces against the BSF Company Headquarters at the Pul Kanjri base, we received orders to get the base vacated and get the BSF troops moving to the main DCB. Meanwhile, the 2 SIKH defences were consolidated on the DCB with strength from two Companies deployed as screens ahead of the drain. From 4–17 December 1971, there was no effort from Pakistan to venture further and engage in any major altercation with the SIKHS. However, it did indulge in sporadic shelling throughout this period, and, in turn, they got back their share of shelling from us in more than equal measure.

In anticipation of the ceasefire between India and Pakistan, which was to be effective on 17 December 1971 from 8 p.m., we received orders from the higher headquarters at 5.45 p.m. to re-capture the Pul Kanjri base which had been vacated by the BSF earlier. Major Koak was tasked once again to muster maximum strength from his 'C' Company at Dhanoya Kalan without denuding its responsibility of keeping adequate strength to hold on to the company defences. Since the time available for this task was very limited, Major Koak made a quick but simple plan to send a section strength under Second Lieutenant Choudhary to the area near the temple[44] for deception purposes and himself led a strength of 30 to move along a drain, going from Dhanoya Kalan

[44] The Pul Kanjri site has a temple, a mosque and a gurudwara, all three symbolic of the secular nature of Maharaja Ranjit Singh, under whose leadership this architectural marvel was built.

to Pul Kanjri, 800 metres away. The fire plan was made hastily.

Pul Kanjri Assault

At 7 p.m., the troops that were to simulate attacks were in position. They opened fire on the enemy along with *jaikaras* (war cries). The josh and high spirits of these troops made the enemy think that the main attack was coming from that direction. Hence, they shifted a few medium machine guns (MMGs) and some other weapons to this direction and opened with artillery and mortar fire. Major Koak had, meanwhile, set off for the task with the meagre strength that he had. While the enemy's attention was diverted by the section at the temple engaging with fire from its location, Major Koak moved with his men frontally. He, and the troops with him, were greeted with the enemy illuminating the area and heavy shelling. Nevertheless, undeterred all kept moving slowly but steadily towards the objective. They came across a mud wall just 20 metres from the objective. Major Koak realised that at that juncture he had only 24 men with him and just ten minutes more before the ceasefire would be effective. He could not afford to lose any more time. He saw a Pakistani MMG detachment close to the mud wall. It could have played hell with our assaulting troops. However, seeing the Khalsas so close, it probably got jittery. The detachment got uprooted and started shooting homewards. In a split second, Major Koak shouted, '*jo bole so nihal*' and led whatever strength that he had for an assault onto the objective, infiltrated into the enemy's defences and started fighting it out with small arms and hand grenades.

In Phase I, section-plus strength was sent to clear the trenches on his left flank and a hand-to-hand fight ensued. It threw the enemy off balance, thus forcing them to abandon their bunkers and flee rearwards, while with the other section, he reached close to the village. It seemed then that the enemy had suddenly woken up from a slumber and opened all their weapons against the assaulting troops. It was at this moment that Lance Naik (L/Nk) Shangara Singh, the 6'4" tall man, pounced at the loophole of the enemy bunker and silenced two machine guns that had been stalling our move further. In doing so, he received a burst of fire in his abdomen, but undeterred he continued to hold the machine gun. The enemy was so terrified that they fled from the bunker. With a pulled-out machine gun from a loophole still in his hands, L/Nk Shangara Singh showed exemplary courage in the face of the enemy and attained a truly heroic martyrdom. During this phase itself, Major Koak got bullet-wounds in his arm while Naib Subedar (Nb Sub) Gurcharan Singh, his Platoon Commander, and Havildar Gurdev Singh who was the Platoon Havildar too, were wounded. This surprise attack had stunned the enemy. Incidentally, the bullet in Major Koak's arm remained lodged for about 17 hours till he mentioned it after the firing had stopped from both sides on 18 December 1971 at 1 p.m.

In Phase II, despite the injuries they sustained, Major Koak and some men kept moving and were able to fool the enemy into believing that a major force had arrived on their defended locality. Having obtained a foothold, Major Koak had managed to get some more men, but they got lost during their move for the attack. Four to five men sustained minefield injuries and thus, they had to be escorted back to the main defences. This further depleted the available strength. Meanwhile, Second Lieutenant Choudhary was directed to move to the Pul Kanjri base location, along with his section strength and the MMG detachment providing fire support from the temple.

By about 8.15 p.m., Major Koak had left only 19 able-bodied men and an MMG detachment at the Pul Kanjri base. Suddenly, a counterattack came from the enemy side. It surprised Major Koak, but he and his men took immediate position and fired back. Artillery and battalion mortars came to their rescue and the attack fizzled out. Two more counterattacks, about platoon-plus strength each, came from 11 p.m. to 1 a.m. These also faded out with accurate artillery and mortar support. It seemed that the enemy had suffered heavy casualties and retreated.

Unknown to Major Koak and his men, Captain Rizvi, the Pakistani Company Commander, with his entire communications intact (both line and radio) was still in his command post. He kept on telling his CO, 43 PUNJAB[45], to counterattack. A renewed attempt was thus made by the enemy at 2 a.m. with about company strength. The enemy carried out extensive shelling, but Major Koak and his men were lucky to survive heavy damage because they were widely disbursed. The brave SIKHS repulsed all attacks. The majority of those injured voluntarily stayed back, manned the bunkers and kept shouting *jaikaras* to simulate greater strength to the enemy. It seemed that the enemy had made it a prestige point. Having failed in their attempt to get reinforcements in form, 15 PUNJAB were sought from Harbanspura near Lahore. A fifth counterattack, with elements from 43 PUNJAB and 15 PUNJAB[46], was launched before the first light. This was a three-pronged attack with a company from each side. In the hour-long fierce battle that ensued, the enemy suffered heavy casualties.

However, the enemy was able to move to some trenches and positions close to us. Our troops holding ground became almost untenable. It was at this critical juncture that Major Koak asked for red-red-red fire[47]. With the ceasefire in effect, it became difficult to get permission for artillery fire. Seeing the delay, unit mortars came to the rescue by firing heavy salvos on the enemy troops that were still in the open. Major Koak started shouting for imaginary companies asking them to surround the assaulting enemy troops from various directions. Maximum artillery and own mortar fire followed and the enemy was caught in the open and suffered heavily. All this rattled

---

45 43rd Battalion, The Punjab Regiment

46 15th Battalion, The Punjab Regiment

47 A distress signal requesting for artillery fire on own location as the enemy is close to penetrating your defence position.

the enemy and by daylight, at about 6.30 a.m. on 18 December 1971, Major Koak saw a Pakistani officer, with raised hands, wanting to surrender. Some others also followed. By about 9 a.m. pressure from the enemy side slackened, though it was only at 1 p.m. that the exchange of fire ceased from both sides. Thus, all counterattacks had been finally repulsed. On 18 December 1971 at about 1.30 p.m., the enemy acknowledged defeat and raised a white flag from their side, wanting to collect a large number of dead bodies. This brought a befitting close to the exemplary display of valour. Brave and courageous men of 2 SIKH[48] had lived up to the prayers of their Tenth Guru and the regimental motto, '*Nische kar apni jeet karon*'.

During a flag meeting a few days after the war was over, Lieutenant Colonel Mohd Iqbal, the CO of 43 PUNJAB of Pakistan, met Lieutenant Colonel S.C. Puri, the CO of 2 SIKH, and told him, 'Well Colonel, from one soldier to another, I would like to compliment you on your excellent outfit. Your men fought heroically and were distinctly superior in the battle'.

Pul Kanjri was handed over to the Pakistani forces on a platter at the start of the Indo-Pak war. In its recapture, the unit suffered over 30 casualties, including the death of five. The company was able to take hold of one officer and 13 ORs of the Pakistani forces as prisoners of war. At the base location, 25 of their dead bodies were handed over to them. The 'C' Company was able to recover 14 machine guns, 17 rifles, 12 Sten guns, two rocket launchers, two platoon mortars, nine radio sets and over 10,000 rounds of small arms (SA) ammunition.

For his courage and gallant action, L/Nk Shangara Singh was awarded Maha Vir Chakra posthumously. Some other awards for this extraordinary action against well-fortified defences were awarded to the battalion as under:

VrC – 1. SM – 2. M-in-D – 4.

On the crucial intervening night of 17 and 18 December 1971, it was to the credit of Major Koak and his handful men that not only

---

48 2nd Battalion, The Sikh Regiment

was the lost territory of several square kilometres regained, but the 2 SIKH troops held on to it tenaciously and courageously. For his bold and gallant leadership of a successful assault against the superior enemy forces, and subsequently holding on to the captured objective despite five counterattacks, Major Koak was recommended for the Param Vir Chakra. His courage was duly commended by the then Defence Minister, Shri Jagjivan Ram, and then Chief of Army Staff, General S.H.F.J. Manekshaw. However, it is very intriguing and vexing to note that while the Pakistani Company Commander who could neither hold on to a well-fortified locality nor dislodge the assaulting 2 SIKH troops despite five counterattacks was awarded the Sitare-o-Jurrat by Pakistan, Major Koak still awaits the much-deserved, long-delayed Param Vir Chakra. This is the tale of a rare soldier, who not only recovered a part of the BSF-held defences that was given away on the direction of higher headquarters but most valiantly recaptured it with a very meagre force despite several counterattacks by the Pakistani forces. What an injustice! The officer is beyond 78 years of age now and does not keep well.

As we celebrate the 50th anniversary of the 1971 war this year, we must take a moment to look back and honour such men from the 1965 and 1971 wars for their exemplary courage. These unsung heroes are the real heroes of the Indian Army and must no longer be neglected.

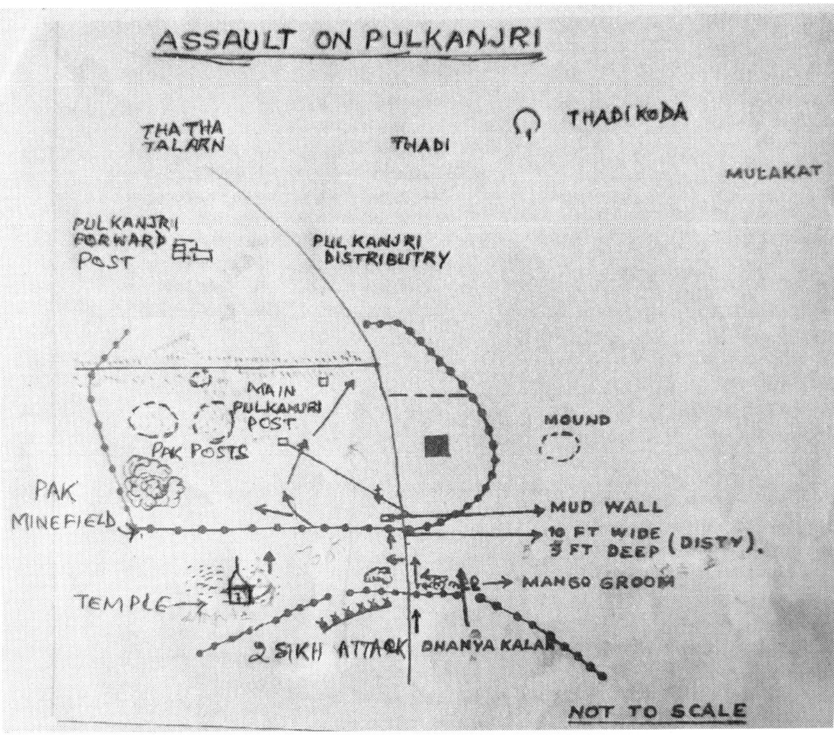

The Pul Kanjri Assault on 17/18 Dec, 1971

L/Nk Shangara Singh,
MVC (Posthumous)

The Pul Kanjri Memorial
at the battle site near Attari

Colonel Tarlochan Singh Kalra (Retired) psc, an ex-NDA, was commissioned on 15 June 1966. He had the privilege of being the Adjutant of 2 SIKH during 1971. He commanded the battalion from 1985 to 1988 and superannuated after a tenure as the Commandant of the Sikh Regiment Centre from 1994 to 1997.

Bloodied on Raising

Lieutenant General P.P.S. Bhandari

Having finished my tenure as Instructor Class 'C' at the Armoured Corps Centre and School, Ahmednagar, I was eagerly waiting to revert to my regiment, Hodson's Horse, in June 1971. Instead, to my utter disbelief, I was posted to be part of a new regiment, the 72 Armoured Regiment, on its raising on 1 July 1971 at Ahmednagar itself.

Consequent to deciding to go to war with Pakistan, Army Headquarters (Army HQ) ordered its raising on an 'Operational-Immediate' basis. Such was the urgency that officers from various regiments who had already received their posting orders, or were on courses in Ahmednagar, were issued fresh postings to form the new raising.

For me, this turning point became the experience of a lifetime—of not only going through the raising of a regiment with no resources in the shortest possible time but also rushing into battle and earning the prestigious 'Battle Honour Chhamb', one of the only two units to be so honoured. Yes, 72 Armoured Regiment was bloodied in the war on raising. While still bonding amongst ourselves, the regiment was rushed smack headlong into the fiercest of battles—the Battle of Chhamb, December 1971.

Despite totally unfamiliar surroundings and terrain, fighting alongside unknown formations and units, the regiment blunted the enemy's offensive, destroying 29 tanks and a Sabre jet in a matter of seven days. That is what earned the regiment the name 'The Little Giant'.

As my regiment's first adjutant, I narrated the challenges of raising it and annihilating the enemy in battle and recorded it in my hand in the regimental Digest of Service and the War Diary.

It was a tall order to be operational in under four months. Due to its importance, besides senior officers from the Army HQ, the Defence Minister, Mr Jagjivan Ram, made a special visit causing further pressure and disruptions in raising.

Amalgamating a heterogeneous lot, I was hard-pressed to set even basics like standard operating procedures, load-tables for tactical echelons and mobilisation. Besides the administration of the regiment, getting soft vehicles and stores, and arranging for ammunition to be released, collected and stored in a matter of days was nightmarish when the depots were yet not geared up.

Such was the workload that I was forever looking for more than 24 hours a day to integrate, convert and train men coming from different regiments with tanks other than the T-55. But then where were the tanks? Still in Poland! The first lot of T-55 tanks arrived only on 17 October, more than three-and-a-half months after the raising commenced.

After a quick traditional *shastra pooja*, we were on our way to Kathua commencing 25 October by special trains on 'white hot priority'. The hurriedly extended railhead from Pathankot to Kathua did not even have the ramps for the tanks and B vehicles[49] to get off

---

[49] A soft-skinned tracked or wheeled land use vehicle, self-propelled or towed, commercial or general service, which is not primarily designed for offensive purposes but may in some cases be armoured for defensive purposes, and which is not otherwise specifically defined.

the train rakes to add to our problems. However, a scary makeshift arrangement of literally jumping off the rakes with mobile girders became a default training event.

Due to such late arrival of the tanks, I could only organise 'battle zeroing' of tank guns by firing on boulders painted white at the Ismailpur ranges between 1–4 November. Despite such zeroing, we destroyed 29 Pakistani tanks in battle later.

Our woes were not over yet. On 5 November, we were ordered to move to Palwan, between Akhnoor and Jaurian, across the Chenab River, under 10 Infantry Division as part of 3 (I) Armoured Brigade.

The deep, fast-flowing Chenab only had a bridge with a load-carrying capacity of 18 tonnes and was unfordable. Tanks had to be perilously ferried across on makeshift rafts. As soon as the front of the tank would mount the raft, it would sink deep down (as would our hearts) before suddenly reappearing once the complete tank mounted the raft. Goosebumps notwithstanding, the regiment was in Palwan by 7:45 a.m. on 6 November.

Organising ourselves at Palwan was the toughest part for me — to ensure that not a speck moved, even as all personnel trained for the expected offensive task, virtually without reconnaissance.

The Battle

On the night of 3 December 1971, Pakistan attacked with the reinforced 23 Infantry Division Group with five infantry brigades (with one in the hills). 26 Cavalry was integral with 11 Cavalry, 28 Cavalry, and 12 (I) Squadron ex-2 Armoured Brigade. It planned to attack with 66, 111 and 20 Infantry Brigades supported by armour. 8 AK Brigade was for the bridgehead across the Manawar Tawi.

On the evening of 3 December, our Commanding Officer (CO), while still in HQ 10 Infantry Division attending an operational bricfing, ordered me to immediately move the entire regiment to a newly designated forward location next to Palanwala, east of the Manawar Tawi.

While on the move at night, we heard the first enemy artillery barrage. The battle had commenced. Hereafter, the regiment was in the thick of the battle, contesting and blunting all three thrusts of the enemy with heavy casualties, delaying him totally, upsetting his plans and eventually stalling his offensive.

Early on the morning of 4 December, along its northern thrust, the enemy's 11 Cavalry Group broke out through the lodgement gained by their 66 Infantry Brigade and captured the strategic Mandiala North Heights.

Till then, the Mandiala crossing on the Manawar Tawi was occupied only by a company of our 9 Para Commandos. In the next 24 hours, the enemy consolidated its position, posing a direct threat to the Mandiala crossing. Simultaneously, an onslaught by the enemy's 111 Infantry Brigade had commenced along the central axis, putting enormous pressure on our 191 Infantry Brigade.

At this stage, the 72 Armoured Regiment was rushed across the Manawar Tawi to reinforce the sector and restore the situation.

While 'B' Squadron was moved across the Manawar Tawi on the night of 4/5 December and placed under the 191 Infantry Brigade in area Chhamb, 'C' Squadron was moved to Chhapreal to checkmate the enemy's northern thrust along the Mandiala Crossing. On 5 December, fighting major actions at Phagla, Goghi and Barsala, 'B' Squadron stabilised the situation along the central axis.

In the north, early on the morning of 5 December, the Pakistani 4 AK Brigade consisting of the 6 AK, 13 AK, 47 PUNJAB and armour, launched an attack in the area of Mandiala Bridge. The enemy's 6 AK lost its way, and with 13 AK having crossed Tawi, blundered into gun areas of our 216 Medium Regiment.

At that point, 'C' Squadron swung into action, and along with 7 KUMAON[50] ex-68 Infantry Brigade, it launched a counterattack and

[50] 7th Battalion, The Kumaon Regiment

pushed the enemy back to the west of Tawi. Thereafter, adopting a counter-penetration position, the squadron blocked the most threatening northern thrust of the Pakistani 23 Infantry Division. The retreating enemy was mauled by the 'B' Squadron elements edging forward from Gurha.

Along the enemy's southern thrust, the advance of Pakistan's 20 Infantry Brigade Group towards the area of Mangotian was fiercely contested by the 'B' Squadron. Despite the officer troop leader having been severely injured and evacuated, the non-commissioned officers (NCOs), who too were successively injured, did not allow an inch to the enemy. After that, the very same troop moved to Goghi, Barsala, to save the day for 5 ASSAM[51] under attack from Pakistan's 111 Infantry Brigade.

On 6 December, a desperate enemy came in with unprecedented heavy air attacks. In our regimental HQ near Palanwala, while away from my tank, controlling actions of the squadrons from the adjutant's van (a modified command B vehicle), I had a providential escape—I had stepped out of the vehicle seconds before it was strafed out of shape. The preserved remains of the radio set and the typewriter still cause a chill in my spine.

In these airstrikes, the 'B' Squadron commander contesting the enemy along its central axis was severely wounded and evacuated. It is to the credit of the troop leader of 'B' Squadron that he shot down an enemy sabre jet to rid the skies of enemy air.

After midday on 6 December, the enemy had captured the tactically critical Gurah Heights making defences rather untenable. Before the enemy could reorganise, 'A' Squadron, which had also been inducted west of the Manawar Tawi by then, launched a counterattack by last light with 'half squadron' and a company of 5/8 GR[52] and successfully recaptured it.

Unfortunately, on 6 December itself, along the enemy's northern

---

[51] 5th Battalion, The Assam Regiment

[52] 5th Battalion, The Eighth Regiment, Gorkha Rifles

thrust, the squadron commander and the second-in-command of 'C' Squadron were killed in action fighting gallantly. However, the squadron continued to block the enemy's northern thrust resolutely.

While the regiment had caused heavy attrition and huge delay to the enemy, yet by then, the Pakistani 111 and 20 Infantry Brigades were able to break through the defences of the forward battalions, which had fought gallantly since 3 December. The General Officer Commanding (GOC) of the 10 Infantry Division, therefore, decided to pull out to a more defensible position east of the Manawar Tawi.

While pulling out, the tank of the OP (Arty)[53] was surrounded by enemy infantry. The driver of the tank was killed while the gunner, Acting Lance Dafadar (ALD) Katar Singh, was captured. Taking advantage of the incessant shelling, the alert and bold NCO freed himself, got into the tank and killed the surrounding enemy with machine-gun fire before driving across the Manawar Tawi. Exemplifying the resilience of our young regiment, the NCO was decorated with a Vir Chakra (VrC).

On consolidating, after tricky replenishment of individual tanks spread all along the eastern bank of the Manawar Tawi, on 8 December, a MiG-21 of Squadron Leader D. Keeler, IAF, was shot down by the enemy. Seeing the pilot parachuting south of Buchcho Mandi between the opposing forces, the officer troop leader of 'C' Squadron daringly waded through the river in full view of the enemy and rescued the injured pilot. Keeler is the guest of honour of the regiment till today. Resuming their offensive, the Pakistani 111 Infantry Brigade launched a two-pronged attack along the Darh and Raipur crossings and established footholds by 6 a.m. on 9 December.

No. 3 Troop 'A' Squadron and 'A' Company 3/4 GR[54] successfully counterattacked at Raipur crossing, preventing a further expansion of the bridgehead.

Along the Darh crossing, one troop each of 'A' and 'B' squadrons

---

53 Observation Post (Artillery)

54 3rd Battalion, The 4th Regiment, Gorkha Rifles

counterattacked and denied expansion of the bridgehead.

By their virtue of being in the right situation, a force of an ad hoc squadron and two companies of the 5/8 GR was formed to launch the deciding counterattack on the Darh crossing on 10 December. The counterattack was approved by GOC XV Corps who had specially flown into the Division sector.

Our nerves and composure were put to the test while coordinating this most critical counterattack. Indeed, its complete success was the final nail in Pakistan's coffin in the Chhamb Sector.

By completely blunting and blocking the enemy's offensive, the 72 Armoured Regiment left no room for manoeuvre to the enemy beyond the Manawar Tawi till the ceasefire on 17 December.

Recognitions

For its exemplary performance, the 72 Armoured Regiment, youngest to be bloodied in battle, was bestowed with the prestigious 'Battle Honour Chhamb 1971', in addition to the award of 'Theatre Honour J&K', one of the only two combat units to be so honoured.

War Memorial

In recognition of the valour of the 'Little Giant' that stood tall in the battle, later, as the then Colonel of the Regiment and GOC 1 Armoured Division, I had a war memorial erected in the battle zone at Kachreal.

Shastra pooja on arrival of
T-55 Tanks on 17 October 1971

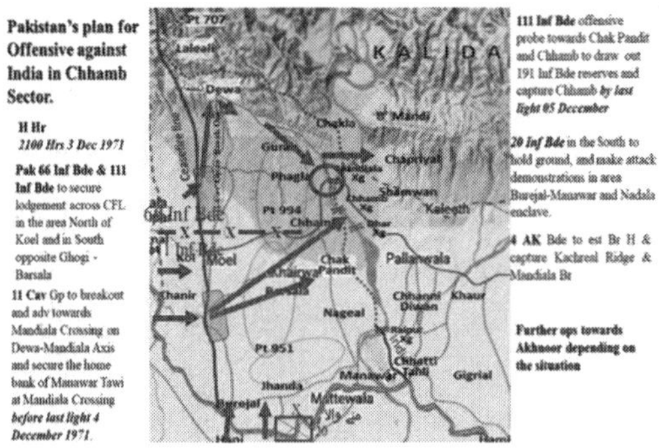

Pakistan's plan for offensive

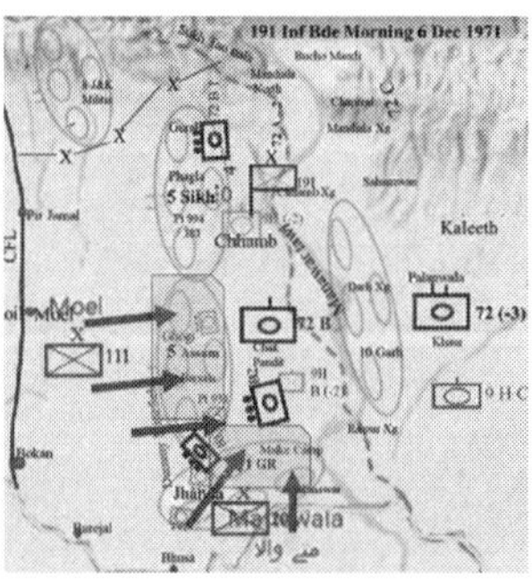

191 Infantry Brigade on the
morning of 6 December 1971

The Colonel of the regiment
pays homage to the fallen comrades

Lieutenant General P.P.S. Bhandari (Retired) was commissioned into Hodson's Horse. He later joined the 72 Armoured Regiment on its raising and commanded it. He is a graduate of the Defence Services Staff College (DSSC), Higher Command Course, and an alumnus of the Royal College of Defence Studies (RCDS), UK, and the Galilee College, Israel. He was a DS in the Armoured Corps Centre and School (ACC&S), Indian Military Academy (IMA), DSSC, and Commander, Senior Command and Higher Command wings. He commanded an armoured brigade, an armoured division and a strike corps besides being the Additional Military Secretary in Army HQ. He retired as Deputy Chief of Army Staff (P&S) in 2006.

The Naval Operations

Action in the Arabian Sea by the Western Fleet

Captain S.S. Sethi

Never since antiquity, in the history of mankind, has a new nation been born as a result of a war between two nations. The jointmanship of the three brave armed forces of India, together with the Mukti Bahini, helped write a glorious chapter of valour, which will be remembered in the footprints of time for future generations. The attack on Karachi (Operation Trident and Python) on the western seaboard and the attack on Dhaka, Chittagong, Khulna, Cox Bazar and Mongla by the seahawks from *Vikrant*, the stealth attack by the daredevils of the Mukti Bahini trained for Operation X by Indian Navy in Plassey, the joint attack by the valiant Indian Air Force's precision bombing and the charged up Army advancing through the Padma and Meghna fronts and the Bangladesh terrain, closing in from all directions into Dhaka resulted in the surrender of the 95,000 Pakistani armed force personnel, 50 years ago. Bangladesh was, thus, created—a new nation came into being! It was a great day for the tri-services of India.

Even as the two nations rejoice the golden jubilee of the momentous grand event of 1971, the alumnus of NDA–28th Course–have come together to reset together the pieces of the jigsaw, fragmented by time, to bring back the events that were the substantial contributor to the war's outcome. I also, having been a member of the prestigious Western Fleet of the Navy, have put together the memoirs, to reconstruct the actions in the Arabian Sea by the Western Fleet.

In retrospect, the Western Fleet had demonstrated complete dominance in the Arabian Sea to ensure sea control for the Indian Navy and a total sea denial to the Pakistan Navy. The fleet had accomplished its stated directives:

1. *Seek and Destroy:* The Pakistani ships patrolling off the Karachi harbour were engaged and sunk.
2. *Attack and Cripple Karachi Port:* The Karachi port was attacked, and the port operations got suspended to a large extent. The fire in the oil farms in Karachi kept burning for days.
3. *Total Blockade:* The operations by the Western Fleet ensured a total blockade of tankers from the Gulf and any other ships entering Pakistan ports.

Naval Scenario Before 1971 and Formation of the Eastern Fleet

Indian Navy had only one fleet till 1971. All operational frontline ships were part of the Indian fleet, under the command of the Flag Officer of the Indian fleet, with its headquarters in Mumbai. In May 1971, the fleet was divided into the Western Fleet based in Mumbai and the new Eastern Fleet at Visakhapatnam.

In June 1971, the aircraft carrier of the Indian Navy, INS *Vikrant*, along with two escorts, INS *Brahmaputra* and INS *Beas*, were transferred to the Eastern Fleet for deployment in the Bay of

Bengal. This was a good move as *Vikrant* played a pivotal role in the operations in East Pakistan.

The Eastern Fleet, with *Vikrant*, was able to enforce a total blockade in the ports of East Pakistan and thwart the escape of the Pakistani forces from the sea. Also, the aircraft from *Vikrant* inflicted heavy damage to Chittagong and various ports in East Pakistan and ensured an early surrender of Pakistan's forces.

My Experience in the Western Fleet During War

I was the Navigating Officer of INS *Betwa*, a part of the Western Fleet, navigating the front-line ship. I was fortunate to have been posted on *Betwa* at the appropriate time. I was undergoing the Long Navigation and Direction Specialisation course in Cochin in 1971. The course was abruptly terminated in mid-October, and I was posted as the ND officer of INS *Betwa*.

The Departure of Western Fleet from Mumbai

The Western Fleet sailed out of Mumbai on Thursday, 2 December. I am emphasising the day as Thursday, since my engagement was fixed for Sunday, the 5 December. This is a separate story and will be related later. However, the engagement ceremony was solemnised on 5 December, in absentia.

When we sailed out of Mumbai, we were 13 ships. INS *Mysore*, the cruiser, was the flagship under the command of Captain R.K.S. Gandhi. The Fleet Commander, Rear Admiral E.C. Kuruvilla embarked with his staff on board. My Commanding Officer for INS *Betwa* was Commander R.K. Choudhry, from the 1st course NDA. The other twelve ships were:

1. INS *Trishul* and *Talwar* of the 15th Frigate Squadron
2. INS *Betwa* of the 16th Frigate Squadron
3. INS *Khukri, Kuthar* and *Kirpan* from the 14th Frigate

Squadron

4. INS *Ranjit* from the 11th Destroyer Squadron
5. INS *Kadmatt* from the Petya Squadron
6. INS *Deepak*, the auxiliary tanker
7. INS *Sagardeep*, the auxiliary supply vessel
8. INS *Vinash* and *Vijeta*, the two missile boats undertow

The Second Group

The second group of six ships, comprising two Petya class ships, INS *Kiltan* and *Katchal*, along with four missile boats, had sailed out to the Kathiawar coast and positioned themselves off Okha. The ships from this formation, took part in Operation Trident, the first attack on Karachi on the night of 4/5 December.

Experience at the Arabian Sea

Incidents on 3 December

Morning

The Fleet, on sailing out from Mumbai on 2 December, had set the course straight for Karachi. During the forenoon of 3 December, a submarine contact was obtained. The Fleet took an evasive turn and our ship, the *Betwa*, along with INS *Trishul* was told to investigate the contact with our sonars. *Trishul* and *Betwa* formed the anti-submarine warfare formation and the contact on the sonar was established intermittently. After about two hours, both ships were signalled to disengage and rejoin the fleet. I believed that this was a confirmed Pakistan submarine.

Night

Our ship, the *Betwa*, was designated as the air picket ship, to search and report all air contacts. It was fitted with LR-960 search radar, with a proven aircraft detection capability. In the late afternoon, the *Betwa* picked up an aircraft on LR-960. After tracking, it was estimated to be a Pakistani reconnaissance aircraft, shadowing the fleet, but at the same time remained outside our gun range. The Fleet Commander was informed accordingly.

The Splitting of the Fleet into Groups

At dusk, on 3 December, we received the signal of hostilities breaking out with Pakistan. The Fleet Commander appreciated that the shadowing Pakistan aircraft would compromise our position. A very smart manoeuvre was executed by splitting the fleet and altering the course southwards. At this time, we were 200 miles south of Karachi. This confused the tracking aircraft, and after some time we lost it on our radar screen.

Tactical Advantage

The smart manoeuvre by the Fleet Commander to split the force and alter the course southwards helped the fleet tremendously for the rest of the operation as the air reconnaissance effort by Pakistan failed to detect the Western Fleet thereafter. This was a huge tactical gain by the Western Fleet. However, the only disadvantage that accrued was that the fleet had moved too far south of Karachi to launch the attack on the Naval base on the very night of breaking out of hostilities with Pakistan.

Fleet Operations on 4 December

The fleet regrouped on 4 December after evading the Pakistan reconnaissance aircraft. It was important to keep the ships topped up with fuel and the tanker INS *Deepak* kept fuelling the ships one after the other.

All this while, the fleet was moving at high speed to avoid any lurking submarines. On the afternoon of 4 December, INS *Kuthar* had a major fire in its engine room, incapacitating the ship. The Fleet Commander decided to detach the three anti-submarine squadron ships—*Khukri, Kirpan* and *Kuthar* back to Mumbai. Also, the missile boat, Vijeta, which had developed machinery defects was sent back escorted by the auxiliary supply ship, *Sagar Deep*. The anti-submarine squadron having departed, the remaining six gun-ships, *Mysore, Trishul, Talwar, Betwa, Ranjit* and *Kadmatt*, along with the missile boat, *Vinash*, and the tanker, *Deepak*, became a formidable surface strike force that was capable of engaging the Pakistani naval ships and shore bombardment as well as inflicting heavy damage to the enemy.

Operation Trident: Attack on Karachi, 4/5 December

The first strike group on Karachi, for the operation that had been code-named Trident, assembled and rendezvoused off Okha in Gujarat on the afternoon of 4 December. The group comprised two Petya class ships, *Kiltan* and *Katchal* as escorts, with three OSA-M missile boats, *Nirghat, Nipat* and *Veer*, loaded with four Styx missiles each.

The force set course towards Karachi on the evening of 4 December; at 6 p.m., it was at a distance of 150 miles from Karachi. At around 10 p.m. when the task force was about 70 miles from Karachi, they detected two targets on their radars. The missile boats closed in and took up positions to engage the targets. The result of this daring attack on Karachi was as follows:

1. The Pakistan Navy destroyer, PNS *Khyber*, was patrolling outside the Karachi harbour. The missile fired by INS *Nirghat* hit the main engine room of *Khyber* and the ship

got engulfed in fire. The next missile fired by INS *Nirghat* was again a direct hit, and within minutes the ship sank, with more than 200 crew on board. The captain and the staff failed to appreciate what had happened. They had earlier radioed that they were under air attack, mistaking the missile attack as an air attack.

2. The missile fired by INS *Veer* hit the Pakistan Navy ship, PNS *Muhafiz.* This was a minesweeper and she sank immediately.

3. INS *Nipat* engaged a ship that was underway close to the Karachi port. The first missile hit the ship, resulting in a big explosion. The second missile hit resulted in the ship breaking into two and sinking. This was MV *Venus Challenger,* a merchant ship carrying a full load of American ammunition for the Pakistan Navy and Air Force.

4. INS *Nipat* fired a missile at the shore establishments in Karachi.

5. The force rendezvoused after the attack and departed for Mumbai. This task force was able to return to Mumbai after sinking three ships outside the Karachi harbour, without suffering any casualties. This attack had a substantial effect on the overall outcome of the war.

Jubilation in the Western Fleet (5 December)

The news of the attack on Karachi by the missile group reached us on the night of 4/5 December after Operation Trident was executed. We, on the *Betwa*, were enthralled with the news; the spirits on board were high and the determination to fight the war boldly only became stronger.

Tactical Picture in The Operations Room of the Betwa

In INS *Betwa*, the operations room and the communication room are next to each other. The teams in the communication room were decrypting all the messages, concerning the operations in the Arabian Sea and forwarding a copy to the operations room. In the operations room, we had the general operations plot, where the movements of all the units in the Arabian Sea were getting plotted and updated. Thus, our ship always had an up-to-date operational tactical picture in real time.

Operation Python: Second Attack on Karachi on the Night of 8/9 December

The Fleet was manoeuvred on 6–7 December and kept fully fuelled up and ready to attack the Pakistan coast, when suitable. The opportunity came on the night of 8/9 December. The Fleet was split into three groups on the forenoon of 8 December. At this time, it was about 250 miles southwest of Karachi and 200 miles south of the Makran Coast. The plan was to carry out a two-pronged attack on Karachi and the Makran Coast around midnight by splitting the force, and thereafter again rendezvous in a position 350 miles southwest of Karachi by the night of 9 December.

The three groups that were formed are as follows:

1. INS *Trishul* and *Talwar* along with the missile boat, INS *Vinash,* took departure for the attack on Karachi.
2. The flagship, INS *Mysore,* along with *Ranjit* and our ship, *Betwa*, took departure for the Makran coast to attack Gwadar and Jiwani.
3. The tanker, INS *Deepak,* along with consort ship, INS *Kadmatt,* sailed towards the African coast with orders to return to rendezvous the Fleet later evening the next day, 9 December.

Attack on Karachi

The attack task force consisting of INS *Trishul, Talwar,* and *Vinash* set course for Karachi, to be in the firing position before midnight. At around 11 p.m., the task force arrived off Karachi and detected a group of ships outside the harbour.

The missile boat, INS *Vinash*, took up the position off Karachi and fired all the four missiles, which scored the following hits:

1. The first missile struck the oil tanks on the shoreline of Karachi and started a huge fire.
2. The second missile hit a ship in the harbour. This was later identified as the British merchant ship, MV *Hamilton.*
3. The third missile hit another ship in the harbour and it sank in a few minutes. This was later identified as the Panama vessel, MV *Gulf Star.*
4. The fourth missile hit the Pakistan Navy tanker, PNS *Dacca.* This ship got severely damaged.

The task force reassembled thereafter and headed back to rendezvous the Fleet at the predetermined position the next day. A few minutes after this attack, the Indian Air Force attacked the Karachi Airfield and the port installations. The blazing oil tanks were easy to home on, and the additional bombing by the IAF aircraft kept the fires burning in Karachi for many days.

Attack on Makran Coast

When the *Trishul* group headed for Karachi, the second group, comprising INS *Mysore, Betwa,* and *Ranjit* proceeded towards Pakistan's Makran Coast. INS Betwa was ordered to bombard Gwadar, whereas INS *Mysore* and *Ranjit* proceeded towards Jiwani.

When the task force was about 70 miles from the target, a merchant ship was sighted. This was identified as the Pakistani merchant ship, MV *Madhumati*. A little later, a radio transmission by

Madhumati to Karachi was intercepted by us. The Fleet Commander felt that the position of the task force had been compromised and aborted the attack on the Makran Coast. The boarding party from our ship was sent on *Madhumati* and the ship was captured. This task group, thereafter, withdrew with the prize catch of *Madhumati*, to rejoin the INS *Trishul* group, thus, returning after the successful completion of Operation Python.

There was absolute jubilation in the Indian Navy after Operation Python, the second attack on Karachi on the night of 8/9 December. However, it was learned that the situation in the Pakistan Navy was extremely different. The warships were not only asked to take shelter in the inner Karachi port but also to de-ammunition the ships, to avoid catastrophic damage in case of a subsequent missile attack by the Indian Navy.

Fleet Operations on 9–10 December

The INS *Trishul* group after attacking Karachi, the INS *Mysore* group after capturing the Pakistani ship *Madhumati* from the Makran Coast, and the third, INS *Deepak* from the tanker group, regrouped on the evening of 9 December. There was overall jubilation in all the ships for completing the missions successfully.

Since all the missiles had been expended, the Fleet Commander felt prudent for the ships to return to Mumbai, carry out emergency machinery repairs, pick up loaded missiles boats and redeploy for operations thereafter. Thus, a southwesterly course towards Bombay was ordered.

The Sinking of INS *Khukri* on the Night of 9/10 December

An anti-submarine squadron consisting of INS *Khukri, Kuthar,* and *Kirpan* had sailed with us on 2 December. At sea on 4 December,

INS *Kuthar* had a boiler explosion and had to be towed back to the Mumbai harbour. The Fleet Commander decided to send the anti-submarine squadron back to Mumbai. These three ships returned to the port on 6 December.

The electronic warfare intercepts had reported a submarine off the Gujarat coast, near the Diu head. The Flag Officer Commanding-in-Chief (FOC-in-C) West decided to sail out INS *Khukri* and *Kirpan* to neutralise this submarine threat.

These two ships sailed out on 8 December and set up an anti-submarine patrol off the Diu head in Gujarat. On 9 December at about 8.49 p.m. while on the anti-submarine patrol, INS *Khukri* was hit by a torpedo. We first intercepted an emergency signal from INS *Kirpan* about an explosion on *Khukri*. A few minutes later, a flash signal was received from *Kirpan*, stating that the radar contact of *Khukri* had been lost. After being hit by the torpedoes, *Khukri* sank in a few minutes, taking down with her 18 officers and 175 men, including the Commanding Officer, Captain M.N. Mulla. It has been reported that Captain Mulla, could have saved himself, but decided to go down with the ship, following true naval traditions.

Fleet Manoeuvres: 9 –16 December

During the return passage to Mumbai, the following facts were evident, and countermeasures catered for:

Surface Threat

There was minimal threat from the Pakistani fleet. Their deployment in the Arabian Sea away from the coastline was unlikely.

Air Threat

Though an air threat was still feasible, the non-detection of our fleet, by the Pakistani reconnaissance aircraft, had gone entirely in our favour. Also, the fleet was now transiting more than 300 miles from Karachi. The likelihood of a Pakistani Air Force aircraft, venturing out at sea was extremely remote.

Submarine Threat

The biggest threat to the returning fleet was from the Pakistani submarines. They would certainly be deployed off the approaches to the Mumbai harbour. On receiving the acoustic warning, they could position themselves to attack the returning fleet.

Given the above assessment, the Fleet Commander decided to continue to proceed in the southeasterly direction. On 11 December, we had reached 250 miles west of Goa by the forenoon. At this time, the course was altered eastwards, towards the Indian Coast. The overall speed of the fleet had reduced due to the slow speed of the captured Pakistani ship, *Madhumati*.

On the evening of 12 December, the course of the fleet was altered in a northeasterly direction to make a landfall at Jaigarh. The shallow water continental shelf from Mumbai, extends for nearly 140 miles to the south, till Jaigarh; thereafter the depths drop quite steeply.

It was appreciated by the Fleet Commander that once the fleet began to transit through the shallow waters, it would not be possible for the Pakistan submarines to close in to attack the returning fleet.

We made landfall at Jaigarh around midnight on 12 December and thereafter proceeded in line astern formation, hugging the coastline. These waters were too shallow for the submarine to operate. Also, we had used the surprise element to make landfall well to the south of Mumbai. This ruse by the Fleet Commander paid off and all the ships, including the captured Pakistani ship, *Madhumati*, entered the Bombay harbour safely on 13 December.

The Pakistan Army in the east surrendered on 16 December and the hostilities were terminated with the ceasefire being announced.

Thereafter, we entered the Bombay Naval Dockyard, to a rousing reception by the Headquarters Western Naval command. I continued to serve on board the INS *Betwa*, till my specialisation course was resumed in January 1972.

Two Personal Experiences

Party Onboard

On the day of the ceasefire, my department sailors organised a small tea party. There was overall jubilation on board, and on being invited, I readily agreed to join the tea party. However, I was totally surprised when my Navigator Yeoman read out my total sleep in 12 days from 2 December to 13 December. He was recording all the winks taken by me on the camp cot in the operations room—my sleeping and resting place. The total sleep recorded in 12 days averaged less than 3 hours per day. It was indeed a very touching gesture from my men and makes me nostalgic even to this day!

Engagement Ceremony in Bombay on 5 December

I desired to get married to my fiancée only after the completion of my specialisation course and had conveyed this decision to my family accordingly. However, since the course had been interrupted and both the families were in Bombay, they insisted we should go ahead with the engagement and the ring ceremony. Thus, the date was fixed for Sunday, 5 December. Before the ship sailed on 2 December, I called up my father and informed him regarding our sailing orders. He was instructed to keep this information confidential and to cancel the ceremony if I did not return on 4 December. When the hostilities broke out on Friday, 3 December, my father realised that I would not be returning for some time. He, therefore, broke the news of my ship's sailing to my father-in-law. My father-in-law was not at all perturbed and felt that the ceremony should be solemnised and not get cancelled. A large number of guests had been invited from both sides. It had been extremely gutsy on the part of both the families to go ahead with the ceremonies, celebrations and entertainment of guests. Later, a small formal engagement took place towards the end of December for both of us to exchange our engagement rings.

The Tribune

2 PAK WARSHIPS, ONE SUB SUNK

KARACHI PORT BLASTED BY INDIAN MEN-OF-WAR

ENEMY NAVAL HEADQUARTERS IN GRIP OF PANIC

Curbs On Our Staff In Pak

Retaliatory Steps Taken By India

RUSSIA WARNS WORLD POWERS TO STAY CLEAR OF CONFLICT

No Cease-fire Line In Kashmir Now

Kosygin Lays

The Tribune (Chandigarh) dated 6 December 1971

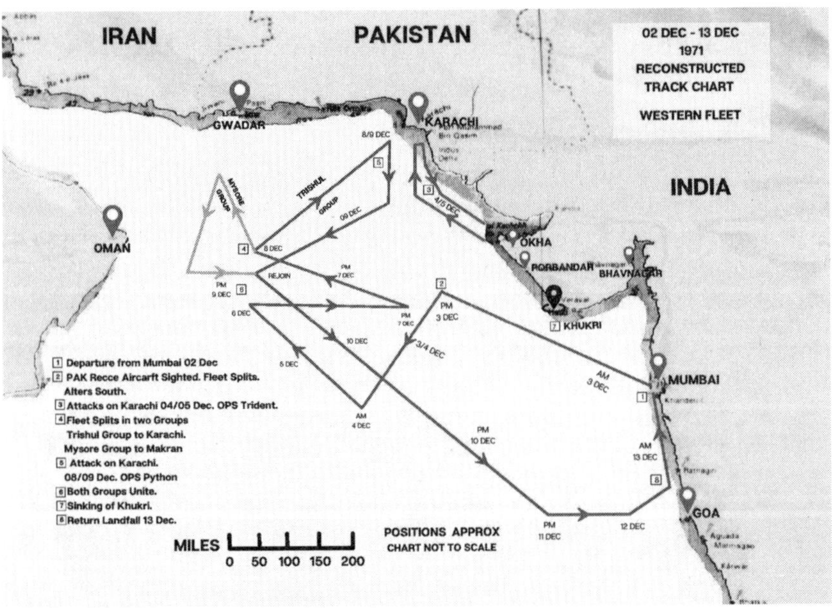

The Western Fleet track chart

Captain S.S. Sethi (Retired) is an alumnus of the National Defence Academy (28th course) and a postgraduate in Military Studies from Defence Services Staff College, Wellington. He has had a remarkable career in the Indian Navy, most of which was spent at sea on various warships—he has commanded INS *Prabal* and INS *Ranjit* and was the Commissioning Captain of CGS *Vijaya*. He was the Indian Naval Commander during the Indian Peace Keeping Force (IPKF) operations in Sri Lanka. He has also commanded the Navigation and Direction School in Kochi. After retirement, he has held senior positions in various shipping and offshore companies. He now leads a retired life in Mumbai.

A Page from My Diary

Wing Commander S. Balasubramanian

4 December 1971

The old Phillips transistor crackled into life late on the night of 3 December 1971. Huddled around it were over a dozen pilots of the Lightning Tribe, No. 20 Squadron of the Indian Air Force. All ears were glued to capture the words as they came along, with the occasional static. Nothing was missed as the voice of our Prime Minister, Mrs Indira Gandhi, came through loud and clear. 'The wanton and unprovoked aggression of Pakistan would be decisively and finally repelled.' Her voice was firm. In the past few hours, Pakistani Air Force aircrafts had attacked Amritsar, Pathankot, Srinagar, Avantipur, Uttarlai, Jodhpur, Ambala, and Agra, as well as some Indian heavy military vehicles, near Sadik, in Punjab. Across the border, their Air Chief had been telling their military's public relations officer not to bother about conjuring up a justification. 'Success is the biggest justification,' he boasted. 'My bird should be right over Agra by now, knocking the hell out of them. I am only waiting for the good news.'

We Were at War

Our location was a small airfield, far from our home base of Pathankot. A pre-emptive strike had been expected. To avoid substantial losses, whenever such a strike came through, our squadron's planes were dispersed to safer havens. Now, it was time to get back to where the action was. We prepared for a take-off at 3 a.m. in the morning. Our planes were most certainly not designed for night flights and operations as they did not have taxi or landing lights. In the absence of any lights on the taxi tracks, the other pilots of the squadron and I had to taxi with the help of airmen guiding us with hand-held torches cycling alongside all the way to the runway! Cycling a few feet away from a hurtling fighter jet, all eight tons of it, takes some courage!

The night was dark. Northern India was invisible due to the strict compliance of black-out norms. At around 4 a.m., our 14 aircraft approached overhead Pathankot, our base, in a formation. With our bright red and green wing-tip lights, it must have been an elegant sight to watch. Then, suddenly, all hell broke loose. The sky lit up with red tracers in hundreds and thousands! Our anti-aircraft guns opened up, mistaking us for an enemy aircraft. One could hear the pop of the exploding shells around. This triggered an unplanned peel off of the planes from our formation in all directions. Unprintable words that followed on receiver/transmitter (R/T) cleared up the skies soon. We had had our first taste of war. One by one, our pilots landed—luckily without any damage.

A fighter squadron usually has 16 single-seaters and two twin-seater trainer aircraft.. The trainer is used for training and is not normally used in combat. Our unit was equipped with Hunter Mk 56A fighters and 66D trainers. These were manufactured by the Hawker Aircraft Company of the UK. We had about 30 pilots to fly these planes. The total manning level of the squadron varied between 250–350. Three technical officers and a medical officer ensured the good health of the aircraft and the unit personnel, respectively. The personnel of other ranks were trained to handle specific trades like technical (mechanical, electrical, and electronics), administrative, catering, and health services. Unlike the Army and the Navy, where almost the entire strength went on to fight, in the Air Force, only the pilots went in for actual combat! Our aircraft needed just one person to fly it, but that person was also its navigator, gunner, and radio operator.

The Hunter Mk 56A was undoubtedly the most docile-looking fighting bird ever built. Powered by Rolls Royce Avon jet engines, the modified first prototype broke the world air speed record in 1953, achieving a speed of 727 mph (1,171 kmph, 632 knots). Initially inducted as a day air defense airplane, these were moved to a ground attack role with the induction of Gnats (Ajeets) and MIG-21s into the Indian Air Force. With its eight underwing weapon stations and four internal 30 mm Aden guns, each capable of firing 20 rounds of ammunition per second, it turned out to be a formidable ground-attack aircraft, something that the Pakistani forces were soon to find out. With fuel in its internal and four external tanks, it had the longest reach when compared to the other aircraft which were then in our inventory. Basing them at Pathankot threatened most of the distant enemy airfields by bringing them within our easy reach.

Back in the crew room of our squadron, the atmosphere was remarkably calm. It was also fun as the pilots exchanged views on the ineffective enemy attacks of the previous evening as we sipped our chai. Frantic shouting and screaming replaced the calm every time the Flight Commander walked in with a strike mission order. Seniority, experience, and whatnot were hurled at each other to be included in the formation for the task! The cell phone's video camera (yet to be invented or available in 1971) would have been best to capture those golden moments —words fail to describe the frenzy. We had, after all, lived for that day.

The squadron was well prepared. We had worked for over months. Maps for various airfields had been meticulously prepared. Navigation consisted of drawing pencil lines to the target and back with running times at important and visible points along the track. The route avoided major cities and dangerous areas. While keeping the fuel requirement in mind, tactical routes were selected so that even if spotted by radars or forward ground observers, the enemy would remain unsure of our target airfield. One had to hold the rolled-up map in the left hand besides controlling the throttle while the thumb was to be locked onto a place one had just flown over the Thumb Positioning System (TPS)—the predecessor of a modern-day GPS had to be invented! From time to time, the thumb was moved over the map as the aircraft travelled ahead. We had been busy for months studying the maps and going over the briefings, possible targets and different eventualities of missions.

Standard operating procedures were created to ensure that every member knew his actions. Thus, it would be easy to maintain total R/T silence through most part of our missions. This would preclude interceptions of our radio transmissions by the enemy that might leak out our intentions. Dummy briefings of the missions were carried out, going down to the minutest detail. These included target descriptions, attack patterns, and actions to be taken if intercepted enemy route or over the target. Escape plans for different sectors, in case of an ejection, too, were covered. In short, nothing was left to a guess. We were ready.

After lunch, I got lucky to be included as a wingman of my Flight Commander in a four-aircraft strike mission over an enemy airfield at a given time. Since the navigation time was known, a take-off time, and thus a start-up time, was calculated. Nearing the aircraft, registered as A-475, I was mobbed by my airmen, the magnificent lot, the unsung heroes, who kept these machines flying. Along with good wishes came a special request from one of them for destroying a 'yellow building north of the airfield'—he would not have any Pakistani living in his grandfather's home! So, working backward for a time over target (TOT), our four Hunters took off on time. Soon, we got into a broad front formation and were on our way. While expecting an air threat from anywhere, this formation provided good 360 degrees view of the skies.

Flying westwards, at a low level, skimming the trees, we hugged the ground in order to avoid radar detection. Total R/T silence was maintained throughout. Crossing the international borders without a passport, as briefed, I fired a short test burst from my guns—the vibration was reassuring. I could defend myself! We were now flying at 420 knots. The speed would increase to 480 knots (almost 900 kmph) as we approached the target airfield.

Closing in onto the target, almost bang on the scheduled time, I could see the control tower and hangar roofs come into view. I craned my neck around to look for enemy aircraft that would generally be on a combat air patrol (CAP), higher up, to defend the airfield and would threaten us. It was time, and my leader pulled up for his attack. I followed after a few seconds. The pull-up point is always to the left or right of the target since the frontal view is blocked with a high nose during the pull-up. A higher altitude provides a better view for target selection on the left or right, as the case may be. This also allows the aircraft to be put into a turn towards the selected target and, thus, achieves the perfect dive angle needed for the accuracy of a weapon impact. The view of an enemy airfield unfurling in front while in the cockpit of a fully armed plane is a fighter pilot's dream, and here I was, actually living it!

The sky started filling up with tracers and black/white puffs of exploding anti-aircraft shells all around us. That is deadly, but in a way beautiful. Through the dense puffs, I located just the nose of an aircraft parked in a concrete pen. It turned out to be even better than a dream.

I rolled the plane almost onto its back to arrest the upward trajectory while turning lowered the nose onto my target. Unmindful of any enemy aircraft and the bursting anti-aircraft shells all around, I knew that now it was me and the target. Correcting my dive angle and speed, I gently eased the gunsight on the visible part of the enemy aircraft. Closing in at the correct range, I pressed the trigger. My ears could not hear anything even as my eyes took in the magnificent view of the aircraft exploding, spewing flames and smoke along with debris! It had been less than fifteen seconds since I had pulled up for the attack. Clearing through the smoke, as I pulled out of my dive, I spotted my leader and soon caught up with him as we headed home.

Actual combat for a fighter pilot, whether on ground attack or air interception, lasts but for a few seconds or minutes. It is generally a do-or-die situation and rarely gives a second chance. However, the skill required can only be achieved through tons of groundwork, hundreds of training missions, and remembering every minute nuance of handling the aircraft and its weapons—all honed over the years. The flight lasting around an hour, and culminating in an attack, is finally the ultimate test of a fighter pilot.

The formation caught up, and with our watchful eyes looking for threats, we headed home. The men were thrilled to see me back. On hearing about the 'kill', I was lifted off the ground and carried on their shoulders to the waiting jeep. It was indeed a memorable welcome. The yellow building, however, remained intact.

Back in the crew room, there were spirited discussions on the day's successes. Post-flight reports were filed. Some of our aircraft had returned with bullet holes in them. Indeed, our squadron had done remarkably well. However, the evening was marred when news came in that we had lost my roommate, Flying Officer Muralidharan, an ace pilot.

Flying Officer Sudhir Tyagi, a very dear friend, and a coursemate operating from the same base, also did not return from another offensive operation conducted the same day. Glory and danger lie before the ones who fight a war. A soldier knows this too well. It takes years of training and raw courage to stand up to your enemies and perform your duty irrespective. It is not easy, but a serviceman craves this opportunity.

As evening fell, I knew I needed my sleep to rest and be ready to perform yet again.

How an airfield looks to a pilot climbing up to an attack run

The author with colleagues

Wing Commander S. Balasubramanian, VrC (Retired) was commissioned in June 1967. He remained associated with aviation for over 50 years. Besides serving in fighter squadrons, he has been a flying instructor in India, abroad, and in the Flight Instructor's School, Tambaram. While in Air India, he had been an instructor and examiner on the Airbus and a simulator instructor on the B-787. He is a trustee with the Indian Development Foundation, an NGO recognised by the UN and involved in humanitarian activities.

A Naval Story from Southern Naval Command

Commander E. Jai Chacko

On 2 December 1971, we set sail from Kochi on INS *Godavari*, under the command of Captain Hardev Singh. I was the Senior Engineer of the ship then. We were accompanied by INS *Ganga* and INS *Amba*, both of which were entrusted with the task of trade warfare and contraband control in the Eight- and Nine-Degree Channels, about 300–400 nautical miles west of Colombo. The task was to choke the traffic of Pakistani merchant and naval ships going to and from the East and West Wings.

On the morning of 4 December, MV *Pasni*, a Pakistani merchant ship disguised as Tokyo *Maru*, was sighted approximately 350 nautical miles west of Kochi. Our ship hoisted the battle ensign and asked the ship to stop. With her not obeying orders, two four-inch salvos were fired across her bows. This brought *Pasni* to a standstill. On close examination, it was found that the ship was transporting many troops to the Western Wing.

The crew of *Pasni* were asked to embark on lifeboats and

abandon the ship. The process was chivvied up by raking the upper deck with 40/60[55] fire. After the crew and troops embarked on the *Godavari*, a boarding party along with the key members of *Pasni's* engine room crew, took over the ship and sailed her to Kochi under *Godavari's* guns.

On interrogating the Pakistani troops, it was revealed that they were from the 23rd Baluch Regiment, the infamous regiment that executed Operation Searchlight, which resulted in the massacre of intellectuals at Dhaka University.

On 6 December, Pasni was brought to Kochi under the command of Lieutenant Commander P.P. Nandi, the Executive Officer of INS *Godavari* and Lieutenant Biswajit Roy. *Pasni's* crew and troops were handed over to the civilian authorities who, after the war, were repatriated.

This article cannot end without a mention of Lieutenant Commander Castelino, the Supply Officer of the ship, who gave a sumptuous meal to the Pakistani crew, who were in a state of shock thinking they would be shot. In fact, the Captain of *Pasni*, when taken to our captain's cabin, had defecated in his pants!

---

55 An anti-aircraft gun

Commander E. Jai Chacko (Retired) is an alumnus of Lawrence School, Lovedale and the National Defence Academy. He was commissioned into the Indian Navy in 1967 and he served on INS *Tir, Kuthar, Delhi, Godavari, Gaj, Sandhayak* and *Darshak*. He studied engineering from INS Shivaji. He worked as Instructor and Commander at the Naval College of Engineering. He retired from the naval dockyard at Visakhapatnam in 1988 and lives in Mankotta, Kerala, where he looks after the family farm.

The author would like to thank Vice Admiral Vijay Shanker (Retired), who was the Assistant Navigating Officer at the time, for his assistance in writing this article.

From the Battle Zone of Longewala

Lieutenant Colonel Ram Chandra Chhetri

Introduction

After the completion of a High Altitude Area (HAA) tenure in Sikkim, pursuant to an immediate operation posting order, I left HQ 164 Mountain Brigade the next day. I drove down to Bagdogra Airport to board IL-76 Transport Aircraft, popularly known as Assam Courier Flight. There were about 85 senior and junior officers, 200 junior commissioned officers (JCOs) and men hailing from the North-East Frontier Agency (NEFA) region and Sikkim. The flight landed at about 5 a.m. at Palam Airport. I rushed to the Delhi railway station to board Jodhpur Mail and reached Jodhpur before noon on 14 October 1971. I reported my arrival at the Rear Divisional Headquarter, where I received instructions to board the vehicle of ASC Transport Company leaving for the operational location that same afternoon. After roughly six hours of road journey, I arrived at the 12 Infantry Division Ordnance Field Park area. The officer whom I had to relieve, Captain N.S. Kandra, and two other officers including my course mate Late Captain S.K. Tiwari and Lieutenant I.S. Rao, were waiting for me. After a brief conversation, we had dinner and retired to our semi underground tented accommodation.

The next morning, while it was 'stand to' time, I, along with Captain S.K. Tiwari, went around the Divisional Administrative Area. Surprisingly, I found that one of the companies of 23 PUNJAB[56] had been deployed for the protection of the flank and the Divisional Administrative Area. The regiment was one of the infantry battalions of HQ 164 Mountain Brigade, where I was posted as the Brigade Ordnance Officer. Lieutenant Colonel M.K. Hussain was the Commanding Officer and Major Kuldeep Singh Chandpuri was the 'A' Company Commander. The regiment had moved out from the HAA for their peace tenure. After a brief conversation with Major Kuldeep Singh Chandpuri approximately 300 metres away from my unit area, we were scheduled to meet the Commander Army Ordnance Corps (CAOC) who was also the Officer-in-Charge of the Divisional Administrative Area. I, along with Captain N.S. Kandra, met the CAOC. After a brief discussion, the CAOC asked his Second-in-Command to take me to HQ 12 Infantry Division for a formal introduction with the staff officers. That liaison visit was extremely helpful as I understood the impending divisional tasks and certain grey areas of logistics. Since it was time for the lunch break, we rushed to the Officers Mess, housed in a large tent covered with a camouflage net. I met all the Service heads who were seated in the modified anteroom.

Ordnance (the Silent Service): Functions in the Combat Zone

Within a few hours of my stay at the operational location and the meeting, I realised the onerous tasks before us—to provide efficient

---

[56] 23rd Battalion, The Punjab Regiment

and responsive material and logistic support to the dependent troops.

Inventory Management and Stocking Process

This entailed detailed provisioning, procurement, storage, and subsequent issue of spares of armaments from small arms to guns, engineering, and signal equipment, 'A' and 'B' vehicles, major assemblies like engine assemblies, expendable stores, tyres, tubes, batteries for mechanical transport and signal equipment. Other important tasks at hand were the receipt of unserviceable and repairable stores from the dependent units and their further disposal to dependent depots.

Each of these functions was critical to the support and success of the campaign. I took over the charge of inventory management and the stocking process, bearing in mind the fundamentals of logistic support, that is the right item in the right quantity at the right place at the right time.

The process of inventory control was to commence on the precedence of the vital, essential and routine nature of requirements of the dependent units. The conventional methodology of inventory control had been very cumbersome, tedious, and time-consuming in comparison to modern computerised control systems which are faster, accurate and devoid of human errors. Now, coming back to the conventional inventory control, which involved vetting of account cards of each item. One account card was assigned to one item which had data like Cat/Part No, nomenclature, accounting unit and other transaction details as well as the total dependencies of equipment and vehicle. There were about 3,500 items of supply responsibility of the Ordnance Field Park (OFP). The process of vetting these account cards continued for 15 days. In case an account card showed a shortfall in quantity, the same was simultaneously covered with operation immediate indents on the dependent depot. After hectic and dedicated efforts put in the earnest and right direction, the stock levels of the total holdings surged to more than satisfactory levels by mid-November 1971.

Traffic Duties

This primarily entailed the receipt or collection of the stores' ex-depots and further issue and dispatch to dependent units. Lieutenant I.S. Rao was assigned the task of organising two outpost detachments to deliver the material at the Unit Repair Organisation (URO) and Light Repair Workshop (LRW) in forward locations. He was also entrusted with the task of collecting indented stores from the dependent depot and Jaisalmer Railhead, for collecting the consignments of sand tyres for 'B' vehicles and heavy-lift stores like engine assemblies.

Unit Administration

Man-management was a very essential aspect, especially in field conditions. Food, clothing and shelter for the men, as well as the safety and security of both men and material, were to take priority over everything else. The responsibility of the administration was entrusted to Captain S.K. Tiwari.

Based on the tactical situation prevalent in the battle zone, 12 Infantry Division was entrusted with the task of overall diversionary tactics in the event of a possible assault by the Pakistani forces. They were also assigned the responsibility of defending the border post of Longewala in the Thar Desert of Rajasthan.

The war started with a pre-emptive air strike by Pakistan Air Force, which was launched on a number of Indian airfields on 3 December 1971. That was seen as a prelude to Pakistan's intentions of declaring an all-out war against India. The partial mobilisation in the initial stages on the western front was turning into a full-blown mobilisation with appropriate scales of reinforcements. Activities in the border post had increased manifold as threat perception from Pakistan's forces seemed imminent.

On the side of Longewala, two Lancers with Centurion tanks were at 'stand to' for a swift move and fire at the intruding Pakistani formation. Major Kuldeep, the Company Commander of 'A' Company of 23 PUNJAB was holding fast in his defensive position with his men. RCL gun-mounted jeep, light and medium machine guns and mortars were all set to take on any attack from the Pakistani formation. Artillery field regiments were deployed to cover the likely axes of the enemy's advance. The troop of Air Defence Regiment, with their 40 mm anti-aircraft guns, was in place to deter the enemy aircraft from intruding into the air space.

Violation of Air Space by PAF on the Intervening Night of 4/5 December 1971

A Pakistani transport aircraft intruded into the Divisional Administrative Area (DAA). The pilot first fired illuminating flare ammunition to enable him to observe the targeted area, and after an interval of a few seconds jettisoned a 1,000 lb bomb, returning home immediately. In the meantime, the troop of the Air Defence Regiment, located in the proximity, started firing 40 mm anti-aircraft ammunition, bringing about a barrage of fire with tracer rounds. The low-flying enemy aircraft, with a large fuselage, was certainly an easy target. Unfortunately, due to the lack of radar equipment for early warning of approaching aircraft with regard to its identification, speed and direction, it survived being hit by our anti-aircraft guns. Undoubtedly, it was a bold move on the part of the Pakistani pilot, who took advantage of the darkness, moving stealthily amidst the DAA and dropping the bomb. However, the bomb did not explode as it struck against soft sand, making a 30-feet deep crater, and laid there live, posing a threat to the lives and assets in the vicinity. The next morning, my friend, Captain Garudacharya, an Ammunition Technical Officer, defused the bomb in situ. However, the Pakistani media was rife with fake news claiming the destruction of an Indian military base in the Rajasthan Sector. In truth, had the bomb exploded, there would have been massive destruction within the divisional administrative area from falling in the vicinity of the Engineer Field Company, which held their mines, explosives and other stores.

Battle of Longewala

After the initial failed attempt by PAF, on 7 December 1971, an enemy infantry brigade, supported by a regiment of armour (mixed T-59 and Shermans), was about to launch a dawn attack on our defensive position held by Major Kuldeep at Longewala. Our Air Controller requested the IAF for direct support of the post at the earliest. In a bold early dawn attack, HF-24 pilots pounded on the tanks of Pakistan's 27 CAVALRY[57], and the IAF started shooting at the moving columns. Sortie after sortie went in to attack and destroy the enemy tanks. We could see the tanks engulfed in flames. Amidst the billowing smoke, we also saw tank crews jumping off the tanks and running helter-skelter to save their lives. A large number of enemy tanks were destroyed. The retreating tanks, moving columns of soft vehicles, and troops were bogged down in the sandy terrain, thereby becoming easy targets for the IAF. After the disastrous offensive in Longewala, our forward border outposts were under continuous shelling by Pakistani artillery and infantry. Our artillery field regiments, and infantry battalions responded with courage, grit, and determination. Our formation could not afford to lower its guard at such a critical juncture because Pakistan's offensives were continuing in other sectors. Within the next few days, it became clear that Pakistan was fighting a losing war.

---

[57] 27th Cavalry Regiment

Conclusion

By and large, it was evident that the strategies of both defensive and offensive postures by the Indian forces as well as a combination of both in various theatres of war during 1971 paid rich dividends. Finally after the surrender of Dacca on 15 December 1971, the war came to an end. The victorious Indian leadership, in politics and military, was accoladed in the various national and international fora. In fact, the victory of India against Pakistan was a direct result of all arms cooperation. The Indian fighting troops displayed a very high sense of discipline, professionalism, resilience and determination during all the campaigns. The conduct of operations, both tactical and logistical excellence, will go down in the military history of the country.

The liberation of Bangladesh was a great achievement because it paved way for sending back hundreds and thousands of refugees home. India's support in establishing an independent Bangladesh was applauded by the member nations of the United Nations. Indeed, independent Bangladesh would forever remember the generosity, moral and material support of the Indian people in their fight for an independent nation during 1971.

Monitoring Progress in Operation Vital Store

A crater from a 1000 lb Pak bomb

Captain R.C. Chhetri explains the functioning of weapons

Lieutenant Colonel Ram Chandra Chhetri (Retired) was commissioned into the Army Ordnance Corps on 15 June 1966. During his service spanning more than three decades, he served in the Northeast as Control Officer, Central Ordnance Depot in Jabalpur and held a number of appointments tenable by officers of his rank.

From Hinterland to War Zone

Brigadier Ujjal Dasgupta

Our course went into the 1971 operations with 5 years of commissioned service, with just the right blend of adequate experience and loads of grit and leadership qualities. We were indeed at the cutting edge of operations by land, sea, and air.

By mid-1971, most schools of military instruction terminated their ongoing courses because the country was preparing for war, and officers were dispatched back post-haste to their units. For some inexplicable reason, our degree engineering course continued. Everything that a military man trains and prepares for culminates in the hope of getting to participate in active hostilities. We were desperate not to miss this opportunity of a lifetime, but 3 December 1971 saw us still chasing electrons in the classroom! With all hope lost, we resigned to our fate. A week later, we received telephonic instructions terminating the course forthwith, and we were asked to choose our posting between the eastern and western sectors. Since my native place is Jessore where my grandfather spent most of his life and my father lived as a young lad, I opted for the eastern sector. But true to form, the Army HQ issued my marching orders for the western sector.

The Hinterland

In the next two days, as we made our way to our units, I got a rare first-hand view of the situation in the hinterland during active hostilities. The spirit of all our countrymen and the way the nation rose as one and stood by the forces is something I have never seen either before, or since. Every man, woman, and child was fully involved, and the rallying cry, '*jai jawan, jai kisan*', given to the nation by Lal Bahadur Shastri, was on everyone's lips.

The next afternoon found us at Indore Railway Station, ready to board the three-tier compartments that would take us en masse to Pathankot and Calcutta. A large crowd had gathered on the platform. They insisted on garlanding us and were eager to shake hands and wish us well. The press also reached there, and the next day's local newspaper covered the farewell of brave soldiers going to war, complete with pictures. All of this attention made us feel special indeed, but also rather silly. We were still at Indore with more than a week of hostilities already over, while the real heroes were those already deep inside East and West Pakistan. It was odd that those heroes were not accessible to the average man on the street while we were. At one point, when I was standing a bit away from the others, a frail old beggar made a beeline for me. He reached me even as I was reaching for my purse. What happened next was unexpected. He appeared to stand a bit taller, his eyes shone with some inner light, his hand reaching out to grasp mine. He held it in a firm handclasp and said, '*Jeet ke aana, Sahib!*' (Emerge victorious, Sahib!) With that, he turned on his heels and walked off. This incident gave me goosebumps, and I felt humbled, proud, motivated, and thankful—all at the same time. In fact, it continues to remain vivid in my memory even to this day. It succinctly sums up the feelings that coursed through the veins of every citizen when the nation was at war.

The New Delhi Railway Station was partly dark by night. The feeble lighting in deference to the blackout just about allowed us to see. People were also talking in muted voices. I embraced my parents and sister who had come from Lucknow to meet me as we passed through.

The first rays of the morning sun found us moving at a sedate pace through Punjab. It was bitterly cold. Nothing prepared us for the onslaught that followed. Even as the train was steaming into a small station, hordes of villagers stormed into every compartment, armed with buckets of steaming dal and baskets of rotis, all the while shouting, '*jai jawan, jai kisan*.' We were unceremoniously made to get up, two to three thick rotis were thrust into every hand, followed almost immediately with a ladle of steaming hot dal on top. We ate the food quickly to keep the dal from spilling. Then the train was off. We were met with such warmth at every stop thereafter—gruff, taciturn hordes of poor villagers waiting impatiently at each station to feed all soldiers en route to the war zone. After nearly three rounds of this, we had no choice but to decline any further generosity because we were so full!

This was a profoundly humbling experience. These villagers, who had so little to start with, were giving us so much more than the food from their tables—we were touched by the warmth in their hearts and overwhelmed with their generosity. They were, quite obviously, very poor. Their womenfolk must have woken up in the wee hours to scrape up whatever was in the house and prepare the delicious food for us. What prompts a person to deprive himself of his meagre fare and unstintingly give it to total strangers? Patriotism? We were to see many more such patriots before reaching our units. We ruminated in silence, each lost in his thoughts.

The railhead at Pathankot was a welter of organised confusion. A non-commissioned officer (NCO) went around asking each of us the names of our units, and we were accordingly led to a long line of civil-hired transport (CHT) and asked to board the respective vehicles. 'Civil' and 'hired' were both misnomers for these scruffy, sleep-deprived drivers and cleaners, who were fully committed to getting us to our units at the earliest; they were as much military as any of us. They knew the locations of the units on the national highway. And 'hired'?

These *thelawallahs* had just materialised voluntarily from everywhere with one single objective—to ferry troops and stores as needed, when needed. No one counted kilometres or litres. No rest, no time for food. All through the hostilities, they kept at this endlessly.

The 'Fog' of War

The Commanding Officer of the Corps Signal Regiment at Samba was at a loss as to what to do with the three of us who had reported for duty on 13 December. It was decided that each one of us would be sent to one of the Divisional Signal Regiments under the corps, to take care of the rearward communication to the Corps HQ.

At last light, I was teamed up with a lineman, a despatch rider (DR) with his jeep, a sackful of daak meant for the Divisional HQ (Corps of Signals was responsible for the scheduled despatch service—SDS) and armed with the assurance from the DR that he knew the location of the Divison HQ. With this, we set off into the night. It was an uneventful trip along the National Highway past Kathua and Pathankot up to Dinanagar, where we had to turn sharply towards the west on kucha tracks. The going became tricky. Trying to follow the tape left by the sappers did not work since it was snapped at many places. We made our way ahead as best as possible.

After an interminable time, the DR stopped the vehicle in the middle of nowhere and announced, '*Sahib, kal to Division HQ idhar hi tha, aaj pata nahin kahan gaya*'. (Sahib, this was the location for the Division HQ until yesterday, but it no longer shows the same!) That was that! The Division HQ had moved on ahead in the last 24 hours. It was pitch dark. With no idea of the new location, I decided to look around the present location, hoping to run into some rear elements to guide us.

Once off the track, it was somewhat forested, and we proceeded single file. Suddenly, out of the darkness came a harsh cry, '*Tham! Kaun aata hai?*' (Stop! Who is it?) We froze in our tracks. Our 'dost' response was met with the next command, '*Haath upar! Pehchan ke lie aage barh.*' (Hands up! Step forward and identify yourself.) Finally, '*Tham. Password?*' (Halt! Password?)

The sudden shock of being thus accosted froze the blood in our veins. It certainly froze our memories, and we remained mum. By now we could make out the shadowy outline of the sentry and his weapon pointed towards us. In a quivering voice that gave away his young years, he repeated, '*Password bolo!*' (Share password!) and simultaneously, the ominous double-click of his weapon indicated it was now cocked. He was trying to steel himself up to press the trigger if he had to. It takes a lot to shoot a person in cold blood. Be that as it may, he was determined to do his duty.

Cold sweat trickled down my shoulder blades. The DR was in the lead and would receive the first bullet. Desperately, he tried to recollect the password. Perhaps in the dim recesses of his memory, he recollected that there was a large animal somewhere in the password or counter-password and decided to take a leap of faith. He blurted out '*ghoda*'. There were a few seconds of silence as the sentry pondered over this—the password was '*kalam*' and the counter-password was '*hathi*'. Perhaps the sentry, too, decided that one large four-footed animal was as good as the other, never mind whether it was the password or counter-password. Peevishly, he said, '*To aisa bolo na!*' (Oh! So say that!) and lowered his weapon. Waves of relief poured over all of us, the sentry included. I assure you; it was not funny at that time!

By first light, we managed to reach the Division HQ just short of Nainakot and thereafter, time passed by in a daze as we were caught up in our tasks. I had become a forced third occupant of a shelter meant for two. When we could get some rest, we would sleep packed like sardines in a can. Any attempt to turn sides resulted in a pile of mud falling upon us!

My rearward radio relay communications to the Corps HQ (we were totally dependent on radio relay) functioned beautifully, even at the extreme ranges from where we were operating, a result of careful siting. In the fast-moving, fluid battle, radio relay was our lifeline. This gave us multiple voice and data channels between Corps HQ and Division HQ so there was no queueing for the important operational calls and messages. An extremely busy three days later, the ceasefire was declared.

One morning, a Pakistani aircraft streaming smoke, flew low over our Headquarters desperately trying to reach its base. Right over the Division HQ, he jettisoned his auxiliary fuel tanks. As these silver tubes came down, everyone dived for the nearest shelter, not knowing whether they were bombs or something else. The tanks landed with a thud, one right into the headquarters and the other a bit further. No one stirred. We were waiting for the bombs to explode. Then two Gurkha johnnies from our defence and employment company ran up smartly to the tank, picked it up under their armpits and trotted back with their war trophy! Senior officers finally crept out from their shelters, feeling very foolish.

There was a Pakistani village, perhaps a little over half a kilometre ahead of us. The very next day after the ceasefire, hundreds of Indian villagers went there and literally stripped and brought back everything they could get their hands on—mattresses, quilts, charpoys, utensils, among others. The villagers on both sides of the border were equally poor, but this was war—no quarter was given, none asked for. It saddened me to see this sight. The next day, a couple of us went to the village. Every possible movable item had been carted away. Only the bare huts remained.

The Aftermath

The ceasefire brought about a sudden reduction of tension. The adrenaline rush that had sustained all of us through many sleepless nights and days now subsided. We were relaxed and had all the time in the world. Then started a flurry of calling on other units in the vicinity to meet friends and make friends, and maybe share a drink and a meal. One day, three of us accompanied the CO to the neighbouring signals unit. We asked for the CO and were directed to his location. We found the gentleman standing inside a small four-by-four enclosure of hessian cloth and bamboo, having a glorious head bath (he was a Sikh) as his helper poured water from just outside the enclosure. The strip of hessian barely covered his unmentionables. He greeted us warmly thus, at ease with himself and the world, and promptly invited us to stay back for lunch. Sundry jawans went by at some distance, quite habituated to this sight. We learned that he was not averse to even giving directions to his Subedar Major from here!

Another minor hilarious episode occurred a few days after the ceasefire. Most of the officers in the unit were smokers, and we ran out of cigarettes. All the local village could offer were 'Kool' cigarettes, a horrible mentholated abomination that we were forced to smoke, with disastrous results on the throat and vocal cords. I was woken up by the exchange one early morning at 4 a.m. on orders of the Second in Command (2IC). He had managed to get the missus online from Mathura with considerable effort, and while her voice came through clearly, his hoarse whisper did not. There followed a hilarious three-way conversation with me relaying what the 2IC said and being an unwitting listener.

A few weeks later, our degree course was resumed and we found ourselves back in Mhow just three months after leaving. Such then were the experiences of this signaller. While they are most mundane as compared to many course mates, I saw the situation in the hinterland and the way the whole nation rallied at that time. I also saw that even war has its funny moments!

Spontaneous send-off for 71 Ops to SODE Course at Indore Railway Station – December 1971

Brigadier Ujjal Dasgupta (Retired) was commissioned into the Corps of Signals. In his career spanning 36 years, he has served in J&K, Sikkim and the western sector. He was the Brigade Major (BM) of an infantry brigade and has held Grade 1 General Staff and Signals Staff appointments at the Army HQ and Command HQ. He has served as an Instructor at the Defence Services Staff College and the Military College of Telecom Engineering. He commanded an Infantry Division Signal Regiment as a Lieutenant Colonel and a Tropo Group as a Brigadier, both in the western sector.

Battle of Shakargarh

Brigadier M.I. Jaisinghani

My regiment, 92 Mountain Regiment, was at Agartala from November 1969, after having come from Dukumpani in the 5 Mountain Division Sector. Our regiment was the only unit in the Indian artillery with 105 mm Italian howitzers. At Agartala, we were part of the 57 Mountain Division, a new division raised at Masimpur.

During our tenure at Agartala in early March 1971, there was unrest in East Pakistan (now Bangladesh). The Mukti Bahini got activated. I had the opportunity to go as an Observation Post Officer with 4 GUARDS[58] and also trained the Mukti Bahinis during April-May 1971. At the end of May 1971, we finally handed over our guns and ammunition to the people whom we trained in April-May.

We left Agartala at end of May and moved to Talbehat, near Jhansi, from Dharmanagar. At Agartala, since we had Sikh troops and had some NCOs/jawans who were unable to get their life partners in Punjab, the CO decided to get them married to local Tripura girls. There were about 10–15 jawans who officially got married to local

---

[58] 4th Battalion, Brigade of the Guards

girls and they travelled in the special train to Talbehat.

At Guwahati, our train was stopped and was surrounded by local sub-area troops with light machine guns (LMGs) and rifles. Someone had complained that we had kidnapped these girls and were moving out of Tripura. However, when we showed them the marriage certificates of the individuals, our train was allowed to move to Talbehat.

At Talbehat, we took over the field guns and trained ourselves with the new field equipment. My unit now moved to the western sector on 12 October 1971. The advance party moved by road. I went with the main party, by train, on 16 October 1971. The train, a military-special, was loaded with guns and vehicles. We left Babina at 4 a.m. on 18 October and reached Chakki Bank railway station on 19 October at 3.30 p.m. On reaching Chakki Bank, the battery commander (BC) and observation post (OP) parties were sent to the battalions of the brigade. We were a part of the 72 Infantry Brigade. Our role was assigned towards the Shakargarh Bulge.

The Shakargarh Bulge juts out like a tongue from the main landmass of Pakistan, between the Chenab and the Ravi. Its southern portion rests on the Ravi, the northern runs parallel to the Shivalik Range, leaving a narrow segment between the International Border (IB) and the hills. Its tip points towards Madhopur Headworks and the Pathankot-Mamun military base. The terrain in the bulge is generally flat and interlaced with numerous nullahs running north to south. 15 GRENADIERS[59] captured Bhopalpur and 922 Field Battery was in direct support. Lamriyal was captured by 1 MAHAR[60].

3 SIKH[61] Light Infantry (LI) was to move along the Chechwal–Giddapur–Khaira Sector and my battery was in direct support. The vanguard was held up due to MMG in area high ground. I was the Operation Officer with 'D' Company of 3 SIKH LI. The nullah where the vanguard was held up, being in depression did not offer the

59 15th Battalion, The Grenadiers

60 1st Battalion, The Mahar Regiment

61 3rd Battalion, The Sikh Regiment

Captain of 65 Operations, Captain B.P.S. Bains, with the observation of the position from where the MMG was firing. Captain Bains crawled out and found out his own position by bringing artillery fire on three prominent villages and finding its bearing and registering the three to four villages. I brought down timely fire and a barrage, and my company moved along the fire barrage and captured high ground with 'D' Company.

On 9 December, 'D' Company' ex 15 GRENADIERS established a firm base in Khaira. 3 SIKH LI had a troop of tanks with the Squadron Second-in-Command (2IC) of 7 CAVALRY[62]. My operation party, along with me, were dug down and just 50 metres behind one of the tanks. The intermittent firing was on, with the enemy and us firing at each other. At about 7 p.m., I saw that one of the tanks, that had begun to move back, was coming right upon my trench. I was very lucky that I was in the trench and the tank passed above my head. After the tank had passed overhead, I got up and ran after this tank to give him a piece of my mind about his driving skills. I gathered that it could have been because the tank commander had been shot when he was standing on the cupola and his body had fallen inside, seeing which the driver had gotten jittery and thus had reversed. I joined back with my operation party and thanked all that we had dug our bunkers as it had saved my life. On 10 December, we attacked Harar Kalan. A fire plan was made by my Commanding Officer (CO), Lieutenant Colonel Santosh Kumar.

The firepower for the brigade attack was with more than 25 fire units and I clearly remember that the amount of pounding the guns gave, the trenches in which we were before the attack and on pre-H hour firing shook like an earthquake. Shahbazpur was captured by 'B' Company ex 22 PUNJAB[63] on 11 December 1971. A company under my command (since the Company Commander of 3 SIKH LI was a casualty) captured Harar Khurd. Captain B.P.S. Bains, my

---

[62] 7th Cavalry Regiment

[63] 22nd Battalion, The Punjab Regiment

senior OP officer and his team were injured near Dusri. For the next 2–3 days, we moved towards the Shakargarh–Zafarwal road and we hit on the second minefield. We had hit on the first minefield where we had launched our brigade attack.

At Dusri, we got the news that the ceasefire was to be effective from 8 p.m. on 17 December. The Pakistani artillery was using a lot of airburst ammunition and thus we got casualties by their airburst ammunition, even though every evening we were halted to be able to dig deeper trenches. We fired nearly 7,500 rounds during this short period.

To recapitulate, the battle was nicknamed Operation Cactus Lily 1971. The night of 3 December 1971 brought the news of the declaration of war with Pakistan. My regiment, 92 Field Regiment, was deployed in Chak Ladwal Sector in J&K in the 72 Infantry Brigade. The battle affiliations were as under:

22 PUNJAB – 921 Field Battery (Fd Bty)
15 GRENADIERS – 922 Fd Bty
3 SIKH LI – 923 Fd Bty

The brigade was launched into action on the night of 5 December. The accurate fire of the regiment assisted in the capture of Village Sukhmal by 22 PUNJAB and Bhopalpur by 15 GRENADIERS. 3 SIKH LI (my battalion), where I was the Operation Officer 75 came under heavy enemy MMG fire during its advance to Khaira. Captain B.P.S. Bains, 65 Operation Officer and 75 Captain M.I. Jaisinghani, with utter disregard to personal safety, brought down accurate fire to silence the enemy during this 13-day war.

We stayed at this location for a year till the delineation talks were on. My boys were Sikhs and we were affiliated with 3 SIKH LI. The 3 SIKH LI CO was our Squadron Commander at NDA, Colonel G.V.E. Masilamani. He used to walk every day where the battalion was deployed. One day, much after the ceasefire, I noticed one jawan of 3

SIKH LI running behind a buffalo, trying to milk it with a utensil for milk. The buffalo was running inside the minefield and suddenly the buffalo blew up since it had stepped on the antitank mine. On seeing this, Colonel Masilamani scolded this jawan very sternly, saying it would be very difficult to account for any casualty after the ceasefire. However, the troops of both 92 Field Regiment and 3 SIKH LI being Sikhs, it was a delight to serve with such fabulous troops. Since we stayed approximately 21 km inside the Pakistani territory for a year, the troops farmed and planted crops in that area.

On all the axes of advance, the Operations Officers never ceded till the end and were instrumental for a safe passage for the infantry's shelling, air attacks and numerous other impromptu measures but were not adequate to halt the intrepid KHALSAS.

Finally, on the eve of 17 December 1971, the order to a ceasefire was received. The triumphant gunners terminated the firing at 6 p.m. The enemy, in defiance of the ceasefire order, continued firing. In retaliation, the unit did not leave any stone unturned and silenced the enemy. As the clock struck 8 p.m., the ceasefire came into force. During the war, a total of 7,407 rounds were fired by the regiment in a short span of 13 days. The regiment also celebrated Shri Guru Gobind Singh's birthday on 24 December 1971, with full fervour, on the enemy soil.

Brigadier M.I. Jaisinghani (Retired) is a veteran with an illustrious career in the Indian Army. He has also served as an Instructor at the School of Artillery for 9 years. In the civil sector, he has had a tenure as the Director and Consultant to some of India's premier security corporations and is a sought-after guest speaker within the industry. When he is not travelling the world to visit his children, he lives with his better half in Mumbai.

From the Diary of a Prisoner of War

Air Commodore K.C. Kuruvilla

The War

On the night of 3 December 1971, Pakistan launched airstrikes on all major western airfields including Halwara. The Indian Air Force (IAF) retaliated quickly by launching counter air strike missions into Pakistan, the first one in the wee hours of 4 December. I was part of one such mission on 6 December 1971. At 6:15 a.m., I took off on a two-aircraft interdiction strike mission, led by my CO, Wing Commander Alan D'Costa. We struck the Dera Baba Nanak Bridge, and on the way back, just two minutes within the Indian airspace, we responded to a forward air controller, who sighted unusual movements southwest of Dera Baba Nanak. To our surprise, we flew over a large convoy of vehicles and other camouflaged equipment and proceeded to interdict those using front guns. Unbeknownst to us, the Pakistani Army's Strategic Reserve Force had been detected moving northeast-wards, and it was here that my fateful sortie ended! After the second attack, I got hit. Within seconds, I had lost control, and my aircraft had caught fire. I ejected at high speed, at about 100 feet, with cross controls, operating just on the left side of the ejection firing handle. Sighting a tree at eye level, after the blackout, I impacted the ground in tall elephant grass, very dazed and winded.[64]

The intense, loud gunfire around me indicated that I was somewhere on the front line. After lying still for about ten minutes, I buried my pistol, hid my parachute and ate some survival pack chocolates, which helped a lot. I crawled towards the sun but encountered a low-wired fence, about six to nine inches above ground level attached with stones inside spaced-out tins. I assumed that this was a minefield, and the rattling of the stones in the tins created a warning. Then I crawled back westwards into the line of fire of a light machine gun (LMG) bunker with a sliding iron door. I also sighted a Pakistani patrol sent out to search for me. I had no option but to wait till dark. Three hours later, as I lay still, very quiet, three soldiers pulled me up from the rear. I was strip-searched, blindfolded, shoes removed, hands tied behind and taken to the same bunker, where my heavy gold chain with a cross around my neck was taken away. Since no officer was present, the agitated soldiers decided to shoot me. Providentially, it was overruled sternly by a Baluch havildar.

Finally, a jeep arrived, and I was driven off through very rough

---

[64] An eyewitness account of the incident as narrated by Colonel Chand (Retired), then the Brigade Major (BM) of 87 Infantry Brigade at BBN: 'I vividly recall the shooting down of young Kuruvilla at Dera Baba Nanak (DBN). I was atop the DBN Railway Station, directing the air support with the Forward Air Controller Flying Officer Aziz, at a rather troublesome Pakistani heavy machine gun nest at JASSAR… The aircraft came down pretty low for the attack. However, the heavy machine guns (HMG) continued to fire at us. The fighter made another low attack, but still the firing continued. Finally, the pilot came down to almost the treetop level! I exclaimed, '*Yeh kaun diler pilot hai? Lekin is baar marega!*' The FAC told me that it was Flight Lieutenant Kuruvilla. 'Oh!' I said. Then the aircraft just sank into the tall *sarkanda*, very close to Kartarpur Sahib Gurduwara. Kuruvilla was taken as a POW. I also told Aziz that he had perhaps been a cadet at the NDA when I was an instructor, because the name was unusual. I had been a Brigade Major of the attacking 86 Infantry Brigade. The HMG was silenced by this young pilot's audacious action. I requested my Brigade Commander to recommend him for a bravery award. I am told that Kuruvilla came back. I hope he received due recognition for his bravery.

terrain. It was a very painful ride with a swollen right ankle and pain in the right side of my neck. We stopped after a long ride, and by nightfall, I was lodged in a cell in the Gujranwala Jail. Around midnight, in the bitter cold, I was collected by men in blue, blindfolded, handcuffed to the back and driven till morning, reaching an Air Force unit. Here, I was put into a cell with one iron grill door, a wooden door and chicks to ensure total isolation. But the air raid sirens and overflying fighter aircraft told me that the war continued.

For the next two days, I was not seen by anyone. Toilet visits were difficult. Guards purposely delayed permission. No medical treatment was provided but lying flat on a hard cemented floor without a pillow helped to heal the injuries to my ankle and neck. On the fourth day, I protested against the solitary confinement, lack of medical treatment and bad food and requested paper and pen to write to the International Committee of the Red Cross (ICRC) since the protocol of the Geneva Convention was not being followed.

Interrogations used to generally commence around midnight, but the enemies could not get proper answers out of me. This resulted in me being left out in the open at 2 a.m. in biting cold, barefoot and forced to stand motionless in attention position. The fear that the guard could shoot and say anything if I moved was daunting! The eventual visit of the ICRC, led by Mr Bablon, accompanied by Pakistani senior officers revealed a lot. My written application was taken by him. Warm clothes, better food and other needs were met and by 23 December, my circumstances had improved.

On 25 December 1971, in a surprise move, I was dressed up and taken to the common room. Here I met the other pilots. We were delighted to learn that the war was over, and India was in a winning position with many Pakistani POWs. The morale was very high—we had, after all, won the war.

Our daily routine comprised being locked up together in the common room after breakfast; we would return to our cells by evening. By February 1972, without any newspapers, radio, or reading material, and without any news of our repatriation, we were beginning to feel very disappointed, and a boredom was setting in. Murmurs of escaping from the POW camp had also started reaching us.

The Escape

On 3 July 1972, the Camp Commandant, Wing Commander Wahiddudin, walked into our common room and pulled out a leading Pakistani newspaper. To our utter disappointment, the headlines read, 'India Returns 5,000 square miles of territory, Pakistani POW to return'. This news upset each one of us as there was no mention of the Indian POW! A part of me wasn't surprised as the Pakistanis never missed an opportunity to take a dig at us. We were very dejected and the resolve to escape strengthened. Later, in a meeting amongst ourselves, it was decided that an escape must be attempted. It was also decided that only the bachelors would participate. Accordingly, three bachelors—Dilip Parulkar, Gary Grewal and Harish Singh volunteered to attempt an escape from the camp. All forms of information gathering for the escape were initiated and money from each of us was set aside. The only escape possible was from the daily gathering at the common room. So, we dug a hole in the wall; it proved to be a perfect way out. On my part, I ensnared Aurangzeb, our lascar, who was very poor. Within days, he smuggled in a bottle of gin and some meat in lieu of some payment. Aurangzeb was now on our side and unsuspectingly, helped us with information on our location, the roads, proximity to the Chaklala Air Force Base, the name of the building behind the common room, bus routes, etc.

The 'hole in the wall' was soon completed and it was decided that the breakout would be done in good weather, over a weekend, executed at midnight. According to the plan, at 11:55 p.m., I would call out to the guard in the common room, demanding a toilet visit. This distraction would require him to walk to the guard room, draw out of the keys to my cell and then walk back to my cell located about 40 yards diagonally opposite to the common room. This process would get the guard to be about ten minutes away from the common room, which would be left unguarded. The trio would, thus, get enough time to get out of the common room and Chati would replace all the bricks to conceal the hole and recheck that the other beds continue to appear as though someone was asleep in them. The breakout had to be executed quietly. Any noise could end up creating a panic and cause the guard to shoot me, as I was out in the open. The escape drill and my distraction routine were attempted four times. Finally, the breakout took place on the night of 13 August 1972.

14 August was Pakistan's Independence Day and our President was rumoured to be visiting Kabul on 15 August 1972. How brilliant it would be if the three officers could make it to Kabul, crossing over to Afghanistan from the Landikotal / Landikhana border, and return to India in the IAF aircraft of the President. The following morning at 10 a.m., all hell broke loose. Three prisoners were missing and the hole in the wall was discovered! All prisoners were immediately locked up in our respective cells by the duty corporal and Chati was put into the adjacent cell next to mine since the common room was now sealed off.

The aftermath of the escape was that the Pakistani Air HQ was informed and a Court of Inquiry was instituted. By noon, all our belongings were taken away. Chati was put into solitary confinement. Later, my involvement in the escape plan was established, deduced from the midnight toilet visits. I was stripped down to my bare skin and made to remain in my cell—everything was taken away. However, by evening, my shirt, pant and toothbrush were returned. Of course, unbeknownst to us, the three escaped officers were apprehended on the morning of 14 August and taken into custody by Squadron

Leader Osman, who was in Peshawar at the PAF Headquarters. On 17 August 1972, we were given back our belongings, bundled into vans with armed escorts and transported to the 'maximum security prison' in Lyallpur.

Return to India

In late November 1972, we were asked to advise on how to set up a helipad. Being the junior-most, I was detailed to assist the Colonel Commandant's team. One morning, we were dressed up and led to a courtyard and seated. Pakistan's Prime Minister, Zulfikar Ali Bhutto, walked in, stood a few feet away, and said, 'Gentlemen, I want you to go home. Tell your country that we want peace with India and please return our prisoners of war.' With these words, he went away!

On 2 December 1972, we were driven to the Wagah Border. At the Wagah Border gate crossing, while near the line for crossing over to the Indian side, stood a motionless Pakistani, in civvies. He was dangling a dark green, moss-covered item in his hand. After I passed him and stepped into the no-man's land near the Indian side, I instinctively turned back and rubbed the chain. It was my mother's heavy gold chain, with a cross at the end. This was unbelievable! I was made to sign for it and ran back to the Indian side. Since the signing process took some time, the others who had crossed over to India were welcomed by the Punjab Chief Minister and left accompanied by his convoy. A car was left behind for me. I caught up and joined the rest. I was safely back in our Punjab.

In 1973, after my wartime films were checked, and International Border (IB) and Air Force (AF) intelligence clearance given, as well as some other processes conducted in March, I was awarded the Vir Chakra.

Air Commodore K.C. Kuruvilla with the Indian Defence Forces Gallipoli Campaign flag

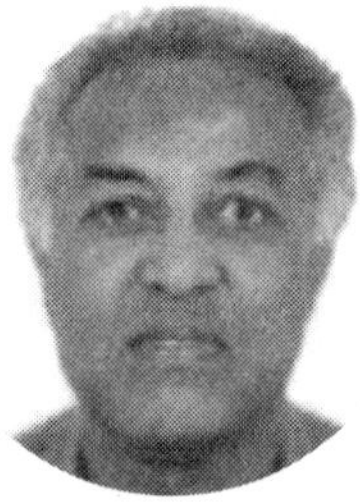

Commissioned as a pilot officer in the Fighter Stream, *Air Commodore K.C. Kuruvilla (Retired)* was placed first in the 97th Permanent Commission and 36th Naval Courses. He received the President's Plaque, the Chief of Air Staff (CAS) Medal for Best All-round Jet Pilot and the Ramchandani Trophy for standing first in academics, which landed him in No. 7 Squadron, Battle Axes at Hindon in 1967. In 1969, he moved on to the latest Sukhoi 7s strike aircraft in 222 Squadron at Ambala. By 1971, with intense training and bountiful operational flying at Halwara, Punjab (western sector) he was ready to be put to the test-space—battle inoculation as a fighter pilot. He was given a befitting tribute by the Air Warrior.[65] Air Commodore K.C. Kuruvilla has the record of surviving three ejections and remained fit to fly the frontline fighter aircraft of the IAF.[66] He went on to re-equip and command No. 9 Squadron, IAF, with the latest Mig-27, ML Swinging Strike Aircraft before he retired from the Indian Air Force.

---

[65] https://www.youtube.com/watch?v=BmDBsSdDG_U&list=PL3rX9_gU5Fjzpkf3Jnl2p_FXXLvuWy5GY

[66] Bird Strike - Indian Air Force Documentary — 1982 https://www.youtube.com/watch?v=ACAG-nesbtE

Some Recollections of 1971

Brigadier Satish Kumar Kukreja

The year 1971 has had a monumental significance for me, due to the major events that took place in my life. At the time, 17 JAT[67] was commanded by Lieutenant Colonel (later Lieutenant General) R. Narasimhan under 36 Infantry Brigade. I was the Adjutant of the battalion. Later, I became a Major and commanded the Bravo Company. I was also newly married and was despatched for the Junior Command (JC) course. Back then, there was no accommodation at the Military Headquarters of War (Mhow). As the war was imminent, I had no choice but to find an unauthorised accommodation in the town. After all, at that time my wife was pregnant, and I had to make sure that she would be okay. I could hardly concentrate on the course, which got truncated by a month, and ultimately, we all left for the unit. So, I found myself boarding the train for Jammu. I precisely remember the date—16 November, my birthday.

Since the unit was already in the deployment area, I took over

[67] 17th Battalion, The Jat Regiment

command of the company at the Jammu bypass. We replaced the D Company, entrusted with the protection of the minefield in front of our battalion defended area opposite to the Pakistan Ditch Cum Bund (DCB).

We were shifted out of 36 Infantry Brigade just before the war as the relations between the Commander of 36 Infantry Brigade, Brigadier D.E. Hayde, (MVC, Dograi fame 1965, Commanding Officer (CO) of 3 JAT[68]) and the General Officer Commanding (GOC) of 26 Infantry Division, Major General Z.C. Bakshi (MVC, VrC, VSM) were not very cordial and it was known to the elements. Major General Bakshi shifted out 17 JAT and one more battalion from 36 Infantry Brigade, which was then left with only one battalion, 9 RAJPUT[69]. My unit was then placed under the command of the 162 Infantry Brigade, which was commanded by Brigadier Ramaswamy (the CO and the new Brigade Commander were both Tamil Brahmins).

Looking back, I recall four key incidents pertaining to the war.

The First Incident

Despite the unit having been shifted out of his command, Brigadier Hayde continued taking interest in our activities and showing up at the unit; he, therefore, visited our location frequently. During one such visit, he was driving along the International Border (IB) in front of my company defended area, in his open jeep with the star plate and flag fluttering, his binoculars slung on the neck, accompanied by his dog. The Pakistanis kept waving at him to go back but he continued driving, till they threatened to shoot him. In a state of panic, he turned inwards, straight in the direction of my company locality, driving through an area where there was supposed to have been a minefield! This compromised the whole game plan of our division, as this area had been earmarked for our tanks to move through to attack Pakistan, if and when required (this was known to some

---

68 3rd Battalion, The Jat Regiment

69 9th Battalion, The Rajput Regiment

formation commanders alone). There was complete chaos as the CO and all of us realised that we were now protecting a non-existent minefield. Overnight, the Divisional Engineer Regiment and others laid mines post-haste. A part of our plan had been compromised due to the foolhardiness of a decorated soldier.

The Second Incident

Second Lieutenant U.P. Singh, one of my platoon commanders, was detailed to go to the enemy DCB to check if mines had been laid, and if there was water in the ditch. The area from the border to the enemy DCB was a cultivable barren field with no bushes or mounds to hide his movement. U.P. Singh set off with his boys for the task. One strand of wire with markings of minefields had been seen by him. He kept moving, looking for signs of fresh digging or mine-laying. In the last 300 yards, he crawled to avoid detection. When he was barely ten yards away from the ditch-cum-bund, he stopped to observe and listen for sounds of enemy activity. He then threw a stone to check if there was any water in the ditch. In the dead of the night, the sound of the stone was magnified, and he thought that he would get detected. Thus, he waited for the enemy to fire bullets or para flare. The mission was still incomplete since neither the sound of stone hitting water or the ground had been heard. He gathered courage and threw another stone. This time there was a clear 'thud' sound, indicating there was no water in the ditch. Relieved, he turned around to get back and saw the moon about to rise on the horizon. Forgetting that the area was supposed to be mined, he just ran across up to the minefield marking wire and made it back to our location without any reaction from the Pakistanis. It must have been such a relief for him to be back home in one piece, especially after seeing the moon rising and then having run across the supposed minefield!

Two days later, he was tasked by the battalion headquarters to again go up to the Pakistani ditch-cum-bund and throw a grenade on the enemy. He was most horrified at the stupidity of being so tasked. When he told me what he had been now tasked for, I realised the futility of it and the danger he would be put to, without any worthwhile gains. I, therefore, gave him a solution and said, 'Take a grenade rifle and fire at the ditch-cum-bund from it'. That is exactly what he did. Even today he wonders what his fate would have been if he had gone up to the enemy ditch-cum-bund to lob a hand grenade at them.

The Third Incident

When the main battle was being fought in the eastern theatre, we were to undertake only holding action(s) on our divisional front. Consequently, commanders in our sector were instructed to engage the Pakistanis in different ways. My company, with four platoons and a troop of newly arrived Missile d'Infanterie Leger Antichar (MILANs) in location during the day, found a gap in the Pakistani DCB, which they had supposedly kept there to assault through, in case required. We had the support of a squadron of Central India Horse (CIH). In one such plan, the CIH was tasked to destroy the bunkers on the Pakistani DCB. The CIH troop commanders came to recce and select their pinpoint target(s). The firing was to be carried out around the last light from my company location. I was to provide illumination for the tanks to engage the bunkers for which I had detailed my platoon nearest to the DCB.

At the given time, the tanks arrived and were ready to shoot, but the required illumination was not forthcoming. I tried to raise this with my platoon commander on the radio but was unsuccessful. Without any thought for safety, my signal operator and I ran towards the platoon headquarters and found the Junior Commissioned Officer (JCO) hiding in his bunker. I dragged him out. He was shivering as he seemed to be scared. No words came out of his mouth. I threatened to shoot him as he was showing cowardice in the battle. He fell on his knees. Anyway, I had something more important to do at that time and told him that I would deal with him later. The platoon provided the illumination for the tanks to start firing, which they did. I returned to my company HQ and the tanks started withdrawing to their location, but lo and behold, barrages of artillery shells started pouring on my company especially in the area from where the tanks had been firing. For the next 20–25 minutes, there was no respite from the intense firing. Later, as the shelling reduced, I started moving to the platoons to check if there were any causalities. Fortunately, there were no major ones. As I was returning to my bunker, a shell fell a few metres from me! My sahayak got a splinter. I was lucky to escape. God was watching.

The Fourth Incident

In this phase of engaging the enemy, all battalions were ordered to select a target for raiding something every night. Since our battalion was facing the Pakistani DCB, there were hardly any targets for planning raids every night, instead, we were laying ambushes. This was, however, not acceptable to our commanders. On 8 December 1971, Captain I.S. Janghu led a raid on Pakistani Putwal post, wherein we lost a soldier, Sepoy Ratan Ram.

Pakistan had one post called Ghug, NW 8130, which was on our side of their DCB. I cannot say as to why the Ghug post was important to Pakistan and why the alignment of their DCB did not include this post (it wasn't our prerogative to analyse reasons at that stage of service). To avoid clashes between their own troops, the battalions used to book the Ghug post for the raid with the Divisional Headquarters. On 11 December 1971, Captain J.K. Sharma raided the post with a platoon and captured a two-inch mortar, three Sten gun magazines and some documents. This was the first raid at Ghug.

Though it was fine initially, the factor of surprise was eventually lost; later, it only became an ambush site for raiding troops.

On 13 December 1971, our battalion again launched a raid at Ghug with two officers and two platoons. In the meantime, unknown to us, Pakistan had laid mines and covered them adequately by fire. Pakistanis started firing on spotting our boys. In the melee, one JCO stepped on a mine; when Captain J.K. Sharma went to help him, his leg was blown.

Major D.P.S. Randhawa, the second officer, was hit with a two-inch mortar bomb (fortunately it did not explode) that broke his jaw and teeth. Two JCOs and four other ranks also got seriously injured. One injured OR was captured by the enemy. One JCO and five ORs were missing after this action; they hid in a *sarkanda* in the Pakistani territory for two nights, before they could extricate themselves. This happened as the JCO was professionally capable—he had earlier served as the intelligence JCO of the battalion. While the intention of keeping the enemy engaged was fine, such actions created a negative impact as nothing tangible was being achieved. However, my CO was not satisfied and wanted to take revenge. The next day, the CO took me to a vantage point and asked me to plan and raid Ghug again the following night to take revenge for our reverses. The conversation between us was as follows:

CO: 'Satish, you know about the results of the raid conducted by Randhawa and J.K., we were found wanting'.

Me: 'Yes, Sir, that was unfortunate'.

CO: 'Now, you have to redeem the prestige of the battalion and raid Ghug.'

Me: 'Yes, Sir, but don't you think we could go to some other place and do some other action to achieve the aim'?

CO: 'The GOC has personally asked me and desired that we raid Ghug. You are an ex-NDA, and a smart officer, that is why I have put you at the most sensitive defended locality in the battalion. I have tremendous faith in your ability'.

Me: 'Right, Sir. If there is no choice, so be it. We will definitely achieve our aim and prove that to the GOC'.

CO: 'That is what I expected from you. We are pinning our hopes on you.'

I did all the planning in that state of mind and readied my troops. The ceasefire came in the way and the plan was dropped! Thanks to the elements.

After the War

As the war got over, we were moved out of wartime deployment to the area of octroi post on the RS Pura–Sialkot Road. There were two posts, one Indian and the other Pakistani, across the IB. These posts were used for the UN observers to cross over to either side under the supervision of officers from both sides. During the war, one of our battalions had captured their octroi post and an area of about one kilometre, after which a new temporary post was established in that area. On one occasion, a Pakistani Major, who had come to escort the UN team, started conversing with me. The dialogue went as follows:

Pakistani Major: 'You all must be feeling very happy'.

Me: 'You all must be feeling very sad about the dismemberment of Pakistan'.

Pakistani Major: 'On the other hand, we are relieved and now the snakes (the Bengali officers in their army) will bite you'.

Me: 'How can you say that?'.

Pakistani Major: 'You will find that out very soon yourself'.

In time, the results became obvious.

Brigadier Satish Kumar Kukreja (Retired) was commissioned into 17 JAT on its raising. He commanded 15 JAT, 10 Sector/Deputy Inspector General B Range (Assam Rifles) in Manipur at the height of the insurgency and held the command of the JAT Regimental Centre as well. He has served in counterinsurgency (CI) areas both in the East and J&K. He was with the JPS (Army) in the erstwhile Cabinet Secretariat (Military Wing). He retired in November 2000 as the Deputy Director General (DDG) of Canteen Services.

A Flashback

Lieutenant General Mohinder Puri

I was posted as General Staff Officer 3 (GSO3) (Operations) in the 25 Infantry Division in July 1971 and my battle account is, therefore, from the perspective of a young staff officer of an operational formation. Following the March 1971 genocide by the Pakistan Army in East Pakistan, which we are all too familiar with, the war clouds were gradually building up in the subcontinent. Our General Officer Commanding (GOC) was Major General Kundan Singh, a diehard infantry officer who kept the formation on a tight leash. Since I was the fresh inductee into the Operations Branch, I had to accompany the GOC on his visits to the subordinate headquarters and units deployed on the ceasefire line (CFL), as it was referred to in those days. There were many posts which were neither connected by choppers nor by any semblance of a road. Visiting these posts was an exhausting experience as at times one had to walk for four–five hours to reach one's destination. While at the road head the GOC and his entourage would comfortably seat themselves on mules, lesser mortals like myself had to be contented by walking behind the convoy of mules, puffing and panting to keep up with the column. With experience, I learnt that the best way to keep up with the pace of the convoy was to hold the tail of the mule, which effortlessly kept you moving with the column.

25 Infantry Division was a large-sized division deployed south of the Pir Panjal ranges, with each brigade having five–six battalions. The area was politically sensitive with the District Headquarters located at the border towns of Poonch, Naushera and Rajouri. The close proximity of these towns to the CFL made them attractive objectives for Pakistan, more so since their capture was denied to them in the first J&K War in 1947–48 and later in 1965. Poonch scored higher in the list of priorities for capture, mainly due to its closer proximity to the CFL, its largely Muslim population with ethnic affiliations with the people across the CFL and its fertile agricultural land. Also, the alignment of the CFL gave Pakistan the advantage of occupying posts on a higher ground, with the ability to observe the town and its military airfield. Both the armies were deployed, more or less, in an eyeball-to-eyeball confrontation with a second tier in the depths in the lesser dominating heights. Over the years, the defences on both sides had considerably improved with proper defence works and a well-coordinated obstacle plan. It was quite apparent to us that Poonch was a lucrative objective as its capture would link up with the Haji Pir Pass and give options to the enemy across the Pir Panjal into the valley.

Co-located with the Division Headquarters was the United Nations Military Observer Group in India and Pakistan (UNMOGIP)—a team of officers and men who were tasked to respond to complaints by the respective hosts against the opposing side. They were free to move around with prior intimation to the Headquarters. A similar team, albeit on a reduced scale, was located with the Brigade Headquarters at Poonch and Naushera. Since the

UN team was not empowered to resolve routine issues like ceasefire violations (CFVs) or the transgression of the CFL, their presence was more of an irritant. Nevertheless, they were there, and we continued to report to them the increase in CFVs from July onwards, without any substantial reduction in the firing.

It was more or less clear that war was imminent, and the probability kept increasing with the increase in the number of refugees from East Pakistan. It was also obvious that while the concentration of the war effort would be in the east, the ferocity of the operations would be matching in the west, if not more. The period from July onwards was spent on planning for the war, which was likely to be fought in the winters when the passes would close and reduce the collusive support of China. 25 Infantry Division was a defensive formation with very limited offensive capability. In the later half of 1971, the intelligence reports indicated that a larger than usual concentration of forces portended an offensive by Pakistan against Poonch. The intelligence inputs led the General Officer Commanding (GOC) to ask for additional troops for the defence of Poonch, a request which was denied by 15 Corps because any reinforcement of troops into this sector would reduce options of the corps in the rest of the corps zone. However, since the GOC was insistent to the extent of telling the Corps Commander that he would not be responsible for the loss of Poonch, 33 Infantry Brigade, ex 39 Mountain Division was inducted into the Division Sector on 25 November.

The war clouds were looming in November and they only got darker when on 3 December 1971, Pakistan launched a pre-emptive airstrike on our airfields which led to the declaration of war. While the border towns in 25 Infantry Division were of strategic importance in the hill sector, the towns of Chhamb and Ahknoor in the 10 Infantry Division sector were of equal importance in the plains of 15 Corps, as their capture opened the option to the enemy to cut-off the hill sector and threaten or attempt to capture Jammu.

From the Indian point of view, the Chhamb Sector was also of significant importance as it was a launchpad for an offensive into Pakistan's soft underbelly by cutting off the main lines of communication on the Grand Trunk Road. However, Pakistan took the initiative, and after a couple of days of bitter fighting, we managed to stabilise the front, although we lost Chhamb in the process.

On the intervening night of 3–4 December 1971, 25 Infantry Division was subjected to heavy artillery fire throughout the sector, with the concentration of ground operations on the Banwat heights held by 6 SIKH and some diversionary actions in the Balnoi sector. Lieutenant Colonel Rattan, the Commanding Officer of 6 SIKH, who later became Major General, was a fearless leader who had well appreciated the importance of his battalion's deployment in the plan for the defence of Poonch. The enemy attack commenced with a heavy concentration of artillery fire followed by a determined attack of a brigade against the Forward Defence Lines (FDLs) of the battalion. Bold leadership exhibited by the Brigade Commander, Brigadier A.V. Natu, who later became Major General, and Colonel Rattan stalled Pakistan's attack and forestalled their third attempt in capturing Poonch. By 6 December, Pakistan had shot its bolt in this sector. The Brigade Commander and the Commanding Officer (CO) were awarded the Maha Vir Chakra (MVC). The award of the Brigade Commander was announced on the radio the minute Field Marshal Manekshaw's helicopter landed at the Poonch airfield while he was on his visit to the station soon after the ceasefire to congratulate the troops for their success. It had, indeed, been good and meticulous staff work.

While the situation had stabilised in the Poonch Sector, 21 PUNJAB launched an attack on a feature called Nangi Tekri in the Krishna Ghati sector, which was dominating the Poonch river in Pakistan occupied Kashmir (POK). The attack was successfully executed by the battalion on 10 December, and they had succeeded in capturing their objective by 11 December. Colonel Sharma, the CO, led the operation from the front and was also awarded the MVC. With this success, the GOC planned a bold raid on the night of 13 December by a team of 9 Para Commando on the enemy's gun-position at Mandhol, a village approximately 19 km southwest of Poonch. This daring and successful offensive operation by the special forces later became a case study in schools of instruction. The commandos destroyed the enemy battery and returned with two dead soldiers and a couple of casualties. A commendable action indeed!

As part of improving our defence posture, limited actions were planned across the CFL. After the capture of Nangi Tekri, 14 GRENADIERS were tasked to capture a feature called Daruchian, which was dominating the Balnoi neck of the Kotli-Balnoi Road between the Poonch river and the CFL. The attack was launched on the intervening night of 13–14 December from three directions, leaving negligible reserves for various contingencies on each of the prongs. After stiff resistance from the enemy, the battalion's attack fizzled out with very heavy casualties, particularly amongst the officers.

The ceasefire was declared to be effective from 17 December. While a number of lessons were learnt, it suffices to say that intelligence continues to remain a weak spot, though our acquisition capabilities have vastly improved since 1971 and 1999.

Lieutenant General Mohinder Puri (Retired) was commissioned into 5/3 Gorkha Rifles (GR) in June 1966. An alumnus of the National Defence Academy, he has served in command and staff appointments in the eastern, northern and western borders including counterinsurgency environments in Mizoram and North Kashmir. He commanded the 8 Mountain Division, which spearheaded the counteroffensive in the Kargil War. He has been a military-attache in Vietnam and superannuated as the Deputy Chief of the Army Staff.

The Capture of Southern Mamdot Bulge

Colonel K.K. Nanda

Prelude to the Capture of Mamdot Bulge, Ferozepur Sector Move and Deployment of 13 PUNJAB[70] (Jind)

Forming part of the 35 Infantry Brigade Ex-14 Infantry Division, my battalion, 13 PUNJAB (Jind), moved from Meerut and reached Ferozepur in early November 1971. We were placed under the 7 Infantry Division for operations and were put alongside Hussainiwala Defences on the twin canal emanating for the Hussainiwala Head Works running in the southwest direction, generally parallel to the International Border.

15 PUNJAB[71] (1st Patiala), one of our sister battalions under the command of Lieutenant Colonel Shastri, was already deployed at Hussainiwala Head Works as part of 7 Infantry Division, with two companies deployed across the Satluj river, two companies on the home side of the river and the Battalion HQ at the Canal House,

---

70 13th Battalion, The Punjab Regiment

71 15th Battalion, The Punjab Regiment

south of the Hussainiwala Bridge. An attack on Hussainiwala by Pakistan on 3 December 1971 at around 5.50 p.m. began with heavy enemy shelling on the Hussainiwala Defences, predominantly on the western side of the bridge. The war had formally begun on the Western Front. My battalion, 13 PUNJAB (Jind), was deployed at the close-by defences, from where we could see the ferocity of the enemy shelling, with the sky full of streaking artillery shells, para light flares and the ground being ferociously pounded by the artillery and both tank and medium machine gun (MMG) fire. The noise was deafening and the scene, when watched from 150 yards, was like a war movie. The battle went on all night and the complete attack was concentrated on 15 PUNJAB (1st Patiala) and the BSF posts under them.

Early next morning the Pakistan Air Force was over us and one of the aircrafts flew very low over our battalion's twin-canal defences. I immediately jumped into a close-by bunker, where a light machine gun (LMG) was placed in an anti-aircraft role and took a shot at the low flying Pakistani aircraft. To my shock, the LMG did not fire. I cursed my luck. We later realised that the LMG mechanism had been jammed. This happens when one does not move the firing mechanism regularly (*'Chal wale purze jam ho gaye'*). What a big lesson we learnt from that episode; it was a great regret for me.

Though 15 PUNJAB (1st Patiala) fought gallantly, the area of Hussainiwala in the Ferozepur Sector on the western side of the Sutlej fell under the control of Pakistan by 5 December 1971. This was after they had launched a brigade attack supported by the regiment of tanks and a large number of artillery guns on the night of 3–4 December 1971, followed by an air attack on 4 December 1971.

Recce Patrol into Pakistan Led by Captain K.K. Nanda

Introduction

To release pressure on the Hussainiwala area, a complete capture of which would have threatened Ferozepur, the 35 Infantry Brigade was tasked to capture the Mamdot Bulge of Pakistan located southwest of Hussainiwala. The Brigade comprised 13 PUNJAB (Jind), 3 GUARD and 15 DOGRA[72]. Our battalion, 13 PUNJAB (Jind), was entrusted to capture the southern portion of the Mamdot Bulge including the Pakistani posts of Pira Kana, Jalloke Hittar and Dona Betu, besides clearing the area along the home banks of the Satluj river. My company was tasked to capture the two posts of Pira Kana and Jalloke Hittar. The senior commanders of our battalion were moved to the BSF border post of Raja Matham around 8–9 December 1971 to prepare for the impending attack.

I was called by our CO, Lieutenant Colonel Kul Bhushan, who was very fond of me, for a briefing on 9 December 1971 while we were both at the border post of Raja Matham. He informed me that I was being sent for a recce patrol into Pakistan to bring information about enemy posts of Pira Kana and Jalloke Hittar, both of which had been proposed to be captured by us subsequently. I was just about getting excited when he added, 'Nanda, you must be wondering why I have selected you and not Suman Sharma, who is younger and junior to you. Well, he is the only son of his parents, and you are three brothers.' I had just about frowned at this remark when he added, 'But let me tell you that if you come back alive and successfully, which I am confident you will, then this experience will be the most exciting and satisfying moment in your career.' He was right.

---

[72] 15th Battalion, The Dogra Regiment

Planning

The recce patrol involved nearly two days of detailed planning by me. I worked out the route-in/route-out of the proposed patrol into Pakistan. I took grid reading from the map, converted it to a magnetic reading for each 'bound' selected by me and memorised the compass bearings. I particularly selected one peacock-shaped tree (*mor pankhi drakht*) as one of my 'bounds' as it was visible from our border post. For calculating the distance to be covered, I kept a couple of pebbles in my para-jacket's pocket and kept putting one in the opposite pocket for every 125 steps taken (depicting 100 yards). In the present day of GPS, all this appears to be such a primitive way to move, but this is a story from 50 years ago. We also studied and worked out the timing of the waxing and waning of the moon so that we could identify the appropriate times when we could see the enemy post more clearly.

I chose three men for the patrol, people I could trust—they had worked under me in various commando competitions earlier. Havildar Kuldeep Singh was a services level X-country stalwart while Bir Singh and Dhan Singh were both ace firers and sharpshooters. They carried specialised sniper rifles and were nominated as each other's *sahayaks* while Kuldip and I carried Sten guns.

It was decided not to leave our buddies under any circumstances and to carry each other back if injured or dead. If we were, we would leave together any which way! We also decided not to become prisoners and planned to retaliate and fire back, full blast, with our weapons and grenades if we got killed or overpowered.

The fear of being taken in as prisoners of war (POWs) by Pakistan sounded more dreadful than getting killed. I briefed all my patrol buddies about the plan, including the route-out objective, the bounds en route task of locating and observing the enemy posts to assess its layout and strength, action on being detected or a possible capture, route in back to our post and others. The peacock-shaped tree was particularly shown to all, as one of the important bounds.

Conduct

We left at 11.30 p.m. on the intervening night of 11–12 December 1971. We were fortunate to reach the approximate area of our destination between the two enemy posts of Pira Kana and Jalloke Hittar, as it was pitch dark and biting cold during our onward movement. We had loaded our weapons in almost a firing position. I was wearing my para-jacket and our woollen trousers were brownish, akin to what Pakistanis wear. I kept four hand grenades in my pocket and kept feeling their release firing pins, just in case I had to pull it out to throw it at the enemy.

We finally sat down together in a huddle, to give the impression of a bush (there were many close to the Satluj river). We sat so close that we could hear each other's heartbeats. The Pakistanis got suspicious and started shouting abuses. When they got no response from us they shouted, '*Koi giddar ya suhar lag rahe hai*' (seems these are foxes or pigs). After a little while, they again got suspicious and fired very light para flares to illuminate the area but could not locate us and remained confused. Fortunately, these para light flares helped us in seeing the post more clearly. We waited for the moon to come up and shine its best so that we could see the layouts of the enemy posts more clearly. Each second was an experience, every minute passing by seemed like an hour.

Then we heard some footsteps towards us; our hearts sank. One of the Pakistani signal line repairs team just went past us by 10 yards! That's the closest we got to them physically. I almost pulled out the pin of the hand grenade in my pocket to hurl at them in case they detected us, but by the strange hand of God, they just went ahead without noticing us, and we heaved a sigh of relief. Surprisingly, my other three buddies were unruffled. They were all battle-seasoned, having taken part in the attack on Mile 13 in the Battle of Dograi in the 1965 war (our unit had put in the first phase of the attack on Dograi on the night of 21–22 September 1965, followed by 3 JAT[73] capturing Dograi in Phase II of the attack). After a while, we heard a jeep passing, about 50 yards away, from us and it went towards Jalloke Hittar. We deduced that the officer in charge could have been returning from his Battalion HQ.

We were to return at 5.30 a.m., keeping the moon phase and moonlight in mind. At around 5 a.m., we heard some troops coming towards us. We had more or less seen what we had to. Though a part of me was panicking within, I put my training to practice and organised our move back, bound-wise. We moved back in quick steps towards the earmarked bound. All of us got separated by a few yards from each other but fortunately got together after moving individually for 150 yards. We could still hear the movement of the Pakistanis. Perhaps they were trying to search for us. I then told our boys to hit for the peacock-shaped tree as our next bound. We reached there after walking for 20 minutes. To our horror, this was not the tree we had selected; we had moved back in the opposite direction, deeper into Pakistan, and not towards our border post!

My heart throbbed from the panic. I composed myself and decided to change directions westwards, towards the Satluj river, so that we could move along its banks towards the Indian side. We, fortunately, hit the riverbank. I took out the compass to identify the directions and began moving along the river.

At about first light, we saw a post to our left, around 150 yards away. Everyone was wearing a khaki-coloured dress (the dress worn by Pakistanis). We froze in our place; it seemed we had hit a Pakistani post. We kept moving along the river hoping for the hand of God, as running back would invite attention. Somehow the Pakistanis were not firing at us; in fact, they did not seem to notice us. When we got

---

[73] 3rd Battalion, The Jat Regiment

a little closer, we saw some guys waving at us. It was actually our own BSF post (who also wore the khaki-coloured dress)! What a sigh of relief it was that we had reached back safely. Our Commanding Officer and all the others awaiting us gave mighty hugs. It was a night of accomplishment, joy and contentment.

Since our battalion, 13 PUNJAB (Jind), had been given the task of capturing the southern portion of the Mamdot Bulge, two more recce patrols besides mine, had been conducted. One had been by Major R.S. Malia in the area of Dona Betu and the other by Second Lieutenant Andotra along the Satluj river.

As part of the brigade plan for the capture of the Mamdot Bulge, based on the information obtained by the three recce patrols, our CO, Lieutenant Colonel Kul Bhushan brainstormed with our unit officers. The final attack plan was based on the collective wisdom of the officers going in for the attack. The attack was to be carried out on the night of 15–16 December 1971.

In Phase I, under Major R.S. Malia, Charlie Company was to capture Dona Betu. Likewise, Alpha Company was to first capture Pira Kana (an outpost) and subsequently Jalloke Hittar from the rear. This was to be done under the command of Major K.S. Sidhu with me as the Company's Second in Command. The Delta Company under Major H.C. Sharma was held as a reserve in Phase I; in Phase II they were to clear the area along the eastern bank of the Satluj river (see sketch). The battalion assembled close to the BSF post of Raja Matham. In the evening, a pep talk by our CO had everybody charged up and ready to go. One havildar wanted to report sick; the CO laughingly told him, '*Shadi wale din dulha bimar nahi ho sakta, sab attack mein chalengey!*' (The bridegroom cannot fall sick on his wedding; we will all go for the attack.) He accompanied the front troops.

Each one of us felt anxious moments before the take-off. I placed myself in the forward-most section with only two scouts in front of me, which is normally the position of a section commander (of havildar's rank). I did this as I knew the route, and I felt that I should be right at the front. I wore a pagri as my company had Sikh troops. The adage that 'the lives of men under you depend on you and your leadership during the war, especially in an attack operation', as taught to us and highlighted by our CO, stayed with me. I was a young officer, single, all of 25 years, bubbling with excitement. Having battle-tested myself in the recce patrol taken in Pakistan four days earlier, I enjoyed the full confidence of our men and that added to my degree of responsibility. Still, there was a thought lurking in my mind: if I were to die in the attack, it would be somewhat sad as I was yet to enjoy the bliss of marriage. Perhaps that would have been my greatest regret of dying, besides the feeling of leaving my parents and siblings. My Company Commander, Major Sidhu, with whom I had a special bond (we were more like buddies) was recently married. He used to kiss his wife's photo and keep it in his pocket. He was a veteran of the 1965 War. He had taken part in the attack on Dograi on the night of 21–22 September 1965 as a 2 Lieutenant, where he was wounded in the battle and Captain Kuljit of our unit, who was just by his side, was killed. He told me, 'Nanda, I am not scared for myself, but I am somewhat worried about my wife, should something happen to me.' We had both pledged to bring each other back in case either one became a casualty and take care of each other's family in case either of us died. In the civil world, it is generally believed that all soldiers are brave and fearless, but very few realise that they, too, have their insecurities, especially about their family and the ones dependent on them.

Due to some last-minute changes in the resource allocation of the Artillery Fire Units to the brigade, there was a delay in our move forward from the assembly area. While waiting, I squatted and decided to have a cigarette; I asked two jawans to cover me with their raincoats (*pani pallas*), so that the enemy may not spot the glow of the cigarette. Suddenly, our CO, with his skeleton protection and the 'O' Group, walked up from behind. Looking at the smokescreen rising out of the *pani pallas*, he probed further and said, '*Oye Nandiya, sharam kar, pagri paa ke cigarette peena!*' (You, Nanda, have some shame! Smoking a cigarette with the turban on). I replied, 'Sir, who knows this could be my last cigarette, please let me enjoy the last puff.' This was war; my request was accepted with a smile.

After the preparatory bombardment of the objectives, we started our move from the assembly area. We first encountered the barbed wire, cut across it and moved forward, with me in the lead. However, the dark cloudy night and the fog reduced the visibility to a few feet; I was intermittently looking at the compass bearing and guiding the two scouts in front of me. Midway, Charlie Company under Major Malia (which was following our company) peeled off to their objective Dona Betu, which was closer to the assembly area than our company objective. We were anxious about wanting to be on the right route and had to requisition the artillery para flares to see the area more clearly. There was pressure from the brigade to ask for the final bombardment of the target area, but the CO held his nerve to hold the fire till he was sure of our own position, lest the artillery shells fell on us. The first platoon of Alpha Company was to capture Pira Kana, an outpost, and the other two platoons were to capture Jalloke Hittar with an attack from the rear. The final attack was planned at first light.

When we reached Pira Kana, we could hear people running helter-skelter, and when we reached the objective, we found the enemy had fled. We quickly consolidated ourselves and then moved to the rear of Jalloke Hittar. While we were forming up and bringing fire on them, the enemy troops were heard running in the northerly direction. By the time we reached the enemy post, they all ran away, leaving behind arms and ammunition. We chased them with some of our boys, using typical 'Punjabi adjectives'.

Meanwhile, the leading platoon of Charlie Company was led by Subedar Bachittar Singh (a war veteran of the 1947–48 and 1965 wars) was moving in the area east of the Satluj river. There were a lot of wild bushes (*sarkanda*) and small dunes in the area. Due to poor visibility and the *sarkanda*, the leading platoon got separated from the rest of the company, while moving forward. Unknowingly and unmindful, they kept moving. At one point in the foggy night, this leading platoon inadvertently entered the outer periphery of their objective—Dona Betu. To their disbelief and horror, they did not find any enemy troops there. Sensing the impending attacks, the Pakistanis had vacated it in the earlier part of the night.

At this stage, an interesting drama unfolded. It was now closer to first light, so Subedar Bachittar started shouting to the rest of the Company—'*Aa jayo! Aa jayo! Ethe koi nahi hai*' (Come on, come on, there is nobody here). Nevertheless, Major Malia, the Company Commander was unmoved and insisted on verifying. He told his company's Second in Command, '*Kahin Bachittar aur party enemy ke kabje mein to nahi hai*' (Check whether Bachitter is in the custody of the enemy and if he is being threatened to shout at gunpoint). He then questioned Subedar Bachittar Singh on the radio set in a typical Punjabi language code to verify. Subedar Bachittar swore by God and said '*Sirji, sanu baabey di souh*'. As the daylight broke, they saw a minefield laid on the outer periphery of the post and wondered how the leading troops had reached the enemy location without a casualty; it was indeed a miracle.

Eventually, the rest of the company reached the enemy post after locating a gap in the minefield. The success signal, red over red, was fired by Alpha Company at about 6.45 a.m., and Charlie Company fired their success signal at 6.55 a.m. The CO caught up with us at the captured post soon after. We were all given a big *shabash* and 'well done' by him. 'D' Company cleared the area on the southern bank of the Satluj river by the morning without much resistance. One of our men lost his leg by stepping on an anti-personnel mine—during the day we realised that the enemy had strewn anti-personnel mines, randomly all over the route. It was nothing short of a miracle that we had only one mine-casualty. Our CO, who always carried a small transistor in his pack switched it on; he then told us that a ceasefire had been declared! We celebrated the victory, with all of us yelling the battle cry—*'Jo Bole So Nihal Sat Sri Akal, Jawala Mai Ki Jai'*.

However, the very next morning, Pakistan violated the ceasefire and launched an attack to reoccupy the post of Jalloke Hittar. We succeeded in foiling their plan and captured 26 POWs with their weapons! Thereafter, there was another encounter with the Pakistanis in the afternoon, wherein a heavy exchange of fire took place. I was almost blown off, when a tank shell missed my head by a hair's breadth and directly hit the recoilless (RCL) gun, which was deployed behind me.

The Aftermath of the Capture of Mamdot

The Capture of POWs – 17 December 1971

After the surrender by the Pakistan soldiers in Dhaka and other places in East Pakistan, on 16 December 1971, a ceasefire was declared. We were rejoicing the victory the next day, when we got a message, that the CO would hold a review meeting at the Battalion HQ at 11:30 a.m. However, at 8:45 a.m., I was ordered to move immediately with a platoon to marry up with Major H.C. Sharma, the D Company Commander, who had observed a Pakistani platoon advancing towards our post at Jalloke Hittar while he was moving in a jeep to the Battalion HQ. I rushed to him along with a platoon of A Company, mustered hurriedly, with a 1-Ton vehicle. Meanwhile, Major H.C. Sharma showed great presence of mind and challenged the advancing enemy platoon. He shouted that they were surrounded by two of our companies, that they should surrender immediately, failing which they would be killed. In actual fact, when he warned them, we had been able to muster only a handful of troops and were numerically inferior!

Somehow, the ruse worked, and one could see them putting down their weapons and raising their hands. However, one soldier with an LMG, disobeying his superiors, placed his LMG in the firing position. As he was preparing to fire, a JCO of theirs pulled out his magazine to abort his attempt, fearing a retaliatory attack by us (though we did not have enough troops to execute a successful attack at that point in time). Soon thereafter, the rest of 'D' Company and I along with my platoon fetched up. We quickly got hold of the POWs and put their weapons in a vehicle (Major Sharma, who managed to snatch the initiative and bluff the Pakistanis to surrender, was an experienced soldier who had led a company during the successful attack at Dograi, in the 1965 war). While the prisoners were being escorted to our Battalion HQ, one of their havildars walked up to me and complained, '*Sahib, aap ka havildar hamara mazaak urhaa raha hai.*' (Sahib, one of your havildars is making fun of us.) I smiled and told him, '*Toh kya wo aap ko jhappi mare?*' (Do you expect him to hug you instead?). Meanwhile, our CO also reached the spot. He ordered that nobody would harm them and got some biscuits distributed to them. Our CO was very humane and fair-minded, besides being brave. We later learnt that the 26 POWs captured by my unit, were the maximum captured by a unit in Western Command!

Confronting the Pakistanis, I was now ordered to remain with 'D' Company along with my platoon and to scan the balance area of the Bulge, to clear it of the enemy, if any. Major Sharma and I started walking in the northerly direction along with a section and ordered the balance of the troops to scan the area platoon-wise. Suddenly, we saw some enemy troops ahead and we halted. We informed our CO and started preparing for a possible attack.

We then saw two Pakistani soldiers waving a white cloth, possibly a handkerchief. We halted our troops, and we, too, waved a white handkerchief; both of us then moved towards them followed by one section of ours. On reaching them, we found that one of them was a 2 lieutenant and the other was a JCO, both from the Baluch Regiment. We then enquired as to why they were there as the area had already been captured by us and was under our control. The officer replied, 'Sir, this is our area.' The JCO further insisted that they had been there for long and showed us their platoon bunkers, which were occupied by their troops. He said, *'Sahib, yeh dekho hamari minefield bhi lagi hui hai.'* (Sahib here is our minefield) We then told them that our brigade had already captured the whole of the Mamdot Bulge including the area occupied by them and that they should immediately vacate it. The officer was nervous, but the JCO insisted that it was their area. We then told them, 'We already had orders to run over you and that our battalion has already formed up behind with supporting weapons.' It is only because of the white flag shown by you that we are giving you a chance to withdraw to the other side of the Satluj river. We also asked our RCL detachments behind to move up and down to make noises to portray vehicular movement in order to scare the enemy. I pretended to take a call on the radio set from the CO and told Major Sharma with a wink, 'Sir, the CO is asking us to commence the attack.' This unnerved them. The officer then asked us to give him 15 minutes as he wanted to speak to his Company Commander. We asked him where his Company Commander was and learnt that he was comfortably across the Satluj river, on their home side. After a while, they agreed to go back across the river. They had a ferry system working with a few boats.

We let them move out from their bunkers with their weapons and let them go unharmed, in conformity with the white flags shown initially. I asked their JCO to show me the exact location of the temporary minefield laid by them, which he did reluctantly.

Unprovoked Firing by the Pakistani Troops

Major Sharma ordered one of his platoons and the company HQs to move forward and occupy defences vacated by the Pakistanis. As directed by him, I took my platoon forward and deployed them near the bank of Satluj, facing the ferry site. The platoon was more or less in the open, watching the Pakistanis crossing over in two boats, each taking three to four persons at a time. I was standing on the bank, with my hand on the hip, watching the scene like a victorious movie hero. As soon as the boats were about to reach the far bank with the last lot of Pakistanis, they started firing at us; my platoon and I were caught in the open.

I had one of my LMG detachments, headed by Naik Issar Singh, deployed next to me. I asked him to retaliate, and he immediately fired at the boat which had almost reached the other side. We could see the occupants scrambling out and felt that perhaps one or two of them were injured. A full-fledged exchange of fire followed, with MMGs, LMGs and even three-inch mortars firing at us. The LMG next to me was particularly targeted by them, and Naik Issar Singh shouted at me to take the lying position. I immediately did so and ordered my boys, who were deployed in the open, to quickly dig trenches next to their positions. Unfortunately, in the din of the battle, we were not carrying digging tools. The boys, thus, started digging with their hands and bayonets, in the sandy area.

The Pakistanis, thereafter, started bracketing the area of the LMG next to me with their artillery/mortar fire. I asked my boys to hug the bank's area—I had known from my experience as Mortar Platoon Commander earlier, that if we do so, the shell would either fall behind us or into the river. The chances of artillery shells hitting the banks were much lesser. Meanwhile, our battalion support weapons, MMGs and RCL guns were deployed at suitable places around by the CO. One of our RCLs got deployed right behind our

LMG position. While the firing was on, I felt a burning sensation in my left heel. I thought it was an insect bite, but when I took my boot off, I found that a small mortar shrapnel had hit the heel of my boot and pierced in to touch my heel.

The thick boot heel had come in handy! The firing continued from both sides, but the Pakistanis had an edge over us as they were firing from bunkers. During this period, I just happened to take my helmet off for a moment to scratch my head, when I suddenly felt something zooming past my hair. When I looked back, I saw that a tank shot had hit the RCL gun deployed just behind me! I had had a miraculous escape! The thought of having my body blown off into pieces by a tank shot haunts me even today. What a proverbial escape—by a hair's breadth! (To date, I celebrate my second birthday every year on 17 December, as for me, it was a rebirth, by the grace of God). Finally, everything went quiet that evening and there was no more exchange of fire. We reorganised ourselves in the area cleared by us.

Later, our battalion handed over the captured area of Mamdot Bulge to the BSF battalion and to our sister battalion, 15 DOGRA, who had bravely captured the northern portion of the Mamdot Bulge. We moved to take over defences in the Hussainiwala Bridge area and our battalion continued to be deployed there during the post-ceasefire period. During this period, I got promoted to the rank of Major in January 1972 and A Company commanded by me was deployed face-to-face with the Pakistani Company on the opposite side of the Satluj river. I had the opportunity to hold a number of 'flag meetings' with Pakistani officers. That itself was a great experience to get an insight into their psyche, behaviour pattern and attitude. I also had an opportunity to organise the opening of the sluice gates of the Hussainiwala Bridge and retrieval of a tank of 3 CAVALRY, which had fallen into the river earlier when two spans of the Hussainiwala Bridge were blown over during the war. We moved back to Meerut in the latter half of 1972, where we were immediately put to guard the Pakistani POW camps that had already been established at Meerut. More about these experiences another time. Looking back, I get a great sense of achievement at having taken an active part in the 1971 War during which I led a reconnaissance patrol deep into Pakistan, later led an attack to capture two Pakistani posts, besides facilitating the capture of 26 POWs. My participation and achievement in the 1971 war have been the high point of my life and has given me the greatest sense of fulfilment for having done something iconic for my battalion and my nation.

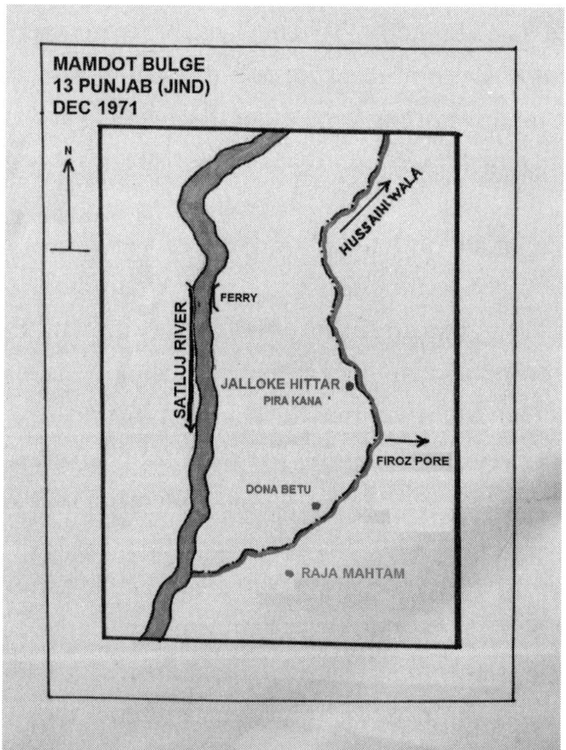

Map of Mamdot Bulge

Capture of arms and ammunition by 13 PUNJAB (Jind) at Jalloke Hittar (Pakistan), December 1971

The author sitting next to MMG post after the capture of Mamdot Bulge of Pakistan

Colonel K.K. Nanda (Retired) graduated from NDA and IMA and was commissioned into 13 PUNJAB (Jind) in June 1966, where he served for a record span of 23 years. He commanded his unit, in both the rank of a Lieutenant Colonel and Colonel from 1985 to 1989. He took an active part in the War of 1971 in the western sector with his unit and has served with them in all the forward areas. He has undertaken various adventure expeditions in high altitudes. Besides, he has served in the Military Operations Directorate, Army Headquarters and as Instructor at the NDA, where his wife, Mrs Puja Nanda, also taught alongside him as a Lecturer and as Deputy Commandant and the Chief Instructor of Women Officers Training Academy, Gwalior.

SIGINT during the 1971 War

Lieutenant Colonel C.P.C. Nath

We were enrolled in the three-year degree engineering course at the College of Military Engineering (CME), Pune, Military College of Telecommunication Engineering (MCTE) and Mhow when the course was terminated midway due to the impending war, and we were posted out to the units.

Peace Posting

I'd had a knee operation some months back at the Military Hospital, Kirkee, Pune, and I was downgraded for a long time in the medical category. Thus, when the Army HQ decided to terminate all courses, they could not post me to a field unit. Hence, I got my posting to a SIGINT unit somewhere in the western sector!

I knew nothing about the signals intelligence (SIGINT) then. So, when I started out, I was a blank slate, without any prior knowledge or experience.

Initiation into SIGINT

Considering the contribution of the Wireless Experimental Unit (WEU) to the war, SIGINT could bear substantial impact. However, my sudden landing at a WEU at a critical time of an impending war without even a general introduction to the SIGINT effort or any training in SIGINT, was neither good for the unit nor me personally.

SIGINT: What is it?

'SIGINT is a broad discipline and can include intelligence collection from various means including communications intelligence (COMINT) and electronic intelligence (ELINT), including radar and electronic warfare.' It is intelligence-gathering by interception of signals, whether communication between people (COMINT) or from electronic signals not directly used in communication (ELINT). Signals intelligence is a subset of intelligence collection management. 'SIGINT can involve the collection of communication data such as call logs, text messages, and geographical location data. Access to SIGINT information provides intelligence analysts with the ability to determine who a target is talking to, when, and where and assess the nature of relationships and their activities, all without being detected.'[74]

Soviet SIGINT

The Soviet Union maintains the most extensive and comprehensive SIGINT capabilities in the world. According to international reports, 'in early 1971, the Soviet Union established two SIGINT stations in Punjab. One stationary operated by some 300 Soviet Air Force personnel, is at Ludhiana; and the other, with some 200 personnel, is at Bathinda. These stations are well-placed to provide SIGINT a

[74] Signals Intelligence: What is SIGINT and How Does It Work? by Ben Stark on 12 November 2016 http://www.intelligence101.com/signals-intelligence-what-is-sigint-how-does-it-work/

coverage of northern Pakistan and southwest China.'

SIGINT Work During the 1971 War

Radio Telephony

We were essentially intercepting the minute-to-minute developments over Radio Telephony (RT) and Radio Tele Type (RTT) on the high frequency (HF) link between Dhaka and Rawalpindi/Islamabad. On RT they were using a secrecy device somewhat like our ITI manufactured the Ultaphone which worked somewhat like an inversion of the audible frequency spectrum. The secrecy provided is minimal in the sense that a trained operator could make sense of the communication whereas an untrained person, like me, could not make sense of the communication. I just had to trust my trained and seasoned operators who have been intercepting this radio link for months together.

Radio Tele Type (RTTy)

Fortunately, most of the information that was passed was sure to follow in the RTTy and we used it more as a confirmation of the Radio Telephony message that had already been intercepted on the RT link.

Interesting Intercepts

Some of the interesting messages passed over to the higher HQ by our intercepting unit were:

1. *Brigadier Khan was in charge of arresting Bangabandhu Mujib code-named Big Bird on the night of 25 March, the account of the arrest of the Big Bird and events leading to the arrest.*
2. *Six months before the start of the war, SIGINT alerted the Indian authorities to the imminent crackdown against the top*

leaders of the Awami League by Pakistani forces; the intercept of the transmission from East to West Pakistan that night was to the effect that '... the bird has been caged' informed them that Sheikh Mujibur Rehman, leader of the Awami League and later the first President of Bangladesh, had been caught by the Pakistanis.[75][76]
3. In early December, radio intercepts that the Pakistanis were 'pulling out' formed the basis of the Indian move to capture the town of Sylhet on 7–14 December.
4. Information obtained through radio intercepts' provided Order Of Battle intelligence on Pakistani forces deploying along the border, although there was little depth to this intelligence.[77]
5. The fall of Dhaka was followed minute by minute from the Pakistani Army perspective as they were continuously reporting to their Western Headquarters about the advance of the Indian Army and the decision to surrender.
6. Speaking on the radio even as the Army began its crackdown, Mujib declared Bangladesh's independence at midnight on 26 March 1971.

All We Knew

All we knew was some of our interceptions were extremely important in some cases to construct the larger picture. However, we did not actually know how this larger picture was constructed or what came of it. So, all we concentrated on was, as soon as anything was intercepted, our responsibility was to ensure that it was conveyed to Delhi SIGINT Headquarters, and once conveyed, our responsibilities were over. How that was used, how significant it turned to be were all outside our horizon. Also, we were not given feedback on the importance of our contribution by the higher headquarters. In the

---

[75] Asoka Raina *Inside RAW: The Story of India's Secret Service* (Vikas Publishing House, New Delhi, 1981), page 54.

[76] The arrest took place well before I arrived at the unit and it was all hearsay for me. All I heard was the message about the bird that had been caged.

[77] General K.V. Krishna Rao *Prepare or Perish: A Study of National Security*, Lancer Publishers, New Delhi, 1991, page 248.

absence of this feedback, it was difficult to keep our men motivated.

How We Kept our Men Motivated

We used to narrate the anecdotal evidence of the effect of an interception of the radio net of Pakistan formation headquarters that resulted in the killing of the Pakistani commanders who had assembled for a meeting of the Divisional Commander in the 1965 war with Pakistan. In the absence of any formal system of passing down the chain of command of the successes of the SIGINT, everything remained just folklore and anecdotal evidence.

Much later, I had read about this in the book on SIGINT that had been brought out by the Australian National University[78]:

'During this first India-Pakistan war (October 1947-December 1948, the Indian Army conducted extensive tactical COMINT operations. For example, on 8 January 1948, based on the information gleaned from the intercepts that the Divisional General Officer Commanding (GOC) was at milestone 35 on the Bhikhiwind road, the Indian armoured troops successfully ambushed the Pakistani force, all of whom (including the GOC) were killed. On 11 September, during the battle at Phillorah, intercepts informed the Indian commanders of Pakistani losses, and it quickly became evident to them that they had achieved a decisive victory and that set a major turning-point in the war.' [79]

It is a tragedy that we had to fall back on such anecdotal evidence to motivate our men to do a better job of whatever they had been engaged in because there was no formal system of conveying the successes of SIGINT to those who toiled day and night in such SIGINT activities. It is difficult to motivate these 'radio spies' without credible stories of successes of SIGINT activities. It is somewhat like:

---

[78] Desmond Ball et al. Signals intelligence (SIGINT) in South Asia: India, Pakistan, Sri Lanka. Canberra: Strategic and Defence Studies Centre, Research School of Pacific . . . , 1996. https://openresearch-repository.anu.edu.au/bitstream/1885/216567/1/117_Signals_Intelligence_(SIGINT)in_South_Asia_India_Pakistan_Srilanka(Ceylon)_Desmond_Ball_P134.pdf

[79] Cited in Major K.C. Praval's *Indian Army after Independence* (Lancer International, New Delhi, 1990), page 283. See also Lieutenant Colonel (Retired) Bhupinder Singh, *1965 War: Role of Tank in India-Pakistan War* (B.C. Publishers, Patiala, Punjab, 1982), page 13G7.

'If a tree falls in a forest and no one is around to hear it, does it make a sound?' It is all about a philosophical thought experiment that raises questions regarding observation and perception.

Post Military Service

After leaving the Army in 1987 on a premature retirement, my work pertained to software using AES-256 encryption with Bouncy Castle that I used in the software product I conceived and designed using a 256-bit key length (any equipment/software with AES key length greater than 64 bit was considered criminally punishable export of munitions by the US Government)[80]. This exposure enabled me to get a position as a software security architect in a leading financial services software company in the USA where I worked until I retired and returned to India.

As an aside, I want to narrate this story as an anecdote for the cryptic humour in it: I did take the AES-256 encryption software with a public-private key pair to RAW[81] and the Army Headquarters where the Major General Signal Staff at the Army Headquarters expressed his apprehension that he was unwilling/concerned to accept the risk of using a public key for encryption/decryption of the software because of the paranoia we in the Corps of Signals had always had for anything public in signals/communication matters. I chuckled with glee and said that he could keep the public key a secret from the public too!

---

[80] 'The US Government had long regarded crypto software as a munition, and thus subject to arms trafficking export controls! At that time, the boundary between permitted ('low-strength') cryptography and impermissible ('high-strength') cryptography placed PGP well on the too-strong-to-export side (this boundary has since been relaxed). The Arms Export Control Act of 1976 (Title II of Pub.L. 94–329, 90 Stat. 729, enacted 30 June 1976, codified at 22 U.S.C. ch. 39: See Link: https://www.law.cornell.edu/uscode/text/22/chapter-39) gives the President of the United States the authority to control the import and export of defence articles and defence services. The H.R. 13680 legislation was passed by the 94th Congressional session and enacted into law by the 38th President of the United States, Gerald R. Ford, on 30 June 1976: See Link: https://www.secret-bases.co.uk/wiki/Arms_Export_Control_Act

[81] Thanks to my erstwhile colleagues and friends, Major General V.K. Singh and Brigadier Ujjal Dasgupta, both of Corps of Signals serving in RAW that time.

SIGINT Today

'The global SIGINT market is expected to grow from USD 12.8 billion in 2018 to USD 15.6 billion by 2023, at a compound annual growth rate (CAGR) of 4.1 per cent during the forecast period. The major growth factors include increasing terrorism, the growing defence budget of major countries across the globe, and the modernisation or the replacement of an ageing defence system. However, the high cost involved in the SIGINT system deployment could restrain the market growth.' [82]

---

[82] Signals intelligence (SIGINT) market by type (electronic intelligence (ELINT) and communications intelligence (COMINT)), application (airborne, Naval, ground (vehicle-mounted, soldiers, and base station), space and cyber), and region-global forecast to 2023. https://www.sdki.jp/reports/signals-intelligence-sigint-market/106540, last visited 4 March 2021

Lieutenant Colonel C.P.C. Nath (Retired) served in the Corps of Signals before he took retirement from the military in 1987. He completed his graduate study in Computer Science at the University of California in 1983. He taught Computer Science at MCTE, Mhow and the Jawaharlal Nehru University. He designed, implemented and presented an implementation of Advanced Encryption System, the AES 256 bit, to the RAW, military and private banking system in India in 2000. He last served as a Software Security Architect for FISERV, a leading financial software company in the US software industry in Los Angeles, California, USA. He dabbles in philosophy, critical thinking, technology, privacy, and law just for the fun of it.

Battle of Jarpal

An Action Journal

Colonel Mahendra Singh Joon

Introduction

This is a day-to-day account of the historic Battle of Jarpal (also referred to as the Battle of Basantar). Please refer to the map to better understand the battles fought by the 3 GRENADIERS.[83]

30 November 1971

On de-induction of the Commando Wing instructors from the sectors around Bangladesh (East Pakistan) to Belgaum, I was moved to the Weapons Leg of the Young Officers' course. I had barely settled, when I received my forthwith posting order to the 3 GRENADIERS on the special request of the Commanding Officer (CO), Lieutenant Colonel V.P. Airy, as he had wanted 'hard core' officers. Brigadier N.L. Poonia was the other officer whose posting, however, did not materialise.

---

83 3rd Battalion, The Grenadiers

1–2 December 1971

Having participated in the training and leading Mukti Bahini missions from the Tura Sector in Meghalaya, I could gauge that Pakistan would start a war any day on our western borders to draw out our forces from the eastern front. I was going to join it as part of the Triumphant Third. My wife, along with my ten-month-old son, Amit, was admitted to Command Hospital in Pune for post-burn surgeries. Hence, on 1 December, as I packed to leave, anxiety, uncertainty and a fear of the unknown occupied my mind. While I could leave it upon the Infantry School staff to take care of my heavy baggage, I had to decide about what to do with my car and my son.

Finally I decided to drive to Pune along with Kim, my Springer dog. I would leave the car there with a friend, pick up Amit and catch a train to New Delhi. Somehow, I was able to contact my elder brother in Faridabad and requested him to meet me at New Delhi Railway Station, so that I could hand over Amit and Kim to him. So, there I was, driving to Pune, at 8 a.m. on 2 December 1971.

3–4 December 1971

Leaving my wife at Command Hospital, Pune, Amit, Kim, and I boarded the New Delhi-bound train. Managing a 10-month-old who could walk but had not started to speak along with my dog Kim was not easy. It worried me to think how Amit would adjust with my parents, whom he was going to meet for the first time since his birth. My father, Major Mehar Singh (a GRENADIER) and my elder brother received me at New Delhi Railway Station. Seeing me worried, my father motivated me and said, 'When I went to fight in the Second World War in Abyssinia, I, too, had to leave behind both your elder siblings. It wasn't easy for me. But we do what is expected of us—we fight. Leave your worries here and do your duty.' They took Amit and Kim away to our village Nuna Majra (near Bahadurgarh, Haryana), and I continued my journey to Pathankot.

In the wee hours of 4 December, I woke up, startled by loud noises. Someone had heard on the transistor that Pakistan had attacked our airfields all along the western front. So, it was no longer just a few clandestine missions, the Mukti Bahini or skirmishes in Bogra, Hilly, etc. (East Pakistan)—it was now an all-out war!

5–6 December 1971

I had no clue about the location of the Triumphant Third. My posting order had mentioned Pathankot as Next Railway Station (NRS). So, on reaching there, I contacted the Movement Control Officer (MCO) who directed me to a group of vehicles with the tactical sign 'W' instead of the regular three numerals. This was the first letter of the General Officer Commanding (GOC) of the 54 Infantry Division, Major General W.A.G. Pinto.

I got into a 1-Ton, and the convoy of 4–5 vehicles left for Sambha. En route, we had to stop a couple of times, dismount and take a position to avoid being strafed by enemy aircrafts.

Late in the evening, the same 1 ton took me to 'B' Echelon of the Triumphant Third, where I was received by Captain D.P. Sharma, who was in command of 'B' Echelon. He briefed me that 1 Corps had been shuttling between Pathankot and Sambha and finally had firmed in Sambha to undertake its first strike. The Triumphant Third was part of the 47 Infantry Brigade under the 54 Infantry Division. On the intervening night of 5–6 December, the Third was to attack and capture the Pakistani Border Outpost (BOP) at Bhairon Nath.

In a pre-dawn attack on 6 December, 'D' Company, under Major Kartar Dalal and Lieutenant Meharban Singh Negi captured the BOP, taking a couple of prisoners of war (POW). The Triumphant Third, with a squadron of Hudson Horse, was then tasked to protect the western flank of the Division and deployed. On 6 December, Captain

D.P. Sharma and I, with lunch and 'F' Echelon vehicles reached the Triumphant Third's location at 10 a.m.

On meeting the CO, Lieutenant Colonel V.P. Airy (MVC and later Lieutenant General), the first thing he did was to ask me to remove my Captain's pips and made me wear the Major's pips. I was then asked to familiarise myself with the deployment of the Triumphant Third and be available at the Battalion HQ. Barring the occasional shelling in the vicinity and the enemy aircraft trying to strafe, everything else was peaceful. In the Battalion HQ, I met the Second in Commands (2ICs), Major P.S. Grewal and Major S.H. Qasim, the Adjutant IO Lieutenant Sarabjit Dhillon, and Lieutenant J.S. Lidder as the Essential Vehicle Column (EVC) Commander (both retired as Lieutenant Generals)

'A' Company was commanded by Major Khazan Singh with Lieutenant Peter Swami as the Company Officer, 'B' Company was under Major S.S. Cheema with Lieutenant B.S. Pathania as the Company Officer, 'C' Company was under the command of Major Hoshiar Singh with Captain Mukul Verma as the Company Officer, and 'D' Company was under Major K.S. Dalal with Lieutenant M.S. Negi and Lieutenant A.S. Chauhan as the Company Officers and Major S.S. Punia was the Mortar Platoon Commander.

On getting back to the Battalion HQ, I dug a trench that was 6 x 2 x 2 ft deep for myself, and after a comparatively hot dinner supplied to us by Captain D.P. Sharma, I tried to take a nap.

7–9 December 1971[84]

On 7 December at 3 a.m., I was woken up by a runner who told me that the CO wanted to see me. When I met the CO, he asked me to go and relieve Major Khazan Singh (3 years my senior) and take

[84] After 6 December, all actions of 'A' Company, that I commanded during the war and in which I physically participated, are facts as I recollect today. Actions of other companies, armour squadrons and the rest of the Triumphant Third's elements are as per information assimilated by me from conversations on the Third's radio net.

over as the Officer Commanding (OC) of 'A' Company. It was after relieving him that I learnt the reason for the change of the Company Commander.

'A' Company's 'F' Echelon truck was parked in a sugarcane field. At midnight, a jawan wanted to relieve himself and entered the sugarcane field. The rustling sound in the field woke up the 1-Ton driver who took it to be enemy activity. In a hurry, he tried to start the 1 Ton, but it misfired. He made a couple of other attempts and every time it misfired. A vehicle misfiring makes a sound like a gunshot. On hearing sounds, the jawan who had gone to relieve himself shouted, '*Re mar diya!*' (Since all this happened in the rear of the Company HQ, the Company Commander assumed it to be an enemy attack and reported it to the Battalion HQ. The CO ordered 'C' Company to move and be ready to counterattack the 'A' Company's location. Fortunately, the faux pas was discovered before 'C' Company had launched the counterattack!

From then on, my company, along with the rest of the 3 GRENADIERS, continued to guard the western flank of the 54 Infantry Division till 7 p.m. on 9 December. Since Bari and Darman, which were further south, had fallen to 16 Dogra and other battalions of 74 Brigade, the 3 GRENADIERS was asked to cross the minefield and redeploy south of it and continue guarding the western flank of the Division.

On 9 December at 7.30 p.m., when we lined up to cross the minefield, suddenly the enemy fired artillery salvo all along our side of the minefield. We were caught in the open and suffered 15 odd casualties. One shell burst very close to me. Stunned, I fell to the ground! When I recovered, I realised that a splinter had hit my back. Luckily I had been carrying a sleeping bag which absorbed the shock and saved me. After evacuating the wounded and the dead, we crossed the minefield and took a defensive position south of the minefield.

10–15 December 1971

We continued protecting the western flank of the Division and dominating the area up to Lahri Kalan and Khurd by patrolling till 15 December.

On the night of 10 December, one of my company patrols, led by Havildar Hawa Singh, reported that the enemy was whistling in front of him. I asked him why the enemy would whistle at him and told him to move left-right and observe. After a while, he again reported about the whistling. The area was full of tall *sarkandas,* a type of grass, a gentle breeze. I realised what was happening. I asked Hawa Singh to cover the flash hider of his rifle and then let me know if the enemy was still whistling! Sure enough, the enemy had stopped whistling. What had happened was that when the air was passing through the flash hider it was making the sound of a whistle.

15 December 1971

After Bari and Darman villages were captured, it was planned to capture Jarpal and Saraj Chak by Hudsons and Poona Horse in a pre-dawn attack on 15 December. The Pakistanis had laid extensive minefields with a depth of nearly 1,500 metres, though these were not dense. However, the armour regiments refused to attack unless a safe lane was provided.

It was, therefore, decided to cross the Basantar Nala and capture Jarpal and Saraj Chak by 3 GRENADIERS and 16 MADRAS[85] (47 Infantry Brigade). At 10 a.m., the 3 GRENADIERS' 'O' Group crossed the minefield near Lohra Kalan and hit another one near Saincha. Just as we hit the minefield, a medium machine gun (MMG), a Pakistani recce and support element, opened fire and bullets started landing barely 20 metres short of us within the minefield!

Even though none was carrying a rifle or wearing a steel helmet (a practice followed by all officers throughout the war), all of us took

[85] 16th Battalion, The Madras Regiment

up positions, aligning our bodies to the direction of fire.

The CO, Lieutenant Colonel V.P. Airy directed Lieutenant Jasbir Lidder to run up to a tank, barely 200 metres to our right and rear and ask it to engage the enemy. While Major Thoru, the Battery Commander, was through to his battery and was getting artillery fired on the MMG position, we all got up and dashed as far back as we could in one sprint.

Now, the bullets were landing at the exact spot where we had taken position earlier. After regaining our breath, we made yet another sprint rearwards. Sure enough, the bullets were now landing at the spot where we had taken the second position. Apparently, the MMG crew had not adjusted the sight to the correct distance and after opening fire, it started resetting the sight, but not before we made the two sprints rearwards. By now, the tank and artillery fire had engaged the MMG position and area around it, and the 'O' Group was able to extricate itself without any casualty.

On 15 December by 7.45 pm, the 3 GRENADIERS had moved to the Forming Up Point (FUP). The 'B' and 'C' Companies were to cross Basantar and capture Jarpal in Phase 1. The 'A' and 'D' Companies were to attack in Phase 2, with 'A' Company capturing Lohal and linking up with 16 MADRAS in the north and 'B' Company in the south, while 'D' was to capture the area southeast of Jarpal, between Basantar Nala and the 'C' Company. The 'B' and 'C' Companies had apparently not hit any recce and support elements and had captured Jarpal without much opposition. But when the 'A' and 'D' Companies launched their attack, they came under heavy enemy MMG fire. Lieutenant M.S. Negi, Company Officer of 'D' Company got an MMG burst in the jaw but the company managed to link up with 'C' Company.

After leaving the FUP, I heard some noise in front of us. Assuming it to be our boys of 'B'/'C' Companies (who had gone ahead in Phase 1), I shouted, *'Oye! Fire mat karna. Hum hain 'A' Company*

3 GRENADIERS' (Hey! Do not fire. This is us—the 'A' Company 3 GRENADIERS). No sooner than I had said that, an MMG opened up!

Fortunately for us, it had tracers, and we could see where the fire was coming from and where it was directed. A few men, including myself, went to the ground but most ran backwards. Subedar Rup Chand crawled up to me and said, *'Sahib, ek MMG hai, ise capture kar lete hain'* (Sahib, we have an MMG, we must capture this position). Seeing only a handful of men around, I replied, *'Sahib, hum is position par to kabja kar lenge par baki company Pathankot mein baithi hogi. Pehle company par kabja karen?'*

We caught up with the company at Jhambian Manhasian. Having rounded up the company, I gave them the choicest abuses in Jatu (it was a Jat company) and again formed up the company for the attack. After going a few steps, everyone halted saying that there was a minefield. I hit the jawan in front of me, asking him to move aside and started leading. I then shouted, *'Mein aage chalta hoon, jo mere piche nahin ayega us saale ko mein goli marunga.'* After some steps, Grenadier Gajendra Sirohi took the lead and said, *'Saalo doob maro! Company Commander aage chal raha hai!'* The boy subsequently got a commission through the Army Cadet College (ACC).

16–17 December 1971

By now, the daylight was breaking and we could see a bunker ahead. An MMG, probably the same one that had fired at us earlier, opened fire. Naik Ram Kumar (Vir Chakra), with his section, rushed to its top and shouted, *'Bahar niklo nahin to grenade andar phaink raha hun'*. I, with the Radio Operator, also reached the top of the bunker. One subaltern, 2 junior commissioned officers (JCOs) and 9 ORs came out of the bunker, with hands raised. Some jawans tried to bayonet them but were stopped by me and were taken prisoners of war. We also captured an MMG and a jeep with a recoilless (RCL) gun. Even to this day, the 3 GRENADIERS has retained the jeep as war trophy and kept it in running condition.

The capture of Lohal village and a link-up with 'B' Company in the south and 16 MADRAS in the north followed. A success signal was given at 7 a.m. on 16 December. Soon, our armour crossed Basantar through a hastily created lane by the engineers of 'A' Squadron, and each of Hudson and Poona Horse were inducted at the bridgehead. Passing behind my company, Second Lieutenant Arun Khetrapal's troop moved south and took up position in the grove between me and 'B' Company.

The enemy reacted very quickly and launched a counterattack, the brunt of which was borne by 'B' Company, led by Major S.S. Cheema and 'C' Company, led by Major Hoshiar. Since the enemy could reach Bara Pind unobserved by ground troops and form-up behind it, the subsequent armour and combined armour and infantry counterattacks also came from the same direction. No counterattacks came on 'A' Company since the area to the west and northwest of it opened right up to Gazipur Forest, and the enemy could not form-up unobserved and attack.

Amidst heavy shelling, the flat end of a splinter hit my forehead above the left eye. Refusing evacuation, I continued with my company after applying field dressing and using morphine. Major Hoshiar Singh got an MMG burst in his thigh. He, too, refused evacuation and continued after a field dressing (finally he was evacuated on the morning of 18 December). There was a total of 6 more counterattacks to recapture Jarpal on 16 and 17 December, but every attack was repulsed by the 'B' and 'C' Companies. To my left, Second Lieutenant Arun Khetrapal's tank was hit in one of these counterattacks after he had destroyed four Pakistani tanks. Both Hoshiar and Khetrapal were awarded Param Vir Chakras posthumously for their gallant action in this battle.

Throughout 16 and 17 December, artillery from both sides

constantly kept firing to support or repulse the counterattacks. Indian and Pakistani Air Forces were also active in strafing each other's troops and tanks. A bullet from a Pakistani aircraft that strafed us, landed just a foot away from me. I had dug it out, and it is still preserved by me. Our air operations in their fixed-wing aircraft were in the air all the time directing the artillery fire.

The last counterattack by 35 FF[86] on Jarpal was also repulsed. By now, Dhaka had fallen, and a ceasefire had been announced, which was to be effective from 8 p.m. on 17 December. After the ceasefire, how many walking-wounded walked back or how many Pakistanis, dead or wounded, were taken away by them on the night of 17 December is not known.

All Quiet on the Western Front

On 17 December 1971, at 8 p.m., there was pin-drop silence, no shelling, no firing of small arms, just stillness—for a good thirty minutes, nobody moved fearing the ceasefire may not last.

On 18 December 1971, at 7 a.m., with no scope to move further southwest, west and northwest of Jarpal, the 'B', 'C' and 'D' Companies stayed put in their locations while 'A' Company advanced in an extended line north of Jarpal and stopped when they came face-to-face with the Pakistanis. This was done to occupy as much additional area as possible.

The Pakistanis and all our Company Commanders and men met, hugging each other like estranged brothers meeting after a long time. Coats and parkas were exchanged. I exchanged my Wills Filter cigarettes with theirs, which was made in Pakistan. On the morning 18 December, the body of 35 FF CO, Lieutenant Colonel Mohmad Akram Raja, two Majors, and 93 others from other ranks were handed over to Pakistan by our CO, Lieutenant Colonel V.P. Airy with a citation for Colonel Raja, based on which he got the second-

---

[86] 35th Battalion, Frontier Force Regiment

highest gallantry award of Pakistan.

Looking back, what continues to astonish me even to this day is how after the war ended, the victors looked beleaguered—unshaven for three days, knee deep in mud, socks still wet, while the Pakistanis (especially the officers) were impeccably dressed, their uniforms starched and their *sahayaks* carrying Thermos flasks filled with steaming hot coffee and tea! This, I think, was the reason for their defeat.

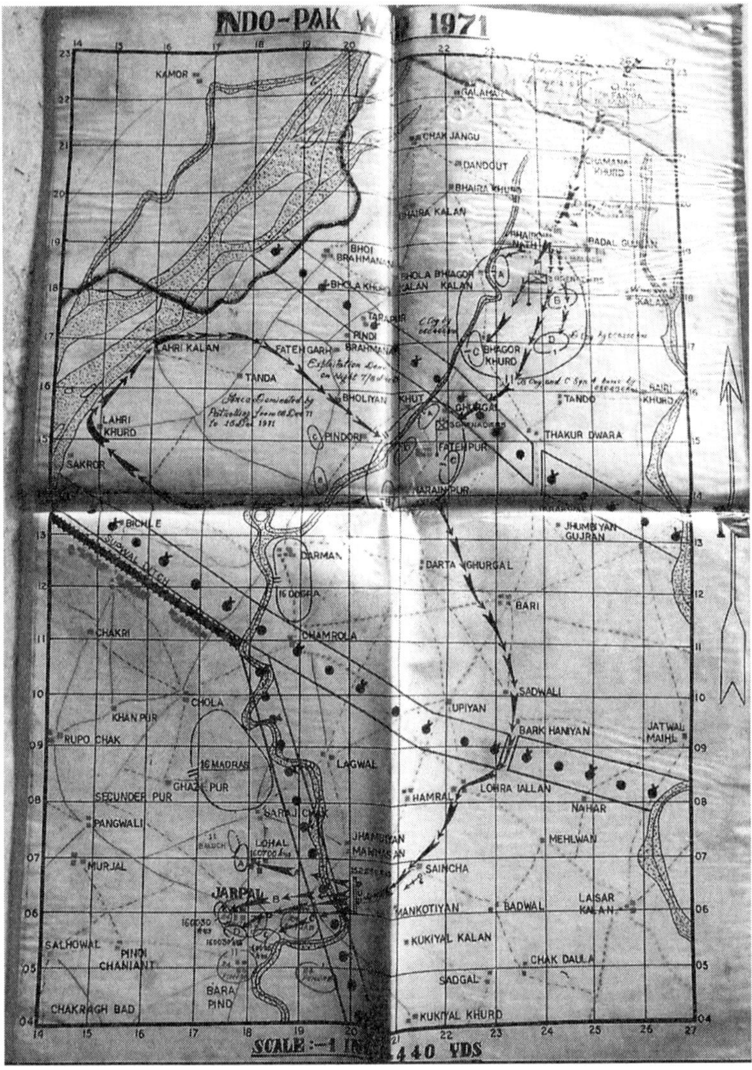

A map of the Indo-Pak War 1971

Colonel Mahendra Singh Joon (Retired) was commissioned into 3 GRENADIERS. A Commando Dagger holder, he served as the Instructor in the Commando Wing, Weapon leg of the YO Wing, General Staff Officer 2 (GSO2 (I)) XV Corps. He also took part in the operations in the eastern sector, commanded 'A' Company 3 GRENADIERS alongside Major Hoshiar Singh (PVC, who commanded 'C' Company) in the Battle of Jarpal. He commanded 3 GRENADIERS, in field and peace, both as Lieutenant Colonel and on in situ promotion as Colonel. After he lost his younger brother, he took premature retirement on 27 August 1990 before his board for Brigadier.

The Capture of Mamdot Bulge

Brigadier Vijay Rai

Some instances in this article throw light on the stellar role of 15 DOGRA[87] in the capture of Mamdot Bulge (south of the Hussainiwala enclave, which was the scene of the intense battle). The area had assumed greater importance as the samadhis of Shaheed Bhagat Singh, Rajguru and Sukhdev are located here and was the direct approach to Ferozepur. Our military planners were of the view that the Mamdot enclave had to be captured to preclude any build-up by Pakistan for opening up yet another avenue of attack or a build-up towards Ferozepur. This assumed even more importance after the fall of Hussainiwala.

Some of the incidents where the unit excelled during the 1971 war haven't been spoken or written about much in our unit's history or war diary (or maybe, I have not read about them). The reader is requested to appreciate that at the time of the war I had served for only 5 years and had been sidestepped from the Adjutant's chair to that of the Deputy Company Commander. Jayant Mohanty had taken

[87] 15th Battalion, The Dogra Regiment

over as Adjutant. Much water has flown since then. However, having experienced varied assignments, the reader may find me disdainful of some decisions taken at the higher command level during the heat of the battle. Nevertheless, this is how battles are fought when higher commanders have to make split-second decisions—while some work, others don't. As junior officers we often criticise and snigger at these decisions without realising the compulsions and pressures that the higher commanders must go through, and vice versa.

The first incident that I wish to cover is a patrol that I had led to the Pakistan position of Amrudwali along the Sutlej river.

Background

Rangewala had been captured on the night of 10/11 December 1971 at a very heavy cost. Twenty soldiers had been martyred and 40 odd men were wounded. Yash Sehgal (27 NDA ex Foxtrot) died on the spot and Ram Rishi Yadav also succumbed a couple of days later, having taken a machine gun burst in the head. Both had been more than friends to me; they had been my family. The grief that one experiences in such circumstances cannot be explained; it can only be felt. Grief is the strongest emotion one feels—anger and revenge follow much later. Bikram Rana, while going on a patrol out of Rangewala, blew his foot on an anti-personnel mine on the morning of 11 December. It happened literally a few yards from me, and when I saw the blood, flesh and bones sticking out from what should have been his foot, it felt hideous. I recall Bikram asking me, 'Sir, is it gone?' What could I have said? Bikram had accepted it like a man, and after getting a prosthetic leg, he served as the Aide-de-camp (ADC) to President Shri Neelam Sanjeeva Reddy.

The General Officer Commanding (GOC) of the 14 Infantry Division, General Onkar Singh Kalkat, came to Rangewala and after offering the perfunctory compliments to the Commanding

Officer (CO), Lieutenant Colonel Keen Tewari, for having captured Rangewala, and then started chiding and berating the CO for having suffered heavy casualties. The CO was one of the most balanced persons I have served with—very humane, practical person with a down-to-earth attitude. However, he was a hard taskmaster, and it was only his maturity that avoided an unpleasant situation. We, the youngsters, who were within listening distance, wanted to tell the GOC to leave immediately and let us run the unit, but then, the GOC must have had his own reasons for doing so.

It was in this backdrop that the CO ordered me to take a patrol to Amrudwali to explore the possibility of attacking and capturing the position from the west, since the map showed Amrudwali on the eastern bank of the Sutlej. One look at the map would indicate that capturing Amrudwali from the west, that is, the rear approach would render Pakistani defences in the Mamdot Bulge untenable. The 'D' Company had been tasked to capture the position. Hence, who better than the Company Commander to lead the patrol. I was to move out after the last light, on 11 December, and be back by the morning of the 12 December. I had my Forward Observation Officer (FOO) Jacob (who, I believe, got transferred to the Pioneer Corps later) and the usual signal support and communications. I remember vividly that Lance Naik Nuklu Ram (who went on to become a Subedar Major) was part of this patrol. We were about 12 men of all ranks in this patrol.

A word about the terrain needs to be mentioned here— there was only vegetation around. The entire region was covered with *sarkandas* or elephant grass, which meant there was practically no visibility at night. Of course, moving along the banks of the Sutlej afforded visibility to the far bank where the main defences of the enemy existed, but it was the same for the enemy as well. So, one had to be careful. The eastern bank of the Sutlej was about 15–20 feet higher than the water level, where there were numerous channels that could be easily crossed by a ferry or even waded through at that time of the year except, of course, the main river. Unfortunately, I don't have the maps of the area. But I did a Google search of the Mamdot area and, to my pleasant surprise, I found the area extensively cultivated with a lot of greenery on the Pakistan side of the border. In December 1971, however, the area only had six to ten feet high *sarkandas*. The Pakistanis had just cleared enough area around their positions to get clear fields of fire. Their observation was equally restricted, which also worked to their disadvantage as you could creep up to the edge of the sarkanda and observe them unhindered.

It must have been around 9 or 10 p.m. when one of my patrol parties slipped on the riverbank, and a fair amount of racket was created. It is surprising how far and swiftly sound travels on a dark winter night. While he was being retrieved, a volley of fire started from the far bank—a couple of light machine gun (LMG) bursts to start with, then longer bursts and in the end, the whole bank lit up accompanied by para flares. Apparently, some sentry got trigger-happy and the entire defence line caught the bug. These were the defences in the area around Attar Singh Wala (While searching on the Internet I could not locate it, but did find Jodh Singh Wala which, I learnt later, was the Pakistani battalion HQ). We witnessed this 'Diwali' for about 15 minutes while lying doggo and hugging the ground. The distance between the two banks was a little more than a kilometre and there was no way their fire could be effective (but this is only in hindsight). During this time, the CO had been trying to get me on an Army Navy Personal Radio Communication 25 (ANPRC-25) set, and we had agreed that once the firing stopped, we would continue our patrol but carefully.

My hunch is that the Pakistanis had no clue about the patrol. After waiting for about 15–20 minutes, when sanity returned, the patrol continued towards our proposed objective. The only problem was how to read the map amidst the *sarkandas* at night. I asked

Jacob, the FOO, to help us locate Amrudwali, which, as per the map, was bang on the eastern bank of the Sutlej. Based on the time and distance, we should have reached Amrudwali by now, but all we saw was elephant grass! Those inch-maps given to us were hopelessly outdated and the compass was not much help either. By then, it was well past midnight, and Jacob and I decided to call for artillery fire to get at least some idea of our objective. After getting in touch with his gun position, Jacob gave the coordinates asking for one 25-pounder to be fired. The gunners responded promptly, but the sound of the shell exploding was too far away, and the echo of the bursting shell confused us even more. We asked for a repeat which was granted. Again, there was no luck. I reported to the CO, who was not amused and asked us to get back by the first light. Despondent for not having completed our task, we started trudging back to Rangewala. It was only later when my company captured Amrudwali on 15 December 1971 that we came to know we had been chasing a wild goose; the place was nowhere near to what had been shown on the maps—there were at least two large creeks (all dry in winters) between the Sutlej bank and the objective. In fact, there had been a few smaller ones as well. Hence, the echo of the shells when they landed seemed to have come from far away. There was no GPS or satellite imagery either those days, which made it tougher. As they say, the time spent on recce is never wasted—this had atleast proved to us that the approach to attack the objective had to be ruled out, and we knew we would have to find another one. Also, little did we know then that there were some more fun and games for my patrol party that awaited.

It must have been around 5.30 a.m. when we were not more than half an hour from the batallion HQ that we suddenly heard a lot of rustling in the *sarkandas* and voices of people speaking Punjabi. They could not have been more than 30 to 40 yards away. The voices seemed to be moving towards the riverbank. We froze, realising that they could not be our troops. However, we needed confirmation.

Soon enough, as the voices started descending to the riverbank, we were certain thery weren't ours. Here was our moment! In military parlance, it was an opportunity ambush. The whispered instructions could not have taken more than 10 seconds and we hurriedly took positions on top of the riverbank. I think it was Jacob who let go of his carbine burst first. Nuklu was next with his LMG. For the next minute or so, we opened up with all we had. As can be appreciated, the visibility of the riverbed was very low because of the early morning fog, characteristic of North Indian winters.

During the split-second pauses, we could hear loud groaning, moaning and splashing in the water. Apparently there was a small boat there being used as a ferry, and these were stragglers lost in the sarkanda after the Rangewala attack. Or they may have deliberately 'lost' themselves to escape the fury and heat of the attack. I was also a listener to some of the choicest Punjabi abuses I have ever heard—most of them unprintable here. After a few minutes, we went down the riverbank; in the sandy bed, we saw two huge pools of blood. They had, however, managed to extricate the wounded (or dead) in the boat which we recovered. We did get one uber machine gun (UMG), six boxes of belted ammunition and about half a dozen blankets. These were displayed to General Kalkat the next day during a discussion of the battalion's attack plan of Jaloke Dhuan and Amrudwali.

The CO had been frantically trying to get in touch with me on the radio, but the situation precluded me from speaking on the radio set. After the incident, we got in touch, and I assured the CO that all was well and would debrief him on arrival at the battalion HQ. This incident also brought out the need for good fire discipline. The indiscriminate firing of all weapons revealed fairly accurately the layout of the Pakistani defences and the improbability of the enemy reinforcing his defences east of the Sutlej. The layout of the defences was also confirmed by an air operation recce flight a day later.

The Attack on Amrudwali

Background

Dhan Singh Adhikari (Danny), who was awarded the Vir Chakra, was tasked to capture Jaloke Dhuan. He had earlier done a splendid job of carrying out a detailed recce of the objective. Taking advantage of the thick sarkanda, he had positioned himself within a few hundred metres during the daytime the previous day and had drawn precise sketches of the defensive layout. This was to stand him in good stead later, and the execution of the attack was indeed praiseworthy.

The plan to capture Amrudwali involved passing through Danny's company after the capture of Jaloke Dhuan (treating it as a firm base). The attack was planned for the night of 14/15 December. My company's attack was supposed to have been completed by the first light on 15 December. However, the attack on Jaloke Dhuan got stretched, and consequently, the attack on Amrudwali also got delayed. The whole night was spent in a trench waiting for executive orders to proceed to the objective. I remember vividly smoking my Panama cigarettes—I must have finished at least a pack of them, all this under the cover of a blanket. My ears were glued to the handset of the radio throughout the night of the 14/15 as Danny went through completing his task most professionally. It was getting close to the first light, and I had this strange feeling that the attack on Amrudwali could well be postponed for the coming night. At that time, though, one was not aware of the advantages of maintaining momentum—I mean, we all knew, that it was an important principle of war but actually executing it in a battle situation was revealing. While mopping up[88] Jaloke Dhuanr, the CO got me on the radio and asked me to execute my company's attack.

Since it was already first light there was little problem in navigating, and within half an hour, we had reached Jaloke Dhuan. After receiving last-minute instructions from the CO, we approached

[88] Clearing remnants of enemy occupied position after capture

the objective; we had some trouble moving through the elephant grass, but by and large, the move was smooth and swift. The CO then sprang another pleasant surprise for me, allotting a troop of Centurion tanks (3 CAVALRY[89]). He, however, told me that they were not to be used for the assault but for fire support alone.

It needs to be remembered that in those days armour was a very precious commodity. It would have taken us about an hour or so to reach Amrudwali, and it was close to 10:30 a.m. When we were about a kilometre away from our objective, I climbed atop Troop Leader Harry Sud's tank, and it was then that I got the first glimpse of Amrudwali. Sprawled over a little more than 500 metres, it had a few huts, which stood out like eyesores. Fortunately, the Medium Regiment Operation Post Officer, Major Sharma, was also on the same tank, and I wanted him to soften up the objective nice and proper before we physically assaulted the defences. I told Harry Sud to use the tank's machine gun (MG) fire, and even the main gun of the other tanks of the troop to blast the area. This was an attack in broad daylight, and I needed to employ all weaponry and firepower at my disposal to make my task easier and reduce casualties!

The rumbling and earth-shaking movement of the 50 tonner Centurions is enough to put the fear of God amongst the most seasoned soldiers with all guns blazing (literally); putting this fear in the enemy had been my intention. In the meanwhile, Major Sharma had carried out ranging of the objective and the 155 milimetre guns were spot on. The observation was really good, and I was convinced that the artillery fire was truly effective; we just could not afford to give any breather to the enemy. With high explosive plastering the enemy and tank guns and MG firing, I jumped down from the tank where I was had been perched watching the neutralisation of the enemy. Shamsher, my company's Second-in-Command, was with me, and the platoon leading the attack was led by Subedar Kirpal Singh.

---

89 3rd Cavalry Regiment

So far so good. Now, we were just 200 to 300 yards away from our objective when a couple of blasts indicated that we were walking through an anti-personnel minefield. We had to get out of this quickly. Fortunately for us, this minefield appeared to have been freshly laid, and hence, wherever we saw fresh earth piled up, or small mounds, we managed to avoid the mines. One wrong step would blow our foot to smithereens. In fact, two of my company jawans had their feet blown off.

As we stormed the objective, it became clear to me that the enemy had been hammered nice and proper. The air was full of the acrid stench of high explosives and the Trinitrotoluene (TNT) of our guns and tanks. Soon enough, we came under artillery and mortar fire of the enemy. By then, we had become 'smart' enough to know whether we were under artillery or mortar fire—the sound of the artillery shell has a peculiar whistling tone while the mortar shell sound is more subdued. Either way, we knew when to precisely get under cover or jump into a trench, and let the shell explode. The enemy had slid into the sarkanda and started firing from within the elephant grass, more out of a false sense of security than any actual effectiveness. Around midday, on 15 December 1971, I was certain that Amrudwali had been captured. It was time for giving the success signal. The feeling that one gets when giving the code word and firing very light flares in actual battle is a different ball game than in training exercises. As we started reorganising the captured objective, my radio operator told me that the GOC would like to speak to me. 'The GOC? Why?' I wondered. Unknown to me till then, apparently the entire command line-up, that is, the GOC, the Brigade Commander, Brigadier Pran Anand (GUARDS) and the CO, Colonel Tewari had climbed up the Pakistani observation post tower of Jaloke Dhuan (the position that Danny had captured the previous night) and were observing and following my attack. The daylight visibility had afforded them a bird's-eye view of my movement and attacking drills as also the effectiveness of tank and artillery fire. The GOC complimented me for the flawless execution and success of the attack and gave me the usual instructions to prevent re-capture by the enemy—dig in, register your defensive fire tasks, be extra vigilant, etc. After responding with a 'Roger' and 'Wilco' to him about half a dozen times, we got down to reorganising ourselves in the objective area.

The warlike stores that we captured at Amrudwali would be documented somewhere in the war diary of the unit. Essentially it was the base from where other positions in the Mamdot enclave were being supplied as was evident from the tonnes of ammunition cartons and boxes of various kinds that we captured. There were numerous boxes of anti-personnel and anti-tank mines which gave us a good idea of the quantum on mines that the enemy had laid in the area. On a lighter note, we also took possession of a large plate, called a *paraat* in our langars (community kitchens), of freshly cut lamb meat for about 30 persons, ready to be cooked. After debating for a short while on whether it could be poisoned and if it could be halal meat, all objections were overruled and the mutton was duly cooked and consumed.

We hadn't eaten anything since 6 p.m. the previous evening, except a few *shakarparas*.

With the capture of Amrudwali, the enemy withdrew from the remaining two positions—Dona Betu and Raja Mahtam—in the Mamdot Bulge. About 20 prisoners of war were captured who could not manage to escape from our sister battalion, 13 PUNJAB[90]. The war was also about to end as Pakistan had surrendered after the fall of Dacca in East Pakistan. It was on 16/17 December that a ceasefire had been declared, just two days after the capture of Mamdot Bulge.

The battalion remained in the Mamdot Bulge for another year or so till the signing of the Shimla Peace Accord when both India and Pakistan withdrew to their own side of the international borders.

---

[90] 13th Battalion, The Punjab Regiment

Other Noteworthy Incidents

At the outset, I wish to state that I was not a part of some other incidents which I want to cover. So, I cannot vouch for their veracity. However, having been part of the set-up and meeting friends, brother officers and men who were present there, it is highly probable that these are correct. As I said earlier, we remained in the captured area for over a year and as part of our lesson learning, we visited many places in and around Ferozepur and Hussainiwala headworks where various actions took place.

Ambiguity in the Allotted Role

Even a rookie officer would have told you that the strategic aim was to go on the offensive in East Pakistan and adopt a defensive posture on the western front. While one can appreciate that even in a defensive role certain limited offensive actions need to be taken for achieving your aim, the articulation of the same was somewhat woolly. 7 Infantry Division was responsible for the defence of Ferozepur and has always been so. To the best of my understanding, it still is. On our arrival in Ferozepur, the first task given to our formation was the defence of the approaches to Ferozepur township and sitting defences around the periphery of the town. We were all asked to recce the area and coordinate such defences. This carried on for about a week after we arrived in the area, in the third week of October 1971. Surely one was not expecting the enemy to make headway up to Ferozepur, and even if he managed to do so, there was a formation in situ whose role was precisely this. It was its primary role. Also, the Hussainiwala headworks was too strategic an area to pass on its responsibility to another formation. My own take on this was that commanders at the higher level were still not clear what our role would be, and hence, we were kept busy by moving around the township. That week after our arrival was totally wasted in moving in and around the township.

Some other odd jobs were additionally assigned to the battalion. One of them was to guard an airstrip close to Ferozepur. I think this was in a place named Kasu Begu. The higher formation HQ was worried that this disused airstrip might be used by the enemy for airborne operations and afford it a base to further build up operations. The reader needs to be reminded that the concept of Strike Corps came into being only after the War of 1971. The Jalandhar Corps was fulfilling both roles during the war. It also seemed to me that there was this fixation, which seemed to be purely personality-based, that 7 Infantry Division would do a better job for limited offensive tasks. With this as a backdrop, the unit deployed in the Hussainiwala enclave was to continue there, making full use of its knowledge of the terrain and deployment but would come under the command of the 14 Infantry Division 'when the balloon goes up'. Now consider this—till the war started, it remained under its parent formation, and as soon as the first shot was fired, its commanders changed and started controlling the battle as the parent formation had to be freed for carrying out offensive tasks. Quite messy, I think. Nonetheless, we were asked to carry out a recce and understand our roles for counterattack and reinforcement in the Hussainiwala enclave. The troops deployed in the Hussainiwala enclave were a thoroughly professional lot, with tremendous esprit de corps and dismissed the possibility of anyone making headway in their defences or needing reinforcements. During the recces, we also visited the samadhis (the originals) of Shaheed Bhagat Singh, Rajguru, and Sukhdev.

Another twist in the tale occurred when the higher commanders (based on some intelligence input) felt that Ferozepur would be attacked from the east of Hussainiwala. This was just days before the war started on 3 December. Thus, we were post haste rushed to the Dulchike village, east of Hussainiwala to take up defensive positions. It took us three to four days to dig up our defences and lay our minefields along the Dulchike bund. There must have been some very authentic source that fed this information, as even the Corps Commander visited us during this preparation time. The question that keeps bothering me, (and this in hindsight), is how on earth could an attacking formation build up and concentrate west and north of the Sutlej river without going unnoticed, and then even assault across the Sutlej. The bridging and engineering requirements would have been colossal. I think we were led up and gave too much credence and capability to this source of information as also the enemy. The proverbial fog of war was clearly evident. Till then, the Mamdot Bulge had never been mentioned by any commander up the chain. We had not even been asked to conduct a map study of the area.

On 3 December, finally, the balloon went up. I remember Colonel K.C. Tewari was with me in my company HQ, sipping tea, when the first shells started landing in Hussainiwala and the township of Ferozepur. It was getting dark, and the artillery shells were pouring in Hussainiwala along with machine gun fire. It was my first experience of actual war and, let me admit, the feeling wasn't pleasant. This feeling got more accentuated as the exodus of villagers in the border area began. The locals came in tractors, trollies, bullock carts, bicycles, on foot and whatever means of transportation they could lay their hands on. Men, women, and children with whatever household assets they could take with them kept moving past us throughout the night, hoping to find safer and more secure areas away from the international border. Panic and fear had gripped the locals, and they just wanted to make a quick getaway.

We had got into a stand-to position expecting to be attacked, but the real action was taking place in the Hussainiwala enclave. The attack never happened; it just couldn't have—not that night or on the days and nights that followed. Feeble attempts were made to reinforce the Hussainiwala enclave, but it was pointless—the enemy had captured the northern end of the bridge and was effectively dominating any and every movement on the bridge by observation and fire. During this reinforcement, one of our tanks fell into the Sutlej river. I learnt later that the crew, or most of it, managed to get away with injuries, but the tank was retrieved only after the ceasefire. To cut a long story short, Hussainiwala fell the same night that it was attacked, on 3/4 December. The unit deployed in the enclave was so confident of holding on to the enclave, come what may, but they had to bite the dust rather unceremoniously. They suffered heavy casualties and several of them were taken prisoners of war while some even jumped into the Sutlej and swam to their safety. I personally met a few such stragglers while deployed on the Dulchike bund, offered them succour and meals and told them to report to their rear location in Ferozepur. Throughout the night, heavy firing and shelling continued in Hussainiwala.

There was some reason for cheer the next morning as the Indian Air Force (IAF) got into action. Countless sorties of aircrafts pounded and strafed the enclave, inflicting heavy casualties on enemy tanks and personnel. I witnessed several scenes where the aeroplanes would fly low, release their bombs (they looked like huge kitbags) and fly out. While all this was on, the anti-aircraft (ack-ack) guns of the enemy would open up aiming to bring down the aircraft. However, to the credit of the IAF, I must admit, I did not see any of our aircraft being brought down over Hussainiwala. During those days, the transistor radio was our constant companion and whenever we got time, we would tune in to find out what the All India Radio was broadcasting (there was no FM, TV or internet then). The major focus was, of course, on East Pakistan and the Hussainiwala battle was being covered by them as '*ghamasan ki larai jari hai*'. This continued for two to three days but the fact of the matter was that this so-called intense battle was all but over on the morning of 4 December, (only a few remnants were left) barring of course the pounding of the enclave by the IAF.

I learnt of another development that took place on the night of the attack on Hussainiwala. This was blowing up of one span of the Hussainiwala bridge. As readers would be aware, strategic bridges are prepared for demolition that are blown up by the defender in the face of the enemy to impede or block his further ingress. The strategic bridge at Hussainiwala was one such reserve demolition wired up with explosives, set to be blown up should the battle situation demand. When the situation became too hot to handle, apparently, some commander and/or senior staff gave the orders for blowing up the bridge. The threat to Ferozepur, it seemed to them, had become real, and the enemy had to be thwarted at all costs. To us youngsters, this seemed too far-fetched and was a knee jerk reaction to an imaginary threat. Ferozepur was still miles away and there wasn't even a shred of evidence to suggest a build-up by the enemy of that magnitude. There was, however, no commander, or senior staff, willing to admit that they had given the orders for blowing up the bridge. Then another theory was propounded—sympathetic detonation. The theory was that with so much explosive material flying around in the vicinity, some shell or shrapnel had triggered off the detonation, leading to the blowing up of one span of the bridge accidentally. It was difficult to swallow this line of argument.

Operation Sluice Gate

This was not codenamed as such but involved the opening of one or two sluice gates in the Hussainiwala headworks. Apparently, some high official of the Government Irrigation Department raised a red flag saying that if this was not done earliest, it would either burst the headworks or flood the villages in the border area, causing great losses citing numerous technical reasons for the same. Accordingly, an operation was planned under the command of Lieutenant Colonel V.K. Dandekar (CO of 3 GUARDS[91], our sister battalion) with

[91] 3rd Battalion, Brigade of the Guards

covering fire and engineer personnel. As can be expected, this ended in a disaster. The enemy sitting on the far bank of the Hussainiwala bridge was very effectively dominating the length and breadth of the bridge (some might remember that Colonel Dandekar was a test cricketer and was the 12th man in one test match). The net result of this operation was that one sapper officer was killed and Colonel Dandekar was wounded in the leg and had to be evacuated.

The sluice gates could not be opened and there was no flooding or any other calamity, as feared, till the end of the war.

The Capture of Anuke and Kassoke

Since the anticipated attack did not happen, we were asked to abandon our defensive positions and capture these two positions in concert with the 7 Infantry Division's offensive operations in the Sejhra Bulge. It needs to be recalled that the command and control of the Hussainiwala sector were no more with this formation—in fact, it was with no one as it had been captured by the Pakistani troops. Pressure had to be built so that the enemy did not become more adventurous. These two positions were captured by our unit on 6/7 December and were a cakewalk. There was practically no resistance as the enemy had gotten embroiled in the advance of the 7 Infantry Division.

After the capture of Anuke and Kassoke, we were again pulled out and it was only then that Mamdot started figuring in our discussions, and we were asked to capture and clear the bulge. We were given just two days of preparation time to commence our attack, which included movement time from the south of Sejhra in Pakistan to Rangewala in the Mamdot Bulge. Just one more day of additional recce would have saved us from several casualties and heavens would not have fallen.

The reader needs to appreciate that in the space of a two-week war, the battalion first occupied defences on the Dulchike bund, cleared Anuke and Kassoke and then cleared the Mamdot enclave.

As I think of concluding this article, the major issue that stands out is relegating the primary role, viz., the defence of Ferozepur and the various approaches to it in favour of making limited gains. Fifty years later, very few people remember Mamdot or Sejhra (except the units or formations who took part in the operations) but the loss of Hussainiwala still rankles our minds. The enemy had removed the statues of the three shaheeds and had paraded them as war trophies in the cities of Kasur and Lahore, as also in other places. The present statues located in the enclave were remade by our artisans and placed after Pakistan had to withdraw from the area, post the Shimla Peace Accord. Another major issue that springs to mind is the reactive nature of operations the formations were asked to perform. The hub of all this was the attack at Hussainiwala headworks. To my mind, had Hussainiwala not happened, the Ferozepur sector would not even have figured in the war. Contingency planning consequent to its loss would have cleared many cobwebs in the military planners' minds. Since no military commander ever thought that the enemy would capture it, not even subconsciously, very little thought or planning was done on this aspect. At best, even if it came up, it must have been glossed over. Today, the formations and units who were major participants in the Ferozepur sector (including my own unit) may pull out their war diaries and try and rationalise their decisions and actions, but soldiers know that in war the first casualty that occurs is truth. Embellishments are added and the kinks are smoothened out to present the positives and paper over the negatives. The area was visited by the Chief, General Sam Manekshaw, within days of the ceasefire. After shaking hands with some of us in the Irrigation Department complex on the home side, he moved aside with a mug of tea and started staring towards the far end of the headworks where the enemy had entrenched himself. The GOC, General Kalkat, came alongside and stated that he was ready to take on the recapture of Hussainiwala if given a chance. Please remember that both shared the same regiment, 8 Gorkha Rifles, and General Kalkat had been handpicked by the Chief to lead and coordinate the operations of the Mukti Bahini in East Pakistan. The Chief shot back at him, 'Don't be silly; the whole world knows about it'. Most of us within earshot distance picked it up. While narrating this, my intention is not to decry the GOC. Most of us will probably do the same with our seniors—after all, who doesn't like to score brownie points. The intention here is only to highlight that the mention of the loss of Hussainiwala touched a raw nerve right up the chain of command.

Conclusion

The nation was in a celebratory mood—we had attained a decisive victory and had created a new nation. Never since World War II had so much been achieved in such a swift and short war. The two-nation theory had fallen flat. The icing on the cake was the 93,000 prisoners whom we had captured after the abject surrender of the Pakistani Army in Eastern Pakistan. The whole world was paying us accolades for freeing millions of people who had been long oppressed by Yahya Khan and his military regime. The political and military leadership of the country were on a high that had never been seen before. All our shortcomings got drowned in the celebrations that took place in India and Bangladesh. Sheikh Mujibur Rehman had been released by Pakistan to become the first Prime Minister of Bangladesh. To summarise, everyone was rejoicing and for a very good reason. The most significant takeaway of the two-week 1971 war, for us young officers, who were in our early or mid-twenties, was that we had been transformed from rookies into war veterans.

At Jaloke Dhuan, a day after ceasefire

General Manekshaw at Hussainiwala
Headworks soon after ceasefire

Brigadier Vijay Rai, VSM (Retired) was commissioned into 15 DOGRA. He later commanded it in the mid-1980s during the counterinsurgency operations. During the 1971 operations, he was a Rifle Company Commander and was awarded the Mention-in-Despatches. During his service, he served on instructional assignments in the Defence Services Staff College, Indian Military Training Team (IMTRAT) in Bhutan and the Counterinsurgency School. He commanded a brigade as part of the Strike Corps. He has carried out operations in staff assignments in the Northeast and has also served in J&K.

The War as I Saw it

Major General P.J.S. Sandhu

I was posted as Staff Captain 'Q' with HQ 16 (Independent) Armoured Brigade (16 (I) AB) which was raised at Faizabad in 1969 and had moved to Patiala in 1970 to take over the regiments of 1 Armoured Brigade, namely 16th Light Cavalry (16 CAVALRY), 4 Horse (4 H) and 17 Poona Horse (17 H). All these regiments were equipped with Centurion Mark VII tanks. Brigadier (later Chief of Army Staff) Arun Vaidya was the Brigade Commander in 1971.

Our Move to the Operational Area and Deployment

It was sometime towards the end of August 1971 that I was suddenly asked to take the brigade advance and harbour parties to Pathankot to marry up with the advance elements of HQ 1 Corps, who were also moving in at the same time. From the beginning of September, regimental trains started arriving at Madhopur, and by the end of October, the brigade had moved into its Concentration Area, which happened to be Kharka Nala, northeast of Sambha. Just before the war, 16 CAVALRY[92] was detached from the brigade, and 18 RAJPUTANA RIFLES[93] (TOPAZ APCs[94]) was allotted to the brigade.

Relief Joins and the War Starts

Sometime in the October of 1971, the posting order of my relief had been received, and he was to reach Pathankot on 3 December. I received him at the Pathankot railway station, and we reached our brigade location at around 7 p.m. On reaching there, we learnt that the war had started. That evening, at dinner in the brigade field mess, a conversation began about a shortage of first line transport with the units. Brigadier Vaidya suggested that the officers' messes could be offloaded in the Concentration Area itself, and these vehicles could be used for carrying ammunition and fuel. Orders were issued immediately that the officers' mess vehicles, including the brigade HQ, would be offloaded and used for carrying ammunition and fuel for the tanks. This was to be Brigadier Vaidya's approach throughout the war.

Further, he had his essential personal kit packed in a kit bag and a haversack which were to accompany him in the tank. It is to his credit that he operated from the Track Group (command and control tanks) throughout the war. He never came back to his HQ and it was always the brigade main HQ that moved up to the location of the Track Group as and when the operational situation allowed. This was the main reason for the success of operations by 16 (I) AB.

The next day, I took my relief around to all the logistics units of the brigade and also completed whatever handing and taking over was to be done. By the afternoon of 4 December, we were able to report to my boss that the handing and taking over was complete; I also sought permission to leave for my regiment, 8th Light Cavalry

---

92 16th Cavalry Regiment

93 18th Battalion, The Rajputana Rifles

94 Armoured Personnel Carriers

(8 CAVALRY). I was ushered before the Brigade Commander. After listening to me, he said 'The war has started. Your relief will be of little use to us and you will be of little use to your regiment. So you better stay on.' A signal was immediately sent to the Army HQ that the officer was being retained as an additional officer till further orders. Naturally, I was feeling quite dejected at being denied a lifetime of an opportunity to fight a war from a tank.

On the night of 4 December 1971, the brigade moved from the Concentration Area to the Forward Assembly Area, a few kilometres north of the International Border (IB) and remained in dispersal during the day. The Brigade 'A' vehicles, numbering about 150, had to be routed through Sambha, which was a big bottleneck as a lot of convoys were moving on the Pathankot Jammu highway that night. My successor and I, with the help of the Brigade Provost Unit, managed to do that without any hold-up. The brigade was grouped with 54 Infantry Division of 1 Corps and was launched into the Shakargarh Bulge along axis Darman –Zafarwal on the night of 4/5 December 1971. On our left flank was 2 (I) AB which was equipped with T-55 tanks.

Foray into the Night

My relief and I constituted the Brigade Rear HQ. Our main job was to control and coordinate the movement of the brigade essential vehicles (EVCs), which had to move every night after last night to replenish the units and be back by the first light. After two to three days, my relief had got a grip on the things and was able to handle all the responsibilities quite effectively. Thus, I was left free to roam around the battlefield and enjoyed doing that very much. It was around 8 December that I was called by the Brigade Major (BM) late in the evening and tasked to go and locate 91 (I) Recce Squadron (equipped with AMX-13 tanks), which had now been placed under command 16 (I) AB. As there was no communication with the squadron, it was to be physically contacted and guided to the Brigade Area of the operations. The area indicated to me was about 20 km to our east and six to eight kilometres into the enemy territory.

So, feeling quite excited for having got a task, I set out immediately in my jeep into the night with a driver and a radio set. After about 10 kilometres, while crossing a nullah, the jeep stalled and would not start. After trying a few times, I got out of the jeep and decided to walk to reach the squadron. I must have walked hardly a kilometre that the jeep caught up with me and we drove on into the darkness. At one place in the enemy territory, we crossed some tank tracks. In torchlight, I was able to identify these as AMX-13 tank tracks as I was from an AMX-13 regiment myself. We followed these tracks without lights. Suddenly, out of the darkness, a voice shouted, '*Thum! Kaun ata ha?*' I recognised the voice instantly; it was Naib Risaldar Sarup Singh with whom I had served in 8 CAVALRY. He was now posted with the 91 (I) Recce Squadron, the sub-unit that I was looking for. It was just providence and some invisible hand that had guided me!

Naib Risaldar Sarup Singh guided me to his Squadron HQ which was located just about two to three kilometres from there. At around 5 a.m., I met up with the Squadron Commander and conveyed to him the orders. During the night, the squadron had taken part in an attack on Chak Masrur Bara Bhai which had just been captured. The Squadron Commander explained that four to five of his tanks had developed leaks in their fuel tanks after firing armour-piercing discarding sabot (APDS) ammunition, and these needed to be replaced. As this was a recurring problem with AMX-13 tanks, an adequate number of spare fuel tanks were being carried in 'B' vehicles which had been fetched and were in the process of being changed. Since this would take about two to three hours, I decided to go round the village of Chak Masrur Bara Bhai which had just been captured. After explaining the mission to the Squadron Commander, I set course for my Brigade HQ. By

11 a.m. I was able to report to the BM as mission accomplished. The squadron also fetched up later in the afternoon.

A Visit to the Regiment

By now I was getting a little frustrated for sitting out of the war. So, on 11 December, I decided to drive up to my regiment (8 CAVALRY) which was about a two-hour drive from our location. I met the Commanding Officer and told him that my relief had been there for a week now, and I wanted to return to the regiment immediately. He straight away sent a signal to the Army HQ saying that the officer was being retained as an additional officer and his services were urgently required in the regiment. Having done my bit, I returned to the Brigade HQ but did not share this information with anyone. Sure enough, two days later there was a signal from Army HQ to relieve me forthwith. It was decided that I could leave on the afternoon of 15 December.

Farewell

On 15 December, I paid a visit to the Regional HQs of 17 H and 4 H who were in their operational locations as there was a lull in the battle and said goodbye to my friends. The Brigade HQ wanted to lunch with me out from the operational location, which was a great honour. While we were at it, I noticed that Brigadier Vaidya and the commanding officers were sitting on the ground a little distance away with their maps spread out. I later learnt that final orders for the establishment of a bridgehead across the Basantar river in the area of Jarpal–Barapind, which was to be carried out that night, were in progress. After a frugal, but most affectionate lunch, I left for my regiment on the afternoon of 15 December and was, thus, to miss out on being part of the famous tank battle of Basantar which took place the following morning.

Back in the Regiment

I reached 8 CAVALRY Regimental HQ near Ranbirsinghpura just as it was getting dark. The regiment had been equipped with AMX-13 tanks when I had left the regiment in November 1969, now they had been converted to Vijayanta tanks. Since I had not done any conversion, I spent the better part of 16 December getting familiar with the new tank. Dhaka fell on 16 December and Mrs Indira Gandhi offered a ceasefire to Pakistan, effective from 8 p.m. on 17 December. On the evening of 16 December, we listened to General Yahya Khan on the Pakistani radio, spewing venom and promising a thousand years of war! The next morning on 17 December, I was told to report to Alfa Squadron and take over as the squadron's Second-in-Command (2IC).

The Short-Lived Thrill and the Ceasefire

I was feeling quite thrilled to be back with the squadron where I had served as a tank troop leader on commissioning and, thus, made haste to reach and report to the Squadron Commander. The squadron was deployed just about one to two kilometres from the IB, and it was a wonderful feeling to be back in the turret of a tank. We could see Pakistani tanks behind an earthen bandh, deployed at a distance of two to three kilometres. In the afternoon, a tank duel developed, and we kept engaging the tanks at long ranges. We did see some flashes but I can't really say if we had destroyed any tanks that day. However, we had suffered no tank casualty, I am sure of. The firing stopped at last light and the guns fell silent at 8 p.m. The ceasefire had been accepted by Pakistan. The rest is history.

Major General P.J.S. Sandhu (Retired) was commissioned into the 8th Light Cavalry on 15 June 1966 and later commanded the 47 Armoured Regiment. During his service, he commanded an independent armoured brigade, an armoured division and retired as the Chief of Staff of a Strike Corps on 31 July 2003. He participated in the War of 1971 as a Captain in the Shakargarh Sector. Post his retirement, he worked as the Deputy Director and Editor of the United Service Institution of India from 2007–2016.

Tribulations of Ammunition Supply Chain in War

Major General Subash Bindra

The Shakargarh Salient is favourable to Pakistan as there are multiple launch pads possible for reasonably attractive objectives in India. Concomitantly, it required the Indian Army (IA) to put on ground a larger quantum of force for its defensive operations.

In 1971, to support the IA operations, the ammunition echelons were located along the line of communication of National Highway 1A Pathankot–Samba–Jammu Road. This is a slender strip of flat terrain with no depth, hence the ammunition stocking units were located practically in the show window. For the protection of these VPs, AD cover had been provided as also few infantry elements.

On 4 December 1971, at the outbreak of hostilities, I was posted at Army Ordnance Corps (AOC) School, Jabalpur. The Adjutant sent for me and informed me that I was to proceed to Unchi Bassi. He didn't say when or give me a reason. Blissfully, I continued to think that since instructors were selected to go abroad for equipment orientation and I had got an AX[95] on a course earlier, that 'mera number bhi aagya'. Military establishments anywhere are in remote unheard of locations; and Unchi Bassi was to be no exception.

Alas, a few hours later, as I collected the move order and the railway warrant, the destination was entered as Unchi Bassi, the clerk explained the details, a station after Jalandhar so we were in India.

This was to be my first separation after marriage. Hence, before I left, my wife and I went to see a 6–9 p.m. movie at the movie hall and then, at 10 p.m., I boarded the train to Delhi. The next night, a change of train and a journey for another 6 hours reached me to my destination. I disembarked at 4 a.m. It was pitch dark, and a straight drop of 7 feet from the rail compartment to the terra firma as there was no platform. The receiving officer handed me a 9-mm Sten gun, as that was to be my personal weapon from then on. On reaching the unit, the first air raid siren at 5 a.m. shook me a kilometre away. That is when I realised: this was no training film from WWII or *The Longest Day* that we had seen at the academy. This was war. For real.

The 18 Field Ammunition Depot (FAD), containing 30,000 tonnes of ammunition, were rightfully isolated. Being far in the rear, there was no threat by enemy action on the ground, other than sabotage. The only damage that could take place was by air raids, hence the emphasis on 'trench drill', rehearsed time and again till the end of operations.

The Commanding Officer (CO) would take frequent rounds in the day and at night to ensure the troops were in their trenches. However, on the night of 6 December at 10 p.m., the siren went off. It was too cold to even move a muscle. But, as certain as death, the CO arrived and shone the torch towards the trench outside our tent. There was no one inside! 'Where were the two new arrivals'—the CO was able to surmise the reality of us not being in the trench but elsewhere.

---

[95] A grading on a training course. Persons with AX grade are recommended to be later posted as instructors on subsequent courses.

The next morning, I left early for the Jalandhar station to escort important items. My tentmate was in front of the CO and his non-military explanation was unhelpful. He said, 'Sir, in the dark, had I jumped into the trench, perhaps I would sustain an ankle injury or land on a snake. Hence, I thought it would be more prudent to remain in bed. I also thought that as the air raids, were either at dusk or during dawn, the alert sound at 10 p.m. was perhaps by accident.'

The CO was peeved—it was not even funny.

By the morning of 7 December, the action on the front seemed to be brewing. I had received orders to move to the next destination at 11 a.m. Just as I was preparing to leave, that afternoon, three junior officers who were dining at the mess with me, decided to host a farewell lunch, as is customary, notwithstanding that I had been there barely for 48 hours—any excuse to enjoy the winter sun in Punjab with a glass of beer in hand. The froth in the second round had just about settled when enemy sabres appeared out of nowhere and flew right overhead; this time there was no warning. Though we heard the siren but it was only when a fly-past by the enemy aircraft had taken place. It was low and deafening. The payload of bombs was released after overflying the mess, 700 metres away and outside the perimeter of fencing. We were just about recovering from the close shave when the CO walked in and once again found that we were not in the trenches! Oh my God—we had committed the same folly yet again. Ignominy, perpetuated, he saw that each of us had a glass of beer in hand. I had wondered, then, if I would land in such kinds of trouble for the rest of my life.

With the IAF Combat Air Patrol by the Gnats arriving in a few minutes, it gave little time to the Pakistani forces to turn around for a second run. Nevertheless, we did have many large craters but all were outside the perimeter. In the words of the Param Vir Chakra awardee, Nirmaljeet Sekhon, 'Gnats in aerial combat were superior to the Sabres.'

I wondered what was with the Sabre aircraft bomb runs, twice a day, both at dusk and dawn, that despite so much effort on one single vital area (VA)[96], there were no hits. This was despite the enemy ground liaison officer (GLO) (a hawker) positioned outside the depot, who was later captured. The interrogation revealed, that whilst the GLO aligned the aircraft run-in with the depot, on arriving at the target area, the pilots could not visually confirm the target. The recently built accommodation was not shown on the maps in their possession either, as it was of an earlier vintage. The topography had changed, new landmarks had emerged, leaving the pilot perplexed about the bomb release line. So, in effect, they would simply unload by approximation towards the end of their run. I guess the lesson learned is the importance of real-time intelligence, as is now available—the Balakot[97] type.

Had even one bomb dropped on the stocks, the entire asset of explosives would have gone off. Its impact would be massive enough to be seen at Jalandhar and even by the enemy across in the Bulge[98]. Needless to say, I would not be alive to recount these events.

Ammunition Sub Depot (ASD) at Pathankot

This sub-unit had been intended to ab initio look after the communication zone sub-area units with about 2,000 tonnes of ammunition. With induction around the Bulge, the dependency of units on this ammunition echelon shot up. Thus, when the build-up started, we had fewer dugouts and plinths and less area to maintain prescribed safety distances as per the UN Hazard Division Classification Safety Norms. In an ideal situation, an ASD is so designed that it can hold 7,000 tonnes of ammunition, with four officers and cater for a corps. But what was happening here was far

---

[96] The area which may need protection of Air Defence guns

[97] The Balakot air strike by The Indian Air Force on February 26, 2019, that destroyed a major terror training camp of the Jaish-e-Mohammed in Balakot, Pakistan.

[98] Shakargarh Bulge is also known as Shakargarh Salient.

from it; we only had one officer, and I had been called to augment the staff. The ground area of an AP, too, was extended to hold an increased tonnage. Everything got stretched. It was quite clear that we were to make-do with what we had.

Now, with a corps plus dependency on the sub depot, it was business akin to pre-Christmas sales at Macy's or Harrods. We were receiving vehicles filled with ammunition to replenish the expenditure in the defensive battle and for a stock build-up for the subsequent offensive.

On any given night, we had about 75 vehicles moving, with no lights switched on, attempting to reach designated plinths in the small area of an ASD. Luckily, we had no accidents, but the density of traffic in such a small area was worrying. The only parallel that I can draw is with Tokyo's Shibuya Crossing, the world's busiest pedestrian crossing, where thousands of people cross the multi-cornered intersection at a time. Despite converging in a mass from all directions, pedestrians skilfully manage to avoid colliding with one another.

The biggest challenge for any ammunition holding echelon is to ensure the safety of stocks. It is guided by the United Nations Organization Hazard Class and Division (HC/D) and consequently, safety distances are to be calculated and maintained across intra-storage sites, such as between magazines and plinth stacks, and outside infrastructure to limit the damage. It demanded watchful manual control on the type and quantity of ammunition, since there were no computers.

The next hot spot was the vehicle-marshalling area outside the depot, where the drivers would rest, prepare hot meals and move ahead. This activity threw up its own set of challenges which could not be imagined and planned for, in advance. The darkness contributed to the confusion. Vehicles that had collected ammunition would await others to complete their numbers and then move out as a convoy. Even if this sounded easy, it wasn't so in reality. At night, the marking tapes that are used to guide vehicles into predefined Arrival and Departure areas, would be run over. This was primarily due to unfamiliar controls set up by faujis. Imagine the T3 Terminal at the Indira Gandhi International Airport, New Delhi, with arrivals and departures happening at the same floor level. Picture the scenario if flights arrive and take-off only at night and the lights in the passenger area are switched off—this is exactly what we had witnessed on each of the 14 nights that the War lasted.

The accounting also posed a serious challenge. The vehicles from supplying at the base depot, loaded with fresh ammunition would arrive at the marshalling area around 2 a.m. At about the same time, the convoy commander of the collection party from the formation up ahead, having finished collection, whilst looking for his vehicles, would commandeer the incoming vehicles that were yet to be unloaded, and merge it along with his departing convoy. For a thela driver, a fauji in uniform was enough authority to concede to; all soldiers looked the same to him. It would be interesting to understand the impact on accounting. Who was to clear the receipt voucher? The vehicle which was to be unloaded had erroneously moved on ahead to the forward Ammunition Point (AP)[99] without entering the ASD and getting duly documented.

Another challenge was posed by the empty vehicles arriving from the formation—though they had to be replenished, these vehicles would wait in the marshalling area as the driver had found a sanctuary of no work and reduced threat there. There were also instances when drivers of vehicles with ammunition loaded from our sub depot would join the convoy comprising the returning empty vehicles to the main depot at Unchi Bassi.

Thus, it may be surmised that there were plenty of unintended opportunities for vehicles to move in and out, and not necessarily to the desired destination, as there were no MPs or traffic control.

---

[99] It is a designated area from where vehicles collect ammunition.

At the forward APs, similar instances were replicated. Such mix-up of convoy vehicles resulted in artillery shells and its matching fuses reaching the neighbouring artillery unit. It so happened that the mines went to an Engineer Regiment and the mine fuses to another. By the time the war ended, our 'Bermuda Triangle' had created so much chaos that we had dealt with a massive number of trucks in and out. A significant number of truckloads of ammunition had been unaccounted for or had simply vanished. We could not find any receipt vouchers for these.

The gravity of the situation demanded that these challenges be addressed. Thus, in late January 1972, we started tracking the journey of each of the vehicles. After linking each vehicle registration number to its entry at a particular ammunition echelon, we still had six vehicles that we could not connect. Where on earth did it reach? Was it at the 36, 39 or 54 Div AP or Corps AP, Amritsar Sub Depot or the units directly? Attribute it to initiative, expediency, and exigency.

The Indian Army also appointed auditors in February 1972, and a second tracking round began. We managed to track the vehicles and their loads and obtain an 'All Clear' in four weeks. Whilst we are proud to have done well, only we can pat ourselves. No logistician returns after the war, with scalps in hand, to be lauded and applauded. Anyways, it was full of experiences previously not encountered, which I am proud to record.

In all fairness, our victory would have been incomplete without the grit and determination of several brave Indian Air Force officers. Group Captain V.K. Bhatia (late) of the 'H' Squadron and his band of pilots, who were located at the airbase in Pathankot, were flying Gnats and provided the Combat Air Patrol (CAP), which kept the Pakistani forces at bay. They were the ones who kept us safe. What a pilot he was! I am glad that our paths crossed during and after the operations, whilst at Pathankot.

Worthy of mention were two more Ordnance establishments

close by, their contribution was equally noteworthy viz. The Mobile Bath and Laundry Unit and the Dry Cleaning Section each with their own war establishment authority. These are mini-units but well thought of as part of Corps Zone entity. The troops would look forward to their visits to these and get indulged upon. Whilst they did not match the creature comforts of renowned bathing houses for troops as Baden Baden in the Black Forest for the Roman soldiers, or the Onsen of Japan, with regular hot water supply, nevertheless they were a welcome indulgence.

Looking back, I reckon that life gives one the opportunity to live on the edge. If one takes head on with the honest commitment of a soldier, the path certainly becomes easier. Nevertheless, destiny has its part too and, thus, what is destined will come your way.

Major General Subash Bindra (Retired) is an alumnus of the National Defence College (NDC 35) and Colcom Higher Command (HC-18) and was commissioned in the Army Ordnance Corps. During his service spanning more than three decades, he has served in J&K and Eastern Command. He has also been in instructional appointments at College of Combat and College of Materials Management, Jabalpur. He has served as Director, Operational Logistics at AHQ. His notable contributions include the Study of Surplus Inventory and Disposal to yield a revenue of 3,000 crores. He was awarded the Vishisht Seva Medal for ensuring accident-free repairs of defective ammunition in remote areas.

Forward Maintenance Area in Barmer

Major General C.P. Tewari

I raised an Independent Supply Platoon in Jodhpur just before the War of 1971. Around October 1971, two Independent supply platoons jointly established a supply depot in the Forward Maintenance Area (FMA) in Barmer in Rajasthan along with other logistic units, namely the Electronics and Mechanical Engineers (EME) workshop and the Ordinance Ammunition Depot. It was the first time that an FMA was established by the Indian Army. All officers used to stay within their respective unit areas and dine from the jawan's cook-houses as no officers' mess had been set up. It was a time when everything was being hurriedly put in place on an ad hoc basis. Very few people knew the plans. The general rumour amongst the men was that we were out on an exercise!

Build Up

Our unit personnel were very hard-pressed—there were heavy

receipts of stores as part of the build-up, everyone was busy sorting out the stocks, and we were, as it is during peace, on a system of accounting. All paperwork had to be completed on a daily basis. The FMA Commander would insist we look into our security, the perimeter defence, trenches, arcs of fire, patrolling, and the like. One often heard the men talking amongst themselves, 'Scheme par ayen hai' (we are on exercise only). Hence, they found the rest of the tactical jobs of no consequence and would, instead, devote more time to their technical jobs. The induction of the formations started—their maintenance had commenced. Now the troops had literally no time to dig trenches, overhead shelters, and crawl trenches.

Induction of the Extra Troops

In October 1971, the FMA at Barmer was a scene of hectic activities. The build-up of logistics, in anticipation of an Indo-Pakistan conflict, had started at a feverish pitch. There were heavy receipts of full railway rakes of rations, petroleum products, ammunition and engineer stores. In November 1971, an infantry division was inducted in addition to the existing paramilitary forces. Units that were already located there and drawing their ration from our supply depot were nearly more than 15,000 troops. The maintenance of troops in a desert is a phenomenal task; every day there were new challenges that had to be resolved by us. There is an old military saying that feeding troops in the desert is a quartermaster's nightmare. The consumption of petroleum products was far more than the estimates. We started moving fuel in road tankers of the Indian Oil Corporation in bulk; the product was decanted into barrels by resorting to ad hocism in absence of proper container-filing machines. The dependent units were all on the field system of accounting, but the supply depot continued on the peace system of accounting. We had to be very careful and meticulous in our accounting procedures, keeping in view the impending audits for later.

The War

On the night of 3 December 1971, the balloon went up. Uttarlai airfield, which was adjacent to our location, about 3 km away, was bombarded by Pakistan Air Force planes. The anti-aircraft guns opened fire when the Pakistani aircrafts began firing machine guns and bombing all over the area around our unit. The whole sky was lit up and general chaos took place. The jawans were running towards their trenches which were half-heartedly prepared. A miracle took place—within a few hours the whole unit was under the ground level, with overhead shelters. The excuses of limited digging implements were all forgotten, people just dug with anything which came in their hands—even plates and mugs were good enough to scoop the loose desert sand out. Someone has rightly coined the adage, 'A week in the battlefield is more than years of training in peace'.

Raja Ram Fires

A raw recruit got hysterical on seeing live ammunition being fired. He went berserk and started running towards Jodhpur. He was caught and had to be slapped a couple of times to get him back to his senses. The next morning there was another air raid, the Pakistani aircrafts flight path was over our depot and everyone was in the trenches. After some time, an all-clear signal was sounded. The Havildar Major came with two kohkhas (fired rounds) and said, 'Sir, Sepoy Raja Ram fired two rounds at the Pakistani aircrafts which just flew over our location'. Here was an example of two opposite psyches—one jawan got hysterical and wanted to run away from the battle zone and the other was brave enough to look up and fire at the low-flying aircraft when everyone was literally hiding in their trenches with their heads huddled in between their knees.

Brave Hearts

I had another singular opportunity of operating a petroleum point for refuelling a company strength of jeeps belonging to the 10 Para Commandos, who were launched from Chachro to go behind the enemy lines on the night of 4 December. It was led by none other than Colonel Bhawani Singh (Maharaja of Jaipur) who was seen off at my petroleum point by the then Army Commander Lieutenant General G.G. Bewoor, who later become the Army Chief. There were about 120 old, refurbished Pakistani jeeps captured during the 1965 war. The 10 Para Commandos were dressed in Pakistani uniforms. It had, indeed, been a very exciting and a thrilling experience.

Move Up of the Logistics

Our ground forces pushed into the enemy territory. Indian Air Force planes mounted unprecedented pressure on Pakistan's land forces, which were facing our troops, and also carried out deep strikes on their ammunition dumps and other logistic installations. Our land forces met good success and were able to go deep into Pakistan. The Army Service Corps (ASC) Battalion had to establish forward supply, petroleum and ammunition replenishment points. We, on our part, as the supply depot, ensured that there never was any shortage of rations or petroleum products.

The Cigarette Packet

Major Krishen Bhatia was the Second-in-Command of the ASC Battalion. Later, he retired as a General and was our Director General Supplies and Transport (DGST). He was an old friend of mine—we had first met in 1969 in Arunachal Pradesh. He was DQ of a brigade, where I had joined as the Composite Platoon Commander. He would often visit us in the FMA to oversee the withdrawal of ration and petroleum products by his unit from our supply depot. One night he came in a tearing hurry and asked us to issue seven day's ration for the entire division. This was in addition to the normal maintenance and reserve ration already held by the units. The requirement was in anticipation of opening a replenishment point further into the Pakistan territory as they were visualising a deep thrust by our troops. The problem was that there were no indents (demands) and also no authority for us to make such an issue. Major Bhatia insisted that we oblige him, come what may because his Commanding Officer (CO) had already committed the Divisional Commander and now Major Bhatia's job was at stake. The other officer sitting with me, Captain Nawal Kishen, said, 'Sir, what if these rations get destroyed in enemy action? Then the noose will be around our neck—we will be questioned as to how this ration leave the Supply Depot for forward areas when there was no authority to make such a huge issue of rations.' Major Krishen Bhatia was exasperated but not be outdone. He pulled out a Charminar cigarette packet from his pocket, threw away the two leftover cigarettes from the packet, tore the packet and flattened it. On its reverse side, he wrote a receipt for the advance withdrawal of seven days of ration for the complete divisional strength and put his signature on it and said, 'Here, Chotu, keep this receipt, it is Krishen Bhatia's word of honour. If anything goes wrong, I will stand by you guys'. I do not know why but suddenly Nawal Krishen and I threw our caution to the wind. Maybe it was the innovative receipt on the packet and the sentimental way in which Major Bhatia gave his word of honour. Also, we were all at war and in war, nobody wanted to be seen as impeding the requirement of the troops. After all, we had been taught that we must uphold the motto of our great corps, '*Seva Asmakam Dharama*'.

All Lights On

A ceasefire was declared after a few days and life became more relaxed, normal maintenance of troops resumed but we had a dependent strength of nearly two divisions. We actually required three times the strength and capability than what we had then. With God's grace, there was not a single occasion when the ASC failed, not only in this sector but elsewhere too. We even arranged to airdrop water, fuel and ammunition in helicopters. Captain Nawal Krishen and I were sharing the same tent. Our *sahayaks* and the jeep drivers use to live in a tent at a stone's throw distance from our tent in the supply depot administrative area.

At dusk, a peculiar silence would descend on our campsite when everyone used to prepare to rest for the night. At times one could hear our drivers and *sahayaks* talking amongst themselves. In the silence of the desert, sound travels far and clear. I remember one day both the drivers were talking and, like all MT drivers of the ASC, they were also gossiping in their typical driver lingo, '*Yaar, jab se ceasefire hua hai mera to 4*4 top gear laga hua hai. Sare din saab forward area mein ghumta hai*'. (Ever since this ceasefire, I am in 4*4 top gear; my sahib tours the whole day in the forward areas.) Yet another oft-heard sentence was, '*Jab sae yeh naya langri (cook) aaya hai, khaana bahut swaad hai*' (Ever since this new cook has come the food is really tasty). The second driver would then interject, '*Khaana to swaad hai, par khate wakt headlight on ho jati hai aur subhah saali taillight on ho jati hai.*' (Yes, agreed, but at night when we are eating, the headlights get switched on and in the morning the damn taillight gets on).

The Noose Tightens

After three to four days, the OC of Charlie Company of the ASC Battalion, Major R.P. Singh, came with a long face and dropped a ton of bricks. The seven days advance ration dumped ahead had been strafed by the Pakistani Air force planes and Major Krishen Bhatia had also been injured during that strafing. It was a calamity for us in the supply depot. The noose which we were dreading seemed to be tightening around our necks. Major R.P. Singh conveyed Major Bhatia's assurance that we need not worry, come what may. He said that indents would be placed on us, and the units would be asked to take the ration on charge and then write them off as destroyed due to enemy action. Relief was in sight but not till we got our indents. After a fortnight of the ceasefire, we did get the indents, post which not only us but our complete staff also heaved a sigh of relief. I wonder, though—what if things had gone wrong? Ah! Never Mind!

Major General C.P. Tewari (Retired) followed his father's footsteps to join the National Defence Academy as an Air Force cadet in the year 1961. Due to medico-technical reasons, he had to change his service choice to the Army. He was commissioned into the Army Service Corps on 15th June 1966 and has served in the high-altitude mountains of both, North and North-Eastern India, also in the jungles of Assam and Arunachal. During the War of 1971, he served in the western deserts. He rendered commendable service in the militant affected areas of Punjab, J&K and Nagaland. He has been an instructor at his alma mater, The ASC School, when it was at Bareilly. He has attended courses of instruction including the Long Petroleum Course with Indian Oil Corporation at Bombay, the Long Defence Management Course at Secunderabad.

IV
Appendix

Captain R.N. Gupta, VrC

Brigadier Mohinder Nath Mahajan

Captain Ravinder Nath Gupta was born in Varanasi on 20 December 1945. He completed Senior Cambridge from the Oak Groves School, Mussoorie, in 1960, where his mother was the principal. He completed inter-science from the Ewing Christian College, Allahabad, in 1962 and soon after joined 28th NDA Course, Fox Squadron, at the National Defence Academy, Khadakwasla, in July 1962, where I had also joined a few days earlier. His father (Late) Shri J.W. Gupta was an officer with the Indian Railways. He had two younger brothers, Virender who joined the Indian Navy (through NDA) and is settled in the USA, and the youngest who joined Indian Military Academy (IMA), Dehradun but unfortunately died in a swimming accident. R.N., as he was affectionately called, was very good both in academics and sports, had a dashing personality and used to stand out among the cadets. It was only after our stay together for about two years that we learnt he was a Christian—his name and conduct gave no such indication! Also, in those days, we never gave a thought to caste or religion. Captain R.N. Gupta was commissioned in the Madras Sappers on 15 June 1966.

During his formative years, after the Young Officers' (YOs) Course 27-C Degree at College of Military Engineering (CME), Pune, he served with the 9 Engineer Regiment in Northeast Frontier Agency (NEFA), now Arunachal Pradesh, as a Platoon Commander (Second Lieutenant). He did his degree engineering course from CME and joined 9 Engineer Regiment again as Captain at Lucknow in January 1971. I was also commissioned in Madras Sappers, and so we were together during the YOs and degree engineering course. I joined 201 Engineer Regiment at Allahabad in January 1971 and both 'The Nine' and 'Two Not One' Engineer Regiments were part of the same formation, that is, 416 Engineer Brigade located in Lucknow.

While 9 Engineer Regiment moved for operations from Lucknow and was allotted to 54 Infantry Division, I, as part of 201 Engineer Regiment, moved from Allahabad and continued to be part of 416 Engineer Brigade. I met R.N. last in October 1971 in Meerut during the road move from our respective locations to Punjab.

During the Indo-Pak War of 1971, Captain R.N. Gupta was one of the Sub-task Force Commanders for breaching a minefield in the Basantar area, which was a part of the Western Sector. The success of the operation depended upon the completion of vehicle safe lanes through the enemy minefield so that an armoured regiment could be inducted into the area before the enemy launched a counterattack. The area was continuously under enemy artillery and mortar fire and information regarding the depth of the enemy minefield was not available. Considering the shortage of time, Captain R.N. Gupta volunteered to lead a small party on foot, on a wide outflanking move, to ascertain the far edge of the minefield. With this move, the party was able to get the final information within an hour.

Subsequently, when the enemy attacked, Captain R.N. Gupta personally guided our tanks through the cleared minefield with complete disregard for his safety. Later, while engaged in the maintenance of the safe lane, he was hit by an enemy artillery shell resulting in his death on 17 December 1971. In this action, he displayed courage and devotion to duty that is beyond words. His gallantry, determination and leadership were, indeed, of a high order. For his bravery, he was awarded the Vir Chakra posthumously.

As per the then prevalent system, he was buried at the Christian Cemetery in Jammu with full military honours. The passing away of a course mate was sad for all of us, but the consolation was that he died defending the borders of our country. I have had discussions with Lieutenant General B.T. Pandit, PVSM, VrC (who retired as the Adjutant General of Indian Army), the then Commanding Officer (CO) of Captain R.N. Gupta, who described R.N. as a dashing, knowledgeable Sapper officer and a 'leader of men' who was always willing to take on challenges.

Colonel Vivek Mundkur, our course mate and a Madras Sapper was posted in Jammu in 1988. He visited the Garrison Cemetery at Jammu and found that the grave was in a state of disrepair and a bad shape. He got the grave renovated with the help of Brigadier Sukhdev Singh, who was commanding an engineer regiment in Nagrota.

Planning for the golden jubilee celebrations of commissioning of the course in June 2016 commenced around March 2016. I hit upon the idea of renovating the grave of Captain R.N. Gupta through his regiment. I decided that I would announce the execution of the work carried out as a surprise to the course during the celebrations.

I requested Major General Surinder Sharma (Veteran), ex-CO of the 9 Engineer Regiment, who had served with me in 201 Engineer Regiment and was later my student at the Defence Services Staff College (DSSC), Wellington. He got things moving but 9 Engineer Regiment was located thousands of kilometres away. Finally, the grave was nicely done up in March 2017 and I informed my coursemates (28 NDA, 37 IMA and 21 Tech), which was a pleasant surprise for all of them. Regular contact was also maintained with Mr Virender Gupta, the younger brother of R.N. and the only living family member, who is settled in the USA. He informed me that the citation and Vir Chakra of Captain R.N. Gupta had been presented to the Madras Engineering Group Centre at Bangalore.

Captain R.N. Gupta at 27-C Degree, CME Pune

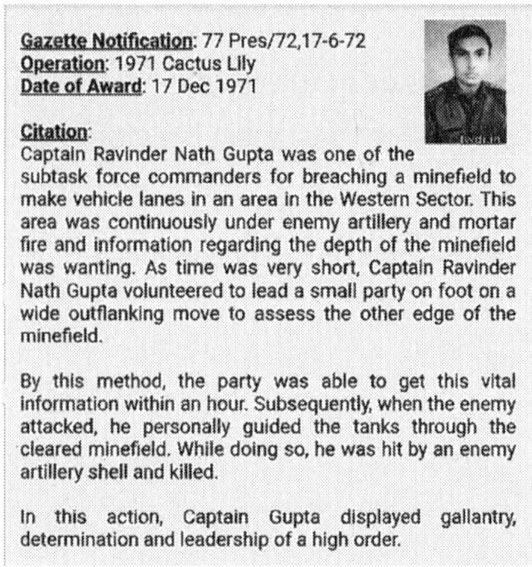

Gazette Notification: 77 Pres/72,17-6-72
Operation: 1971 Cactus Lily
Date of Award: 17 Dec 1971

Citation:
Captain Ravinder Nath Gupta was one of the subtask force commanders for breaching a minefield to make vehicle lanes in an area in the Western Sector. This area was continuously under enemy artillery and mortar fire and information regarding the depth of the minefield was wanting. As time was very short, Captain Ravinder Nath Gupta volunteered to lead a small party on foot on a wide outflanking move to assess the other edge of the minefield.

By this method, the party was able to get this vital information within an hour. Subsequently, when the enemy attacked, he personally guided the tanks through the cleared minefield. While doing so, he was hit by an enemy artillery shell and killed.

In this action, Captain Gupta displayed gallantry, determination and leadership of a high order.

Gazette Notification OP Cactus Lilly

Lieutenant General B.T. Pandit at the War Memorial saluting the plaque of IC 16871 Captain R.N. Gupta, VrC, 9 Engineering Regiment

Brigadier Mohinder Nath Mahajan (Retired) was commissioned into the Madras Sappers on 15 June 1966. During his service, he served in Ladakh, J&K and the Thar Desert (Rajasthan). He commanded an Engineer Regiment Bridge (PMS). He introduced computerisation in the Border Roads Organisation (BRO), has been an Instructor at the DSSC, Wellington and has been the Chief Engineer of a corps. Before superannuation, he served in the Quarter Master General Branch in the Army Headquarters.

Captain G.G.K. Panicker

Major Pradeep Sharma

History and its recording are both vital. Especially during war. The validity of the above precept could not be better proven than by recounting the story of our course mate, Captain G.G.K. Panicker, a Bengal Sapper. Panicker joined 37 Indian Military Academy (IMA) in June 1965, after completing his pre-IMA qualification as part of the 7 Operational Training Unit (OTU) course. Panicker, as he was usually called, and I, did the 38 Young Officers' (YOs) course at the College of Military Engineering (CME), Poona in 1967–1968. We reported back to the CME for the degree course and were part of the 27-C Engineer Officers Degree Course between 3 January 1968 and 2 January 1971. We were also roommates at the CME for several months during the course.

Panicker got married to Padmini in 1969 while undergoing training. Their son, Prasanth, was born on 16 July 1970. The family was last together in July 1971 in Alleppey (now Alappuzha) Kerala, when Panicker went on leave from 74 Independent Field Company where he had been posted after the degree course. It was early in January 1972 that we got the very tragic and sad news of Panicker having become a war casualty on 17 December 1971 in Kargil. His wife, with an 18-month-old son, was unable to even be present for his last rites. There is absolutely nothing available as history in 74 Field Company, or in Bengal Sappers HQ and Centre at Roorkee to record how this brave officer passed.

Prasanth, his son, later joined NDA (Golf Squadron) and was commissioned into the Indian Navy in 1991. While leading a mountain biking expedition of the Navy, he managed to locate a memorial that had been dedicated to Panicker and two other sappers who were martyred in a minefield clearing operation. The memorial was located within the Army Service Corps (ASC) Battalion ('B' Company) supporting 121 Infantry Brigade, at the time.

Pieced together with excruciating delay, and tinged with both pride and grief, the apparent sequence of events, in Prasanth's words is:

'On 17 December 1971, during the demining operations after the ceasefire (according to the accounts that I have heard from various persons, including family members and my mother), my father undertook to rescue two jawans who had been trapped in a minefield. In the absence of the officer designated for this task, he volunteered to do this urgent rescue. During this action, one of the trapped Sappers stepped on a mine that exploded. My father suffered grievous shrapnel injuries. Yet, he refused evacuation until after the two soldiers, who were part of the mine-clearing team, were first evacuated for treatment. He died shortly thereafter, and an eyewitness reported to my mum that he went down gallantly with a smile on his face. The watch that he was wearing on his wrist got punctured with holes and debris and stopped at 3.30 p.m. (time of the explosion). This watch is now with us in Thrissur. We had limited and occasional contact from the Bengal Sappers following his valiant death for the next couple of years before things went silent. Contact was maintained with us by a couple of his

friends and course mates through visits and letters all this while. Sometime in the late 1990s, late Colonel Ramachandran (Signals), who was my father's good friend, managed to find his memorial in Kargil while travelling at great personal risk of getting shelled by the Pakistani Army and sent us some photographs. Thus, we knew that there was a small monument in my father's name. Colonel Ramachandran maintained constant contact with us till his untimely death in 2007. In June 2008, I managed to locate the same memorial (which also named 2 other jawans of his unit) in the unit lines of 'B' Company in the ASC Battalion supporting 121 Infantry Brigade in Kargil. I offered to pay for the maintenance of his memorial to the Brigade Commander. The latter was kind enough to tell me not to worry and that that he will ensure it from his end.'

It is indeed tragic and sad that a son managed to locate some detail of his father who died a martyr to the nation after nearly 37 years! I would say that this is all because we do not bother to record history as it happens. There is no effort to post history as known to some on the internet for posterity. The media (mainly the print media in the previous millennium) was never present or embedded with units in the field. Lessons are seldom or never learned and those who gave their lives for the nation go unsung, unrecorded and unremembered.

We are fortunately now in an age of the ever-present and proliferating smartphones where photographs are instantly taken and can be electronically sent in minutes. Hopefully, this lack of history and an authentic and useful record will become a thing of the past. May your soul rest in eternal peace, dear Panicker.

Captain G.G.K. Panicker at the start of the
Degree Course in January 1968

Captain Daljinder Singh

Brigadier Gautam Tandon

Daljinder, known to most of his close friends as Dallu, was a strapping six-foot two-inch 200-pounder who lived life king size. He studied at the Lawrence School, Sanawar and the Rashtriya Indian Military College (RIMC), Dehradun. He joined NDA, like all of us, in July 1962, however, somewhere down the line, he earned a one-star, if I am not mistaken, for passing a PT test for someone else and subsequently passed out with the 29th Course.

Daljinder and Surinder Kaushik (Kalakar), both ex 28th Course, were commissioned in the Deccan Horse in December 1966 and joined the regiment at Firozepore. Thus, there were three of us from the same course as budding young troop leaders. I joined the regiment in June 1966 in Babina where the regiment was converting to T-54 tanks after having shed their Second World War vintage Sherman tanks. These were the same make of tanks that had served the regiment in its advance to Rangoon during the Second World War and in the Khem Karan Sector in September 1965.

In 1970, both Daljinder and I were posted at the Armoured Corps Centre and School (ACC&S) where there was a large contingent of captains from the 27th, 28th, and 29th Courses who were posted as instructors. A major part of our leisure hours was either spent on the golf course or at the annexe bar. Amongst our group, Jiti Mann and Dallu were really good golfers, and Dallu could, by his sheer size, outdrive us by at least 30 yards. Since Vijay Krishnan (16 CAVALRY) and I were the only course mates who had made the early plunge into matrimony, we were constantly being raided by the likes of Dallu, Kutbab Hai, SAG Gulati etc.

Being a great foodie, Dallu never found the mess bill of fare upto his standard in terms of quality and more so, in quantity. In the latter part of the 1960s when the regiment was in Ambala, the officers' mess ran a piggery. In those days we had a veteran waiter called Gopal, who in good humour, announced one day that the two things that were troubling in the mess were the Yorkshire pigs and Daljiner Singh sahib—both had enormous appetites! Those were the days when he was on a weight reduction diet of boiled food. After grudgingly eating his boiled food, he would order Gopal to serve what was on the platter for the others.

Daljinder is best remembered as a fun-loving person who loved having his leg pulled. It was difficult for him to be serious about anything—it was just not part of his nature.

In March 1971, DECCAN replaced 8 CAVALRY as the division regiment AC of 10 Infantry Division, which was operationally responsible for the Akhnoor Sector. The regiment less 'B' Squadron, was located at Pahun Da Chak (PDC), while the 'B' Squadron moved to Pathankot where the 10 Infantry Division, less the 191 Infantry Brigade, was located. In those days, as per the 1950 Karachi Agreement, only one infantry brigade and a squadron of tanks could be located in Chhamb-Jaurian. During the odd time that a UN representative visited, the RHQ (Regional Headquarters) and the 'C'

Squadron would disappear into the nearby khud!

With the situation rapidly deteriorating in erstwhile East Pakistan and the large influx of refugees, by early October the conflict with Pakistan was appearing more than likely. Towards the end of October, or early November, 'B' Squadron joined up with the regiment and the balance of the division moved into the sector.

With our courses almost coming to a standstill, a number of officers including Dallu were posted back to their respective regiments. It was some time in the third or fourth week of October 1971 that Simran and I bid farewell to Daljinder at the Nagar Railway Station. Dallu was affectionately referred to as the 46th tank of the regiment which no Pakistani tank shell could penetrate. How prophetically wrong we were.

Dallu, on his return, was appointed as the Second-in-Command of the 'B' Squadron where he had earlier served both as a Troop Leader and the Second-in-Command. I was to move a little later to re-join the regiment. Prior to the outbreak of hostilities, 191 Infantry Brigade and 'A' Squadron were deployed west of the Munawar Tawi in the Chhamb salient while the rest of the division was located to the east of the Tawi. The overall plan was that the 191 Infantry Brigade was to provide a firm base for a limited offensive through the Chhamb salient towards Jhelum/Gujarat. On 30 November, Lieutenant Colonel J.S. Bal met with a serious jeep accident and had to be evacuated. Major H.N. Hoon took over as the Officiating Commandant, and on 8 December, was promoted to command during the war.

On the night of 3/4 December, as we were in the process of moving into the forward posture for a subsequent offensive, there was intense Pakistani artillery shelling all along the front and in the depth areas, followed by multiple attacks on the FDLs of 191 Brigade by the enemy infantry, while being supported by armour.

The initial deployment of the brigade was better suited for

providing secure launch pads rather than a sustained defensive battle. It was a repeat of 1965. Pakistan had launched an offensive with an infantry division and an armoured brigade. The offensive came as surprise in view of the prevailing intelligence. Considering the prevailing situation in the early hours of 4 December, Bravo Squadron was inducted across the Munawar Tawi to augment the Alpha Squadron. At around 7 a.m., 'B' Squadron came under the tank and heavy artillery shelling. In the ensuing skirmish, Dallu's tank sustained a direct hit by an artillery shell and he suffered fatal shrapnel wounds. Daljinder was one of the first casualties that the regiment suffered on that first day of the 1971 war.

On the morning of 4 December, we lost two brave hearts – Captain Daljinder Singh and the 2 Lieutenant, S.S. Gill, the Troop Leader of 'A' Squadron. Within a matter of hours of the start of the 1971 conflict Daljinder had made the supreme sacrifice for the nation and the regiment. Alas, the regiment lost a brave soldier and, for me, I lost a dear friend and a comrade in arms. It is difficult to believe that in another few months it will be fifty years since Dallu left us—it still feels like yesterday when Daljinder, Kalakar Kaushik and I were sitting on the saddles in the Drunken Horse bar sipping our whiskies.

I salute you, my friend.

Captain Daljinder Singh

Deccan Horse War Memorial at Pahun Da Chak (Jaurian)

Brigadier Gautam Tandon (Retired) studied at the Welham Preparatory School and Doon School, Dehradun. He was commissioned in the Deccan Horse and was part of the regiment during the 1971 Indo-Pak war in the Chhamb Sector. He subsequently commanded 42 Armoured Regiment. He is an alumnus of the US Armor School, Fort Knox and the Defence Services Staff College (DSSC), Wellington. His more than three decades of service included instructional tenures at the Armoured Corps Centre and School and the College of Combat. His staff tenures included stints as the Brigade Major of an infantry brigade in Poonch, colonel administration of a desert division, Brigadier General Staff (BGS) (Operations) of the Western Command during Operation Vijay and brigadier administration Southern Command. He has also commanded the Mountain Brigade (Chindits) in the northeast. Post his retirement, he has settled in Pune.

Honours, Awards and Achievements

Lieutenant General Arvind Sharma

On 15 June 1966, one of the largest courses, comprising 416 gentleman cadets of the 37th Regular and 21 Technical Graduates Course, were commissioned as officers of the Indian Army from the Indian Military Academy, Dehradun. Their contemporaries at the National Defence Academy, Khadakwasla were commissioned as officers—21 in the Indian Navy on 1 January 1967 and 79 in the Indian Air Force on 4 June 1967.

The 28th Course had joined the National Defence Academy, Khadakwasla in the second week of July 1962 and was under training there, when the 1962 Indo-China war took place. The 1965 Indo-Pak war passed by us as we were still under training at the Indian Military Academy, Naval Academy and the Air Force academy. During the 1971 war, we all were in the four to five years of service bracket and the ranks of a captain in the Army, lieutenant in the Navy and flying officers in the Air Force. A fairly large number of officers of our batch were in Schools of Instruction attending specialist courses of long duration, and by the time they rejoined their units, the war was almost over.

In the 1971 war, some of our colleagues laid down their lives in service of the motherland; some were given gallantry awards and recognised for having rendered distinguished service. Besides, several of our course mates were given due recognition in a similar manner for their performance in counterinsurgency operations, aid to civil authority and other operations. The Kargil operations in 1999 were conducted under the dynamic and charismatic leadership of one of our colleagues—Mohinder Puri. Besides, a few of our colleagues gained recognition at the national level in other fields of excellence.

During the 1971 war, some of us fought on the western front and while others in erstwhile East Pakistan, where the Pakistani Air Force was knocked out of the skies in the first three days of the war. In 1968, when a battle was fought with the Chinese at Nathu La, Sikkim, one of us, the then 2 Lieutenant (later Colonel) of Signals, N.C. Gupta performed creditably and was awarded the Sena Medal for gallantry. During Operation Blue Star in June 1984, one of our colleagues, Major H.K. Palta of the Kumaon Regiment, led his company from the front and made the supreme sacrifice. For his act of bravery, he was awarded the Kirti Chakra. Yet another colleague, Major G.S. Khanuja of the Corps of Electronics and Mechanical Engineers (EME), during the Bhopal Gas Tragedy in December 1984, did meritorious work for which he was awarded the Vishisth Seva Medal. Unfortunately, he suffered a total loss of vision due to the disaster.

Martyrs

The following officers of our batch made the supreme sacrifice in the 1971 war and the counterinsurgency (CI) operation(s):

Captain Ravindra Nath Gupta, Engineers, 1971 war
Captain Daljinder Singh, Armoured Corps, 1971 war
Captain Manjit Singh, Artillery, 1971 war
Captain G.G.K. Panicker, Engineers, 1971 war
Major Gurdeep Singh Badalia, MAHAR, CI Operations Nagaland, 1970
Major H.K. Palta, Kumaon, PUNJAB, Operation Blue Star, 1984
Brigadier V. Sridhar, GUARDS, J&K, CI Operations, 1994

Gallantry Awards

Uttam Yudh Seva Medal

Lieutenant General Mohinder Singh, PUNJAB, CI Operations Assam, 2003
Major General (later Lieutenant General) Mohinder Puri, 3 Gorkha Rifles, Operation Vijay, 1999

Kirti Chakra

Major H.K. Palta (posthumous), KUMAON, Operation Blue Star, 1984

Vir Chakra

Captain Ravindra Nath Gupta (posthumous), Engineers, 1971 war
Captain Manjit Singh (posthumous), Artillery, 1971 war
Flying Officer (later Air Commodore) K.C. Kuruvilla, Indian Air Force, 1971 war
Flying Officer (later Wing Commander) S. Balasubramaniam, Indian Air Force, 1971 war
Wing Commander Sudhir Tyagi (posthumous), Indian Air Force, 1971 war

Yudh Seva Medal

Colonel (later Lieutenant General) T.P.S. Brar, MARATHA LI, Operation Pawan, 1987
Colonel (later Lieutenant General) T.S. Pathak, PARA, Operation Pawan, 1987
Colonel (later Major General) Basant Singh, 1 GORKHA RIFLES, Operation Pawan, 1987
Colonel (later Brigadier) P.S. Gurung, 4 GORKHA RIFLES, Operation Meghdoot, 1987
Air Commodore R.V. Kumar, Indian Air Force

Sena Medal (Gallantry)

Major (later Brigadier) A.B.S. Kundra, DOGRA, CI Operations Manipur, 1969
Captain (later Brigadier) NR Naidu, RAJPUT, High Altitude Warfare School (HAWS), J&K, 1971
Lieutenant (later Colonel) R.K. Ganapathy, GUARDS, CI Operations, Nagaland 1970
2 Lieutenant (later Colonel) N.C. Gupta, Signals, Sikkim, 1968

Mention in Despatches (1971 war)

Captain (later Lieutenant General) Mohinder Singh, PUNJAB
Captain (later Brigadier) B.S. Mehta, Armoured Corps
Captain (later Lieutenant Colonel) V. Malhotra, Armoured Corps

Distinguished Service Awards

Param Vishisht Seva Medal

Lieutenant General Arvind Sharma, 4 GORKHA RIFLES, 2006
Lieutenant General P.P.S. Bhandari, Armoured Corps, 2005

Lieutenant General Mohinder Singh, PUNJAB, 2005
Lieutenant General Mohinder Puri, 3 GORKHA RIFLES, 2005
Lieutenant General T.P.S. Brar, MARATHA LI, 2005
Lieutenant General R.S.K. Kapur, Engineers, 2005

Ati Vishisht Seva Medal

Lieutenant General Arvind Sharma, 4 GORKHA RIFLES
Lieutenant General P.P.S. Bhandari, Armoured Corps
Lieutenant General Mohinder Singh, PUNJAB
Lieutenant General T.S. Pathak, PARA
Lieutenant General Rajinder Singh, Artillery
Lieutenant General R.S.K. Kapur, Engineers
Major General V.S. Budhwar, KUMAON
Major General Basant Singh, 1 GORKHA RIFLES
Major General Rajendra Singh, Corps of Electronics and Mechanical Engineers (EME)
Major General R.S. Batra, Corps of Electronics and Mechanical Engineers (EME)
Rear Admiral M.S. Bedi, Indian Navy
Air Vice Marshal J.S. Grewal, Indian Air Force
Air Vice Marshal H.S. Sidhu, Indian Air Force
Brigadier T. Mukherjee, Rajputana Rifles
Commodore A.A. Chacko, Indian Navy
Commodore A. Sachdeva, Indian Navy
Air Commodore A.D. Karandikar, Indian Air Force

Sena Medal (Distinguished Service)

Lieutenant General R.S.K. Kapur, Engineers
Major General Satbir Singh, Artillery
Colonel Kiran Krishan, Engineers

Nao Sena Medal

Commander A.S. Lazaro, Indian Navy

Sena Medal (Distinguished Service)

Air Commodore A.D. Karandikar, Indian Air Force
Air Commodore P.C. Chopra, Indian Air Force
Wing Commander V.M. Bhatia, Indian Air Force
Wing Commander V. Pashupati, Indian Air Force

Vishisht Seva Medal

Lieutenant General Arvind Sharma, 4 GORKHA RIFLES
Lieutenant General Rajinder Singh, Artillery
Lieutenant General R.S.K. Kapur, Engineers
Major General V.S. Budhwar, KUMAON
Major General Basant Singh, 1 GORKHA RIFLES
Major General R.N. Suryavanshi, 11 GORKHA RIFLES
Major General K.B. Kapoor, Engineers
Major General D.K. Bewtra, Signals
Major General Subhash Chander, Signals
Major General Lalit Chopra, Signals
Major General Rajendra Singh, Corps of Electronics and Mechanical Engineers (EME)
Major General R.S. Batra, Corps of Electronics and Mechanical Engineers EME)
Major General Subhash Bindra, Army Ordnance Corps(AOC)
Major General Amrik Singh, Engineers (MOGSGS)
Rear Admiral M.S. Bedi, Indian Navy
Air Vice Marshal H.S. Sidhu, Indian Air Force
Brigadier V. Sridhar (posthumous), GUARDS
Brigadier M.S. Ruhil, GRENADIERS

Brigadier M. Dutta, 9 GORKHA RIFLES
Brigadier Parvez Cawasji, Artillery
Brigadier R.D. Singh, Engineers
Brigadier B.M. Bakshi, Engineers
Brigadier Pradip Mehta, Engineers
Brigadier S.M. Joshi, Corps of Electronics and Mechanical Engineers (EME)
Brigadier V.P. Singh, Military Farms
Air Commodore A.D. Karandikar Indian Air Force
Colonel P.S. Bhandari, Bihar
Group Captain Om Kumar, Indian Air Force
Lieutenant Colonel G.S. Khanuja, Corps of Electronics and Mechanical Engineers (EME)

National Awards and Achievements

Colonel K.S. Garcha

He was conferred the Rajasthan Shree in 1986 and the Arjuna Award in 1987 for excelling in polo. He captained the Indian Polo Team for the World Cup in 1995 and has played the game in about 30 countries across the world.

Colonel Vivek Mundkur

He achieved national recognition for his pioneering efforts to introduce hang gliding in India. His innovations in power generation, by designing and fabricating windmills with local resources, have been adopted by some states in interior areas. His innovation of a portable solar power pump won the World Innovation Challenge organised by Greenpeace in December 2013. This pump was so designed that it would provide water to small marginal farmers who do not have electricity and cannot afford diesel pumps.

Air Commodore A.D. Karandikar

On being commissioned as a pilot in the transport stream on 4 June 1967, he was awarded the Chief of Air Staff Trophy and the Flying Trophy, for being the best cadet. In 1972 he was given a commendation by the Chief of Army Staff (CAS) for safely landing a fully loaded Dakota, following an engine fire after take-off from Lilabari, Assam, on an air maintenance sortie. He was one of the first three pilots who was cleared for VIP operations on the Boeing 737-200 aircraft on its induction in the Air Force.

In 1995, his outstanding performance of recording 12,990 hours of military flying, accident and incident-free, was recognised by an entry recorded in the Limca Book of Records. After taking voluntary retirement from the IAF in June 1997, he was appointed the Chief Pilot of the Eastern Region, in Alliance Air, flying B737-200s. On 26 December 2004, when the earthquake and tsunami struck Port Blair, he was the first one to land on the runway, which was reduced to half its length by the calamity. Thereafter he led the relief efforts, flying multiple sorties from dawn to dusk.

He also holds the distinction of being the first to land at Thoise, Ladakh on Boeing 737-200, for commercial operations. Subsequently, he flew B737-700, 800, 900NG aircraft with Sahara and JetLite/Jet Airways. When he finally hung up his flying overalls, he had logged in a total of 24,680 hours of flying sans a mishap. A record indeed!

Citations

CAPTAIN R.N. GUPTA, VrC - Engineers

On the night of December 17, Captain Ravinder Nath Gupta volunteered for the task of conducting a recce along the wide frontage of the enemy minefield across river Basantar. Despite the grave risk involved and very intense enemy fire, he and his party brought back vital data which enabled 17 Horse to be inducted into the bridgehead well in time to take on the enemy's counter attacks and eventually led to the destruction of his armoured formation west of river Basantar. Determinedly working on improving the crossing, Captain Gupta was among those killed on December 17, by enemy fire. For his exemplary courage, he was posthumously decorated with the Vir Chakra.

CAPTAIN V. MALHOTRA - 17H Recommended for MVC

On the night of 13/14 December 1971, The Poona Horse was inducted across the mine field at Lohara, with a view to carrying out a night approach march and securing an encounter crossing over the Basanter River. Captain V. Malhotra was selected to lead and navigate the Regiment column. The entire night approach march, which was over a distance of approximately six kilometer, was through an enemy held area. From the moment the Regiment was inducted across the mine field, it came under accurate and intensive shelling which continued throughout the night. That apart, once the enemy got wind of what was happening, they employed every means at their disposal to block the Regiment's advance. Undeterred by all these adverse factors, and with an utter disregard for his personal safety, Captain V. Malhotra continued to navigate and lead the Regimental column during its approach march. In the execution of this task, he had often to dismount and lead the column of foot, through an unknown and reconnoitred area infested by the enemy, but he took all this in his stride in spite of great personal risks to which he was continuously exposed.

On the morning of 16 December 1971, during the battle of the Basanter River, the Regimental pivot at Jarpal held by two troops of `B; Sqn under heavy enemy counter-attack. Captain V. Malhotra, along with No 3 troop `A' Squadron, was ordered to reinforce this pivot. The bridge head across the Basanter River had not been fully cleared of enemy troops and, as this task force moved towards their assigned positions, they came under fire from enemy strong points and RCL gun nests that were still holding out. As time was at a premium, Captain V. Malhotra threw caution to the winds and started attacking the impending strong points by literally charging them, over running the defense works with his tanks and capturing the enemy infantry and weapon crews at pistol point.

Overcoming all enemy opposition by a series of such daring attacks, Captain V. Malhotra and 2/Lt AS Ahlawat, commanding no 3 Tp, joined up with 2/Lieutenant Arun Khetrapal and deployed on the Northern flank of B Squadron. These officers had barely got into position when the enemy reformed and launched a major counter-attack. This time, they selected the sector held by Captain V. Malhotra, 2/Lieutenant Arun Khetrapal and 2/Lieutenant A.S. Ahlawat as the point for their main effort: they launched an entire armored squadron against these three tanks in order to effect a breakthrough. A fierce tank fight ensued and a number of enemy tanks were hit and destroyed. At this critical juncture, Captain V. Malhotra's gun became inoperative due to mechanical failure but, nevertheless, this officer stuck to his post and continued to direct the battle in his assigned sector of responsibility in a cool and unruffled manner. During the later stages of the same battle, 2/Lieutenant Arun Khetrapal was killed in action and 2/Lieutenant A.S. Ahlawat wounded. Though the enemy attack had been halted and beaten back by the intrepid valour of these three officers, they could be seen reforming fora fresh onslaught. Captain V. Malhotra's tank was the only surviving tank in this area, its gun was inoperative: reinforcement had been ordered for this sector, but it would be some time before they could fetch up. The only impediment between the enemy and his cherished goal of a breakthrough were the resolute courage and steel like nerves of this officer: he boldly continued to face the enemy, fully knowing that should the enemy decide to press home their attack, there was little that he could do to stop them. It was also quite evident that in such an eventuality, his tank would be destroyed and he and his crew killed. Under these circumstances, Captain V. Malhotra would have been fully justified in pulling back us, because of his defective gun, there was little he could do to stop the enemy. However, this officer decided to hold his position in the face of almost certain death on the outside chance that by his mere presence he may succeed in holding the enemy at bay till such time as the expected reinforcements arrived. This was an act of courage and resolution far beyond the call of duty, and it paid handsome dividends. The enemy, who had received a severe mauling in the earlier attack, saw this officer's tank in position and remained at a healthy distance, making no determined attempt to close in and breakthrough. Captain V. Malhotra, by a calculated act of his courage, had averted a crisis.

From the day he joined action, Captain V. Malhotra has displayed the highest qualities of leadership, a calm and unruffled temperament under stress, great nerve and daring, and courage bordering on recklessness. His valour and his exploits have been beyond the call of duly and in the best traditions of our Army. For his outstanding performance, I recommend Captain V. Malhotra be awarded the Maha Vir Chakra.

Hanut Singh
Lieutenant Colonel
Commandant
17 Poona Horse

Captain V. Malhotra

CAPTAIN B.S. MEHTA, 45 CAVALRY RECOMMENDED FOR MVC

AWARDED: Mention-in-Despatches

1. Captain B.S. Mehta was the 2IC of 'C' Squadron 45 Cavalry. At about 6 a.m. on 21 November 1971 when the Squadron moved to a suitable location to counter the threat posed by the enemy tanks, Captain B.S. Mehta was in command of the right-hand group of the Squadron.
2. He effectively controlled his group of two troops on the right flank and opened fire, knocking down one tank with his own tank. In this tank-to-tank battle when one enemy tank tried to encroach further into the FDL's Captain B.S. Mehta again engaged the tank and knocked it out. The enemy also brought down heavy concentration of artillery and small arms fire, Captain B.S. Mehta held his ground and kept on directing his group to effectively continue engaged by two enemy tanks.
3. It was at this critical stage of the battle that the sudden news of the demise of the Squadron Commander Major D.S. Narag reached Captain B.S. Mehta. The Officer was undaunted and unnerved by this loss and promptly assumed command and control of his Squadron. He encouraged his troops with fine example of personal courage and leadership and led them on to the final destruction of the enemy squadron. The task was completed within a short period and the Squadron accounted for 10 enemy tanks. The Officer displayed fighting spirit, courage and leadership qualities in keeping with the highest tradition of the Armoured Corps and the Army.

In Fond Memory...

In 2006, during the reunion of 28 NDA course an idea was mooted that the Course should present a memorial to the alma mater, that would have visibility before every visitors to the National Defence Academy. The idea was unanimously accepted; suggestions and proposals for the memorial were tossed around and it was finally agreed upon to build a memorial to the battle of Tiger Hill. After consultation with the NDA authorities, it was decided to construct the memorial in front of the Cadet's Café as a tribute to the brave hearts. It was inaugurated by Lieutenant General Arvind Sharma, of the same batch while GOC-in-C, Headquarters Eastern Command.

Coursc mates of 28 NDA, 37 IMA, 21 Tech, along with their wives, attending the inauguration of Kargil Memorial

Lt Gen Arvind Sharma, GOC-in-C HQ Eastern Command inaugurating the Kargil Memorial

OTHER OCCAM MILITARY TITLES

March to Justice: *Global Military Law Landmarks*

Navdeep Singh and Frank Rosenblatt

An anthology of twenty-five short essays and commentaries by eminent jurists, judges, and academics from around the world.

March to Justice: Global Military Law Landmarks is a unique work in governance, military law and human rights. An anthology of twenty-five short essays and commentaries by eminent jurists, judges, and academics from around the world, this book throws light on some of the pathbreaking judicial decisions that changed the course of military law in several jurisdictions. Not only does the book enlighten the reader on the diverse course taken by military law, justice and reform in various nations, it also brings to the fore some noteworthy lessons from these experiences, in addition to facilitating a comparative analysis. The contents are articulated in simple, non-scholarly language for a layperson. This book is a must-have for the intrigued reader of texts on military, law, politics, public policy, governance and human rights.

Once Upon a Time in RIMC

Brigadier Jasbir Singh, SM

A humorous book that brings alive the tales of mischievous teenagers before they turn into valiant soldiers and leaders.

Boys of RIMC never really grow up, and happily, the spirit of adventure and mischief lives on, even after many winters have passed. Fatty and Kajla were to procure the digging implements surreptitiously. Tota, Soli, and Tinda were to help spread the mud! They were to make holes in their pockets, fill them with mud and go for walks all along the track from Ranjit Section to the mandir, spreading the mud so no one would suspect that we had been digging the 'Shoe'. HS Vaid, the 'giraffe', was to stand as a watch tower and warn us of any approaching threat, by making sounds like the confounded owl that used to inquisitively follow us during our night-time mischievous adventures!" For nearly a century, Rimcollians have done the three Services proud, and the civvy street too. Known for their camaraderie and spirit of never accepting defeat or yielding to any adversary, whether in the battlefield or the playground, Brig Jasbir's humorous book brings alive how mischevious teenagers are forged into soldiers.

***The Fighting Fourth:** A Personal Narrative of the History of 4 Kumaon*

Brigadier Jasbir Singh, SM

An intimate and personal account of the glorious history of the 4th Battalion, The Kumaon Regiment

Fighting Fourth or 4th Battalion, The Kumaon Regiment (4 Kumaon), raised in 1788, has fought with distinction and etched its name in the annals of Indian military history with honour and pride. From fighting the Pindaris to quelling the Boxer Rebellion in Hong Kong, the battalion saw extensive action in both the World Wars and the Indo-Pak war of 1947–48, where the gallant actions of the unit saved Kashmir Valley for the Indian Union and changed the course of history in the region. Major Somnath Sharma was posthumously awarded India's first PVC, the highest award for gallantry, while Brigadier Pritam Singh emerged as the Saviour of Poonch. The unit was awarded Battle Honour 'Srinagar' and 57 awards for bravery, including one Param Vir Chakra, three Maha Vir Chakras, 13 Vir Chakras, one Bar to VrC and other awards. In the Indo–Pak War 1965, the battalion was awarded Battle Honour 'Sanjoi–Mirpur', while in the 1971 operations, it was awarded Battle Honour 'Shamshernagar', along with three VrCs, one SM and other awards. Brigadier Jasbir presents an intimate, personal account of the glorious history of this fine battalion that has contributed no less than two Chiefs of Staff of the Indian Army and is among the most highly-decorated ones.